Answer Key for

Linguistics
An Introduction to Linguistic Theory

written by Victoria A. Fromkin (*editor*), Susan Curtiss,
Bruce P. Hayes, Nina Hyams, Patricia A. Keating,
Hilda Koopman, Pamela Munro, Dominique Sportiche,
Edward P. Stabler, Donca Steriade, Tim Stowell, and
Anna Szabolcsi

BLACKWELL
Publishers

Contents

2

Morphology:
The Structure of Words

General Notes on Answers

Many of the answers provided here include more detail or background information than would be expected in student answers. This material is included to stimulate class discussion or the individual reader's thinking.

In addition, many of the questions do not have only one acceptable answer. In some cases, more than one acceptable answer is provided, but in others, the answers given are only models of what might be acceptable.

The goal of the exercises is to stimulate linguistic thinking and analysis. In many cases, more than one analysis is fully acceptable.

Analyze the following English sentences and phrases by **segmenting** them – putting hyphens between all morphemes you can identify. Identify each morpheme as bound or free, lexical or grammatical. For the first occurrence of each bound morpheme, give another word that contains that same bound morpheme. Some words are hard to divide into morphemes – discuss any problems you encounter. For example, *day* is certainly a separate word (morpheme); should the *yester* of *yesterday* be considered a morpheme? If so, what does it mean? Similarly, how many morphemes are there in the verb *told*, which refers to the past?

EXERCISE 2.1

1. Yesterday Ophelia picked wildflowers in the churchyard.
2. He told me that Desdemona had married a Moor.
3. Aren't you going to show me your newest quiver?
4. Portia argued her case long and well.
5. My horse! My horse! My kingdom for a horse! (*Richard III*, V, iv, 7)
6. All the perfumes of Arabia will not sweeten this little hand. (*Macbeth*, V, i, 56)

7.   I'll put a girdle round about the earth in forty minutes. (*A Midsummer Night's Dream*, II, i, 163)

8.   Merrily, merrily shall I live now, under the blossom that hangs on the bough. (*The Tempest*, V, i, 88)

EXERCISE 2.1 ANSWERS

1.   *Yester-day Ophelia pick-ed wild-flower-s in the church-yard.*

yester- bound; lexical (a rare morpheme; cf. *yesteryear?*)

day free; lexical (all nouns are lexical morphemes)

Ophelia free; lexical (all names are lexical morphemes)

pick free; lexical (all verbs are lexical morphemes)

-ed bound; grammatical (kiss-ed)

wild free; lexical (all adjectives are lexical morphemes)

flower free; lexical (is it possible to analyze this as *flow-er*? Doesn't seem like!)

-s bound; grammatical (girl-s)

in free; grammatical (prepositions are considered to be grammatical morphemes here)

the free; grammatical (all determiners are grammatical moprhemes)

church free; lexical

yard free; lexical

2.   *He told me that Desdemona had marri-ed a Moor.*

he free; grammatical (all pronouns are considered grammatical morphemes)

told (hard to analyze: a lexical combination of a free morpheme (*tell*) plus a bound morpheme (*-ed*; see above); such cases are discussed further later in the chapter)

me free; grammatical (as with *he*)

that free; grammatical (a **complementizer** or subordinating conjunction, in traditional terms; these are all considered grammatical morphemes)

Desdemona free; lexical

had free (hard to analyze: *have* plus *-ed*, as with *told* above. *Had* can be lexical (as in *Desdemona had a tiara*) but here it seems to be grammatical, since it is an **auxiliary** that helps the hearer understand the tense (or the relationship between the telling and the marrying).)

marry free; lexical (spelling shouldn't worry us; this is the same word as *marri-*)

-ed (as above)

a free; grammatical

Moor free; lexical

3.   *Are-n't you go-ing to show me your new-est quiver?*

are free (an irregular complex morpheme, containing *be* plus indications of present tense and either 'you' or plural reference; such cases are discussed further later in the chapter. Like *had*, *are* can be either lexical (as in *You are the king*) or grammatical (in the auxiliary use here).)

-n't (a **contraction** (shortened form) of *not*). *Not* is free, *-n't* is bound. Both are grammatical. (Another instance of *-n't* is in *can't*.)

you free; grammatical (as with *he*)

go free; lexical (in general – but in this usage *are . . . going to* might be seen as an auxiliary, since it helps the hearer understand the time of the showing)

-ing bound; grammatical (*sing-ing*)

to free; grammatical

show free; lexical

me (as above)

your free; grammatical (we might segment this as *you-r*, with a possessive morpheme *-r*, as in *her* and *their*)

new free; lexical

-est bound; grammatical (*pretti-est*)

quiver free; lexical (although this word probably was originally segmentable, modern English doesn't seem to provide any *quiv-* to relate it to)

4. *Portia argu-ed her case long and well.*

 Portia free; lexical

 argue free; lexical

 -ed (as above)

 her free; grammatical (this could be segmented as *he-r*, as suggested in the discussion of *you-r* above. But the relationship to *she* is not clear, so this doesn't necessarily seem desirable from the viewpoint of modern English.)

 case free; lexical

 long free; lexical

 and free; grammatical (like all **conjunctions**, words that join together other words and phrases)

 well free; lexical (as discussed in the text, *well* is an irregular adverbial form of *good*, seemingly containing the meanings of *good* plus *-ly*) (Another example of *-ly* is *cheerfully*.)

5. *My horse! My horse! My king-dom for a horse!*

 Repeated words in the same sentence are discussed only once.

 my free; grammatical (although this word seems parallel to *your* and *her*, it does not contain their *-r*. We might compare it to *me* – but it is certainly irregular.)

 horse free; lexical

 king free; lexical

 -dom bound; lexical (this **bound lexical morpheme** (see Sidebar 2.2, p. 34 of textbook) means something like *realm* and is related to *domain*) (Another example of *-dom* is in *dukedom*.)

for free; grammatical

a (as above)

6.   *All the perfume-s of Arabia will not sweet-en this little hand.*

all free; lexical (though some might argue that **quantifiers** like *all* should be considered grammatical)

the (as above)

perfume free; lexical

-s (as above)

of free; grammatical

Arabia free; lexical

will free; grammatical (*will* is a **modal**, an auxiliary verb like *can, may, should, must, would*, and so on, which indicates the speaker's view of the likelihood or possibility of an event's occurrence. All of these are generally considered grammatical.)

not (as above)

sweet free; lexical

-en bound; grammatical (*-en* is a **derivational morpheme** (discussed further in the text below) used to form verbs from adjectives; these are all considered grammatical) (Another example of *-en* is *tight-en*.)

this free; grammatical (like *that* above)

little free; lexical

hand free; lexical

7.   *I-'ll put a girdle round about the earth in for-ty minute-s.*

I free; grammatical (like *he* above)

-'ll (*I'll* is a contraction of *I* plus *will* (discussed above). Both *-'ll* and *will* are grammatical; *-'ll* is bound, *will* is free.) (Another example of *-'ll* is in *he'll*.)

put free; lexical

a (as above)

girdle free; lexical (this is related to the verb *gird*, but there doesn't seem to be any justification for recognizing a derivational morpheme *-le* (in contrast to *girder*, productively formed from *gird* plus *-er*). However, maybe this is a cranberry morpheme! (see Sidebar 2.2, p. 34 of textbook).)

round free; lexical (like all adverbs)

about free; grammatical (if all prepositions are indeed grammatical morphemes; while this analysis seems well justified in the case of *in* and *of*, longer prepositions like *about* seem more lexical!)

the (as above)

earth free; lexical

in (as above)

four free; lexical (unless quantifiers like *all* are considereded grammatical morphemes, as discussed above) (Note that spelling changes between *four* and *forty*.)

-ty bound; grammatical (*-ty* is used to derive names of decades (another example is *sixty*). Thus, it seems to be related to *ten*. However, note that *-teen* (as in *fourteen*, clearly not the same as *forty!*) must also be related to *ten*, so we don't want to propose too hasty an analysis of these words.)

minute free; lexical

-s (as above)

8. *Merri-ly, merri-ly shall I live now, under the blossom that hang-s on the bough.*

merry free; lexical

-ly bound; grammatical (see discussion of *well* above)

shall free; grammatical (as with *will*)

I (as above)

live free; lexical

now free; lexical

under free; grammatical (but see discussion of *about* above)

the (as above)

blossom free; lexical

that free; grammatical (This word is homophonous with the complementizer *that* discussed above. In this sentence it functions (in traditional terms) as a **relative pronoun**; some might consider it a complementizer here also. In any case it is a grammatical morpheme.)

hang free; lexical

-s bound; grammatical (this is the singular present ending on verbs, which is homophonous with but not the same as the plural ending on nouns) (Another example is in *marries*.)

on free; grammatical

the (as above)

bough free; lexical

Consider the following list of actual and possible words in English. Segment them into their component morphemes. Comment on each word: is it a 'real' word (does it occur in your mental dictionary)? Is it a possible word (an item that you don't know but which you think could be a word)? Is it an impossible word (one that could not be in any English speaker's lexicon)? (You might want to discuss the contexts in which words whose existence might be debatable could be used, and any other difficult cases.) **EXERCISE 2.2**

anti-Trotskyite, beautifully, boys, children, children's, childrens, disenchanting, girled, hims, hors-d'œuvres, lovelily, morphologist, nounize, overs, postpositional, stealize, sweetie, unman, unwoman, verballiest

Since these answers refer to the student's own individual mental dictionary, they will vary from student to student. Many answers could be correct (though most student answers will not be as detailed as those below). The conclusion is that most words listed are in fact possible words.

anti-Trotskyite – This word is probably in few people's mental dictionaries, but it certainly is a possible word, in that its formation follows regular rules of English.

beautifully – A real word of English in most speakers' mental dictionaries, following the regular word formation rules of English.

boys – A real word of English, in all speakers' mental dictionaries.

children – A real word of English, in all speakers' mental dictionaries.

children's – A real word of English, the possessive meaning 'belonging to the children'. Possessive forms like this are not listed in normal (written) English dictionaries, though plurals are. (Some of the reasons for this practice are suggested by Sidebar 2.10, pp. 72–3 of textbook.) Similarly, such forms may not be in speakers' mental dictionaries, though exactly what a mental dictionary should be assumed to contain is a matter for theoretical discussion.

childrens – An impossible word of English (in general), since *children* is plural and need not have plural *-s* added to it. (*-s* is also a verb ending; similarly, however, *children* is not a verb.) However, there are contexts in which the word *childrens* might be used, for instance if someone was counting the number of occurrences of the word *children* in a document. Even given this restricted context, however, it seems unlikely that anyone's mental dictionary would include this word.

disenchanting – Not a real word of English for most speakers of English, but a possible word of English. *Enchant* is a real verb of English, and *enchanting* is a real word, both a regular form of the verb (as in *The sorcerer is enchanting the king*) and an adjective (as in *Your dress is enchanting*). The prefix *dis-* is used both to form adjectives from other adjectives (as in *ingenuous/disingenuous*) and to form verbs from other verbs (as in *enfranchise/disenfranchise*). So if *disenchanting* was a word of English, it would be formed either by adding *dis-* to the adjective *enchanting* or by adding *dis-* to the verb *enchant*, and then adding *-ing* to this derived word *disenchant*. Adding *dis-* to an adjective is not a regular process, however: most adjectives do not have *dis-* forms: **disred*, **dispretty*, **dishappy*, etc. Similarly, adding *dis-* to a verb is not a regular process: most verbs do not have *dis-* forms, and there is no verb *disenchant*. Thus, although **disenchanting** is a possible word of English, it is not a real word in most speakers' mental dictionaries.

girled – Not a possible word of English. *Girl* is not a verb, and *-ed* is a verb ending. (*Girled* would be a possible verb if speakers began using a verb *girl*.)

hims – Not a possible word of English, given that *him* is a pronoun and *-s* is either a noun or a verb ending. However, *hims* could be used in the same context described for *childrens* above.

hors-d'œuvres – *Hors-d'œuvres* is not an English word originally, but a word borrowed from French. Many speakers have this borrowed noun in their mental dictionaries, but certainly not all.

lovelily – Not a real word of English, but a possible word of English. *Lovely* is an adjective, and *-ly* is used to form adverbs from adjectives (such as *beautifully* above), so *lovelily* is a possible word. However, not all adjectives have derived adverbs formed by adding *-ly*; *lovely* is one of these adjectives. (It is probable that the fact that *lovely* ends in *-ly* makes such a derivation unlikely: other adverbs formed from adjectives ending in *-ly*, such as *cowardlily* and *leisurelily*, are also not used.)

morphologist – This is a real word of English, though it is probably in few speakers' mental dictionaries. A morphologist is someone who studies morphology (either in linguistics or in other fields, such as biology); the word is formed regularly by adding the suffix *-ist* 'specialist in' to the noun *morphology*, as with *botanist* or *organist*.

nounize – A possible word of English, but not a real word of English (for most speakers!). *-ize* forms verbs from nouns; since *noun* is a noun, it follows that *nounize* (meaning something like 'make into a noun') is a possible verb. (The usual term for 'make into a noun' in linguistics is *nominalize*.)

overs – Like *hims*, *overs* initially does not seem to be a possible word, since *over* is an adverb, and *-s* is added only to nouns or verbs. Of course the word could be used in the same counting context described for *childrens* above, but in addition, *over* might be used as either a noun (meaning something like 'instance of being over') or a verb (meaning something like 'go over' or 'cause to go over'); any speaker who had *over* as a noun or a verb in his or her mental dictionary could use the word *overs*.

postpositional – Like *morphologist, postpositional* is a real word (a technical term in linguistics, referring to elements that function oppositely to prepositions, going after their associated nouns – in a phrase like 'house in', the word meaning 'in' would be a postposition). However, this word is probably in few English speakers' mental dictionaries. Like *prepositional, postpositional* is formed by adding the prefix *pre-* and the suffix *-al* to the noun *position*.

stealize – Initially *stealize* seems like an impossible word. *Steal* is a verb, and (as discussed for *nounize* above) the suffix *-ize* is added to nouns to form verbs. However, *steal* can also be a noun (as in the phrase *It's a steal*), so it is possible that a speaker might form the word *stealize* to mean 'make into a steal'. This derivation seems unlikely, however; although *stealize* might be called a possible word, it is not likely to appear in any speaker's mental dictionary.

sweetie – A real word of English. Because many speakers might find the diminutive noun *sweetie* informal (formed by adding *-ie* or *-y* to the noun (rather than the adjective) *sweet*), they might be surprised to find it in a dictionary. Probably some dictionaries list this word, and others do not. Since all speakers are probably familiar with this word, though, it is probably in all their mental dictionaries.

unman – A real word of English. Although the usual meaning of *un-* is to form adjectives and verbs from other adjectives and verbs, *un-* is also used to form verbs from nouns (generally deriving a verb that indicates depriving someone or something of the noun or a quality associated with it, as in *unearth*). Probably some speakers do not have *unman* in their mental dictionaries, however, since it's a relatively uncommon word.

unwoman – A possible word of English: if *unman* is a real word, certainly *unwoman* is possible. This is not a word (so far) used by speakers, however, so it does not occur in any speaker's mental dictionary.

verballiest – A possible but unlikely word of English. *Verbal* is a standard adjective; *verbally* is a standard adverb derived from it (like *beautifully* above). Certain adverbs have superlative forms in *-est*, such as *slowliest*, though many speakers consider these forms awkward. *Verballiest* is thus possible but highly unlikely to be used or to occur in any speaker's mental dictionary.

EXERCISE 2.3   Consider each of the following groups of words, and answer questions (a–d) below about each group. Looking the words up in a dictionary is not necessary, but may be helpful.

(i)   badness, fairness, goodness, insurmountableness, wellness
(ii)   incorrigible, incongruous, indefinite, inflexible, insurmountable
(iii)   cowardly, daily, fatherly, lonely, lovely, womanly
(iv)   fifth, fourteenth, sixth, thirtieth, seventieth, seventy-seventh
(v)   dependent, descendant, defiant, prudent, reverent, servant
(vi)   democracy, idiocy, jealousy, monarchy, photography, victory

(a)   Is there any morpheme that occurs in all the words in the group? If so, what is it?
(b)   If your answer to (a) was yes, give three additional words containing that morpheme.
(c)   If your answer to (a) was yes, tell the meaning of that morpheme.
(d)   If you can, tell what class of words the morpheme you found in (a) is added to, and what the class of the words formed by its addition is. Discuss any problems you have arriving at these answers.

Spelling is often a clue to morpheme relatedness, but it may be misleading. Don't assume that two morphemes are necessarily different because they are spelled differently. For example the *-ly* in *lonely* and the *-li-* in *loneliness* represent the same morpheme.

The words in (vii) are a special case:

(vii)   glare, gleam, glimmer, glisten, glitter, glow

These words beginning with *gl* seem to have something in common semantically (what is it?). However, *gl* does not seem to be a morpheme like *-ness*, *-er*, *-ly*, or any of the others you found above. Explain why. (Hint: look at what is left of each word in (vii) when you eliminate the *gl*.)

Once again, answers will vary considerably.

(i)   *badness, fairness, goodness, insurmountableness, wellness*
  (a)   Yes; *-ness*.
  (b)   *helpfulness, soreness, tidiness*
  (c)   'quality of being _____'
  (d)   *-ness* is added to adjectives to form nouns.
(ii)   *incorrigible, incongruous, indefinite, inflexible, insurmountable*
  (a)   Yes; *in-*.
  (b)   *incomplete, indifferent, indistinct*
  (c)   'not   '
  (d)   *in* is added to adjectives to form adjectives.
  (Note: Students may note that *in-* is identical in use to the prefix *im-*, as in *imprecise, impossible*.)
(iii)   *cowardly, daily, fatherly, lonely, lovely, womanly*
  (a)   Yes; *-ly*.
  (b)   *leisurely, motherly, monthly*
  (c)   'having the quality of (a) _____', 'characteristic of (a) _____', 'characterized by (a) _____'
  (d)   *-ly* is added to nouns to form adjectives.
  (Note: Students may note that this *-ly* is not the same as the much more common *-ly* used to form adverbs from adjectives.)
(iv)   *fifth, fourteenth, sixth, thirtieth, seventieth, seventy-seventh*
  (a)   Yes; *-eth*.
  (b)   *fourth, seventh, tenth*
  (c)   '_____ in a numerical sequence'
  (d)   *-eth* is added to counting numbers (technically called cardinal numbers) to form numbers used to specify ordering (technically called ordinal numbers). Both types of numbers are quantifiers, generally functioning like adjectives.
(v)   *dependent, descendant, defiant, prudent, reverent, servant*
  (a)   No.
  All these words end in *-ent/-ant*, but they do not appear to have a common meaning.

Dependent, descendant, and *servant* all are nouns formed from verbs, meaning 'one who _____s'.

Dependent, descendant, defiant, and *reverent* are all adjectives formed from verbs, meaning '_____ing'.

Prudent may be related to *prude,* but the connection does not seem obvious.

(vi)   *democracy, idiocy, jealousy, monarchy, photography, victory*

(a)   No.

All these words end in *-y,* but they do not have a common meaning. *Monarchy, photography,* and *victory* are all nouns formed from other nouns, meaning 'something associated with a _____, state in which there is a _____'.

Democracy and *idiocy* are similar, but in the case of these words, there is an additional change: the final *-t* in the nouns *democrat* and *idiot* is replaced by *c* (pronounced with the sound of [s]) before *y* is added. (Brackets – [] – are used to show pronunciation, as opposed to spelling.)

Jealousy is a noun formed by adding *-y* to an adjective, although the general meaning seems similar.

(vii) *glare, gleam, glimmer, glisten, glitter, glow*

(a)   No.

All of these words seem to refer to light, but it is not true that the *gl* contained in each word is a morpheme like *-ness, -li,* or *-y.* If the *gl* is removed from these words, what is left (*are, eam, immer, isten, itter, ow*) doesn't have any meaning at all, so there is no sense in which a morpheme is being added here to form a new class of words.

EXERCISE 2.4

(a)   Decide whether each of the bound morphemes you discussed in Exercise 2.3 is inflectional or derivational. Explain your answers.

(b)   English has fewer inflectional morphemes than many other languages. List as many of them as you can. (You'll be reminded of a lot of them by going through the previous part of this chapter.)

EXERCISE 2.4 ANSWERS

(a)   The morphemes identified in (i)–(iv) of Exercise 2.3 are *-ness, in-, -ly,* and *-eth.* Of these, *-ness, in-,* and *-ly* are all derivational morphemes. They function to derive base words from other base words, and their use is not required by sentence structure (as the plural *-s* or past tense *-ed* are, for example).

The number suffix *-eth* probably should be regarded as an inflectional suffix. Numbers with and without *-eth* do not have different meanings or belong to different classes. Numbers above 1 have different frames for use with and without *eth*:

(number above 1) PLURAL NOUN (as in *thirty girls, four flowers, twelve nights*)
(number above 1) + *eth* SINGULAR NOUN (as in *thirtieth girl, fourth flower, twelfth night*)

This shows that *-eth* is an inflectional suffix.

(b) (i) Noun suffix: *-s* (plural)
     (ii) Verb suffixes: *-s* (singular present), *-ed* (past), *-ing* (present participle), *-en* (past participle)
     (iii) Adjective suffixes: *-er* (comparative), *-est* (superlative)
     (iv) Adverb suffixes: *-er* (comparative), *-est* (superlative)

As noted above, the number suffix *-eth* is also inflectional.

(a) The following Swahili sentences use many of the same morphemes you encountered above, p. 36 of textbook.

Ninasema.	'I am speaking.'
Tulisema.	'We spoke.'
Atasema.	'He will speak.'
Watasema.	'They will speak.'

Rewrite the sentences with hyphens separating the morphemes, as in the text. These sentences contain two new morphemes. What are they, and what do they mean?

(b) Translate the following sentences into Swahili:

'They read' [past]; 'I will speak'; 'He is speaking'

(c) The verbs of Swahili sentences can include an additional morpheme to indicate the **object** of the sentence, as with

Nilikisoma. 'I read it' (where 'it' refers to an item like a book).

How many morphemes does a verb like *Nilikisoma* contain? What order do they come in?

(d) Here are some new Swahili sentences. (They contain two additional morphemes you have not seen before.) Analyze them (separate them into morphemes), explaining what each morpheme means.

Anamfukuza.	'He is chasing him.'
Ananifukuza.	'He is chasing me.'
Tulimfukuza.	'We chased him.'
Walitufukuza.	'They chased us.'

(e)   Translate the following sentences into English:

Ninamfukuza; Nitamfukuza; Anatufukuza.

(f)   You've seen that Swahili verbs change to indicate present, past, and future tense, and that certain English verbs have different forms for present and past tense. Can a single English verb change to show the future?

EXERCISE 2.5 ANSWERS

(a)   Ni-na-sema.   'I am speaking.'
Tu-li-sema.   'We spoke.'
A-ta-sema.   'He will speak.'
Wa-ta-sema.   'They will speak.'
The new morphemes are -*sema* 'speak' and *wa-* 'they'.

(b)   'They read' [past] is *Wa-li-soma*.
'I will speak' is *Ni-ta-sema*.
'He is speaking' is *A-na-sema*.

(c)   *Ni-li-ki-soma* contains four morphemes. *Ni-* is the subject prefix 'I', *li-* is the tense prefix for past, *ki-* is the new object prefix for 'it', and -*soma* is the verb.

(d)   The completely new morphemes are *m-* ('him' object prefix) and *fukuza* 'chase'. These sentences also show *ni-* being used to show an object 'me' and *tu-* being used to show an object 'us'.
   Below the sentences that follow is a simplified representation of the order and meaning of each morpheme (a **gloss**; see Sidebar 2.4, pp. 42–3 of textbook):

A-na-m-fukuza.   'He is chasing him.'
he-present-him-chase
A-na-ni-fukuza.   'He is chasing me.'
he-present-me-chase
Tu-li-m-fukuza.   'We chased him.'
we-past-him-chase
Wa-li-tu-fukuza.   'They chased us.'
they-past-us-chase

(e)   *Ni-na-m-fukuza* means 'I am chasing him.'
Ni-ta-m-fukuza means 'I will chase him.'
A-na-tu-fukuza means 'He is chasing us.'

(f)   No. In order to express the future in English, we need to add extra words. Thus, the (singular) future of *chase* in English is either *will chase* or *is going to chase* – there is no way to add a morpheme directly to *chase* to show the future.

(a)   Here are some additional sentences that help demonstrate that Tolkapaya is a polysynthetic language. State what two additional morphemes these sentences contain, and explain how they change the meanings of the words to which they are added:

**EXERCISE
2.6**

'ich-'-chthúl-ma.   'I wash something.'
'ich-'úu-ch-ma.   'They see something.'
M-'úu-v-ch-ma.   'You guys are visible.'
Chthúl-v-ma.   'He is washable.' (or more sensibly 'It is washable')

(b)   Now translate the following sentences into Tolkapaya:
'I am visible'; 'You guys wash something'; 'You are washable'; 'He sees something'.

(c)   *Tpóqma* means 'He pours it'.
Divide the following Tolkapaya sentences into morphemes, and tell what they mean: *'tpóqchma; 'ichmtpóqma; Tpóqvchma*.

(a)   The sentences have two additional morphemes that are not present in the text above this, the prefix *'ich-* 'something' and the suffix -*v* 'is able to be _____ ed' or 'is _____ +able'. The first morpheme adds an object to the translation of the sentence. The second is more complicated, expressing a meaning that seems more like the meanings of English derivational affixes.
      The prefix *'ich-* goes before the subject prefix; the suffix -*v* follows the verb.

*EXERCISE
2.6*

ANSWERS

(b)   'I am visible' is *'-'úu-v-ma*.
'You guys wash something' is *'ich-m-chthúl-ch-ma*.
'You are washable' is *M-chthúl-v-ma*.
'He sees something' is *'ich-'úu-ma*.

(c)   *'-tpóq-ch-ma* means 'We pour it'.
'ich-m-tpóq-ma means 'You pour something'.
Tpóq-v-ch-ma means 'They are pourable' ('They are able to be poured').

You already saw the prefix *'ich-*, which indicates the object 'something' in a Tolkapaya verb. As in Swahili, Tolkapaya verbs can indicate other objects as well as subjects, all in the same word. First of all, *'úuvma*, 'He sees', could also be translated into English as 'He sees him' (or 'He sees her' – in other words, a third-person subject sees a third-person object), and *Mchthúlma*, 'You wash', also means 'You wash him' (or 'You wash her'). Thus, just as there is no Tolkapaya prefix to indicate a third-person subject, there is no prefix to indicate a third-person object. Other

**EXERCISE
2.7**

objects are indicated with prefixes. Here are some examples with 'me' objects:

Nychthúlma.   'He washes me.'
Nym'úuvma.   'You see me.'

You've seen that a *-ch* suffix can make a Tolkapaya subject plural. Plurality of an object is indicated somewhat similarly in Tolkapaya:

Paa'úuvma.   'He sees them.'
Paamchthúlma.   'You wash them.'
Paanychthúlma.   'He washes us.'
Paa"úuvchma.   'We see them.'

(a)   Translate the following English sentences into Tolkapaya: 'I wash them'; 'They see me'; 'We wash him'; 'You guys wash them'. Present each new Tolkapaya sentence with hyphens separating the morphemes and a gloss underneath the word showing what each morpheme means, as explained in Sidebar 2.4, pp. 42–3 of textbook.

(b)   It is claimed above that Tolkapaya has no prefix to indicate a third-person object. On the other hand, someone might say that *paa-* was such a prefix. Explain why this is not so (you might want to compare *paa-* with *-ch*).

EXERCISE 2.7 ANSWERS

(a)   Paa-'-chthúl-ma.
       plobj-1-wash-nonfut
       'I wash them.'

       Ny-'úu-ch-ma.
       1obj-see-plsubj-nonfut
       'They see me.'

       '-chthúl-ch-ma.
       1-wash-plsubj-nonfut
       'We wash him.'

       Paa-m-chthúl-ch-ma.
       plobj-2-wash-plsubj-nonfut
       'You guys wash them.'

       New abbreviations: plobj = plural object, 1obj = first-person object, plsubj = plural subject.

(b)   *Paa-* is not a third-person object prefix, because it is used with plural objects of other persons, such as 'us' and 'you guys' (object).

(a) Make a template for Swahili verbs, incorporating the material introduced in the text and in Exercise 2.5.

(b) The template in (20), p. 44 of textbook, reflects the fact that a Tolkapaya verb like those introduced in the text must contain two morphemes, VERB and TENSE, and may contain either one or two additional ones. The Tolkapaya verbs in Exercises 2.6 and 2.7 are more complex, however. Make a more complete template than (20) for Tolkapaya verbs, incorporating every morpheme introduced in Exercises 2.6 and 2.7. You have not been given enough information to be sure of the relative ordering of every Tolkapaya morpheme, but you may be able to deduce that certain morphemes are incompatible (they would not make sense if used together). Discuss the template you come up with.

EXERCISE 2.8

(a) Here is a Swahili template:

SUBJECT - TENSE - (OBJECT) - VERB

(b) Here is a fuller Tolkapaya template:

(*paa*) - (OBJECT) - (SUBJECT) - VERB - (*v*) - (*ch*) - TENSE

EXERCISE 2.8 ANSWERS

This template shows that the only required parts of a Tolkapaya verb are still VERB and TENSE, and that sometimes it makes better sense to refer to specific morphemes in a template than to general categories. However, if category labels seem more appropriate, this new template could be rewritten as:

(OBJECT PLURALITY*)* - (OBJECT) - (SUBJECT) - VERB - ('able'*)* - (SUBJECT PLURALITY) - TENSE

The order of the morphemes above is justified by the data in the text and in Exercises 2.6 and 2.7. There is one indeterminate case, however: we have not seen any examples that demonstrate the relative ordering of the '*ich*-'something' prefix and either *paa-* or the object prefixes. However, since '*ich*- is always an object, we can infer that it will appear at the same position as the other object prefixes, in the OBJECT slot of the template, and that it would be incompatible with other object prefixes.

Consider the three analyses of Tolkapaya -*i* presented on p. 46 of the textbook. Rewrite each one to include a specific rule expressed as an *if . . . then* statement. Then consider the template describing Tolkapaya verb structure in (20), p. 44 of textbook (and modified in Exercise 2.8), in which VERB and TENSE were presented as required categories. Is this template compatible with each of the suggested analyses? Discuss your answers.

EXERCISE 2.9

EXERCISE 2.9	Here are restatements of the three analyses of Tolkapaya -*i* given in the text:

ANSWERS

- if a verb ends in a consonant, its absolutive form is made by adding -*i*. If a verb ends in a vowel, its absolutive form has no suffix.
- if a Tolkapaya word ends in two separate vowels, the second of these is deleted. (Note that we must assume here that long vowels like *ii* are not two 'separate vowels', even though they are written with two vowel letters in Tolkapaya orthography.)
- if a Tolkapaya verb ends in a consonant, -*i* is added after that consonant. If the templates in (20) and Exercise 2.8 are correct, TENSE is a required category in Tolkapaya. The first and third analyses above are incompatible with this template, if required categories are required to be filled by actual morphemes (rather than by zero). This must in fact be true, unless Tolkapaya tense suffixes can occur as words on their own (which would be the case if the VERB slot could be unfilled). Therefore, given these assumptions, the second analysis above must be most appropriate.

EXERCISE 2.10	Consider the following verbs from Chickasaw, a Muskogean language spoken in Oklahoma, and their corresponding first-person plural ('we') subject forms (in Chickasaw orthography, underlining a vowel indicates that it is **nasalized**, or pronounced with the air released through the nose rather than the mouth):

afama 'meet'	ilafama / kilafama 'we meet him'
bashli 'cut'	iibashli / kiibashli 'we cut it'
hilha 'dance'	iihilha / kiihilha 'we dance'
impa 'eat'	ilimpa / kilimpa 'we eat'
loshka 'tell a lie'	iiloshka / kiiloshka 'we tell a lie'
oochi 'kindle'	iloochi / kiloochi 'we kindle it'
<u>o</u>loshka 'tell a lie about'	il<u>o</u>loshka / kil<u>o</u>loshka 'we tell a lie about him'
paska 'make bread'	iipaska / kiipaska 'we make bread'

Analyze the sentences into morphemes; then answer the following questions:

(a) What do these sentences suggest about the way a third-person singular object is indicated in Chickasaw?

(b) What are the allomorphs (the different forms) of the first-person plural prefix in Chickasaw?

(c) The allomorphs of the first-person plural prefix illustrate both free and conditioned variation. Explain which allomorphs are in free variation. Then tell which allomorphs illustrate conditioned variation, and explain the conditioning factor.

Here are the sentences segmented into morphemes:

afama	'meet'
il-afama / kil-afama	'we meet him'
bashli	'cut'
ii-bashli / kii-bashli	'we cut it'
hilha	'dance'
ii-hilha / kii-hilha	'we dance'
impa	'eat'
il-impa / kil-impa	'we eat'
loshka	'tell a lie'
ii-loshka / kii-loshka	'we tell a lie'
oochi	'kindle'
il-oochi / kil-oochi	'we kindle it'
o̲-loshka	'tell a lie about'
il-o̲-loshka / kil-o̲-loshka	'we tell a lie about him'
paska	'make bread'
ii-paska / kii-paska	'we make bread'

(a) The data suggest that there is no morpheme to indicate a third-person singular object in Chickasaw. (However, the prefix *o̲-* appears to mean 'about him'.)

(b) There are four allomorphs of the first-person plural prefix: *ii-*, *kii-*, *il-*, and *kil-*.

(c) The allomorphs beginning with *k* are in free variation with the corresponding allomorphs without *k*. The data suggest that any time *il-* is used, the speaker may choose to replace this morpheme with *kil-*, and that any time *kii-* is used, it could be replaced with *ii-*, for example.

   The allomorphs *ii-* / *kii-* and *il-* / *kil-* illustrate conditioned variation. The allomorphs ending in *l* are used before vowels, while the allomorphs ending in *ii* are used before consonants.

Substitute a blank into sentences (28) and (29), p. 49 of textbook, to create subject and non-subject frames, similar to those in (4–9), pp. 31–2 of textbook. Most English noun phrases work like *Bianca* in these frames: they look the same whether they are subjects or non-subjects. What other English words can you find that work like *I* and *me*?

Subject (nominative) frame:

_____ promised to inquire carefully about a schoolmaster for the fair Bianca.

Object (accusative) frame:

The fair Bianca promised to inquire carefully about a schoolmaster for
_____.

For most English data, we could generalize these somewhat complex frames
as follows:

SUBJECT VERB OBJECT
SUBJECT VERB OBJECT.

   Here are some other words that have separate forms for subject and object:

subject (nominative) words: I, he, she, we, they
object (accusative) words: me, him, her, us, them

Some speakers make a similar distinction between (nominative) *who* and
(accusative) *whom*, but many speakers do not follow this one most of the
time.

**EXERCISE
2.12**

Consider the following verbs from Lakhota, a Siouan language spoken in
South Dakota:

Pajája.	'He washed him.'
Wapájaja.	'I washed him.'
Yapájaja.	'You washed him.'
Mapájaja.	'He washed me.'
Nipájaja.	'He washed you.'

(a)   Find one lexical and four grammatical morphemes in the Lakhota
      sentences above. What are they, and what do they mean?
(b)   How are third-person singular subjects and objects marked in Lakhota?
      Consider these additional Lakhota sentences:

Mayápajaja.	'You washed me.'
Chipájaja.	'I washed you.'

(c)   The first sentence contains three morphemes, as expected according
      to the analysis you developed in (a) above (discuss the analysis of this
      sentence). The other, however, contains a portmanteau morpheme.
      Identify the portmanteau morpheme, explain its meaning, and tell what
      sentence you would have expected instead of the one containing the
      portmenteau.
(d)   Can you tell what the rule is for where the accent mark is placed in
      Lakhota, according to these examples?

(a)   The lexical morpheme is *pajája / pájaja*, 'washed'.
The grammatical morphemes are *wa-*, 'I', *ya-*, 'you', *ma-*, 'me', *ni-*,
'you (object)'.

(b)   According to the data, there is no morpheme to mark third-person
singular subjects and objects.

(c)   *Ma-yá-pajaja*, 'You washed me', has a morpheme for subject and a
morpheme for object, following the list in (a).
   Chi-pájaja, 'I washed you', however, does not. *Chi-* is a portmanteau
morpheme meaning 'I' subject + 'you' object.
   According to what is given in (a), and following the order of
morphemes suggested by *Mayápajaja*, we would expect 'I washed you'
to be *Wa-ní-pajaja*.

(d)   The examples suggest that the second vowel in a Lakhota word will
be accented.

Irregular forms can often be analyzed as portmanteau morphemes. Consider
the underlined words in the following English sentences, each of which
might be considered a portmanteau. Describe the different morphemes that
contribute to the meaning of each word, and the form you would expect
the word to take if it was regular.

Take Antony Octavia to his wife, whose beauty claims no <u>worse</u> a husband
than the <u>best</u> of men.   (*Antony and Cleopatra*, II, ii, 136–7)

In Aleppo once, where a Turk <u>beat</u> a Venetian, I smote him thus.
                              (shortened from *Othello*, V, ii, 354ff)

The fault, dear Brutus, is not in <u>our</u> stars.   (*Julius Caesar*, I, ii, 134)

Mice and rats and such small <u>deer</u> have been Tom's food.
                              (*King Lear*, III, iv, 142)

Take Antony Octavia to his wife, whose beauty claims no <u>worse</u> a husband
than the <u>best</u> of men.   (*Antony and Cleopatra*, II, ii, 136–7)

worse – this contains comparative *-er* plus *bad*; the expected form would be
badder.
best – this contains superlative *-est* plus *good*; the expected form would be
goodest.

In Aleppo once, where a Turk <u>beat</u> a Venetian, I smote him thus.
                              (shortened from *Othello*, V, ii, 354ff)

beat – this contains past *-ed* plus *beat*; the expected form would be *beated*.

The fault, dear Brutus, is not in <u>our</u> stars.   (*Julius Caesar*, I, ii, 134)

our – this contains either *we* or *us* plus possessive *'s*, apparently, so the expected form might be something like *we's* or *us's*.

Mice and rats and such small <u>deer</u> have been Tom's food.

(*King Lear*, III, iv, 142)

deer – This contains *deer* plus plural *-s*; the expected form would be *deers*.

EXERCISE 2.14

(a) If you can, show that the irregular forms in (30–31), pp. 51–2 of textbook, illustrate sub-regularities by finding an additional verb or noun that works similarly (or relatively similarly) to each of these cases if you can. You may have trouble with some of them.

(b) Find a list of fifty or more English verbs with irregular past tenses (like all but the first group of verbs in table 2.2, p. 31 of textbook) – one good place to look for such a list is in a bilingual dictionary, which may list them for the convenience of non-native speakers of English. Organize the verbs you find into groups of words that work similarly, and formulate a description of how their past tenses are derived. You may include verbs that have been discussed so far in the chapter. (In organizing your results, it is probably best to focus on similarities of pronunciation rather than spelling.)

EXERCISE 2.14 ANSWERS

These answers will vary from student to student, though there are not too many possibilities for most of (a).

(a) (30)

sing —— sang, ring —— rang: additional verb spring —— sprang. Some speakers may also use wring —— wrang. Somewhat similar are verbs like sink —— sank, drink —— drank.
tell —— told, sell —— sold. There do not seem to be any additional verbs like this.
swear —— swore, wear —— wore: additional verbs bear —— bore, tear —— tore.
(31)
mouse —— mice, louse —— lice. There do not seem to be any additional nouns like this (but for spouse —— spice, see Sidebar 2.7, p. 66 of textbook).

alumnus —— alumni, locus —— loci: additional nouns focus ——
foci, tumulus —— tumuli. (Nouns following this singular–plural paradigm are all borrowed into English from Latin.)
sheep —— sheep, fish —— fish; additional nouns deer —— deer, elk
—— elk, and various other animal names.

(b)   Groups of verbs loosely organized according to the way the past
tense is formed (based on American English pronunciations).

1.   Some verbs do not change at all in the past tense:
hit —— hit, hurt —— hurt, put —— put, beat —— beat

2.   Many irregular verbs do not add anything, but only change the pronunciation of the (last) vowel of the verb. There are many different
possible types of changes, which are organized below on the basis of
the sound of the vowel in both forms of the verb:
run —— ran
find —— found
sit —— sat, begin —— began
know —— knew, blow —— blew, grow —— grew
sing —— sang, ring —— rang, spring —— sprang
write —— wrote, rise —— rose, drive —— drove
swear —— swore, wear —— wore, tear —— tore, bear —— bore
wake —— woke, break —— broke
come —— came
fall —— fell
hold —— held
fly —— flew
choose —— chose
cling —— clung, swing —— swung, wring —— wrang (for those who
don't use wring)
dig —— dug
meet —— met
drink —— drank, sink —— sank
eat —— ate
fight —— fought

3.   Some verbs seem to add what sounds somewhat like the regular past
suffix *-ed* (or a similar *t* sound), but also change the pronunciation of
the verb's vowel:
tell —— told, sell —— sold
say —— said, lay —— led
buy —— bought
creep —— crept, dream —— dreamt, keep —— kept
do —— did
hear —— heard

4. Some verbs add something like -*ed* (as in (3) above), but also make a more drastic change in the pronunciation of the preceding verb:
    teach —— taught
    bring —— brought
    catch —— caught
    have —— had
5. Other verbs seem to have totally irregular past tense forms:
    be —— were

EXERCISE 2.15

Although some of the SLQ Zapotec verb forms in (34), p. 53 of textbook, illustrate partial and full suppletion in their roots, the distribution of habitual and imperative prefixes follows rules. Consider the examples in (34) and the additional examples below:

ràann 'looks'	gwàann 'look!'
ra'uh 'eats'	bda'uh 'eat!'
rcwààa'ah 'throws'	bcwààa'ah 'throw!'
rde's 'lifts'	bde's 'lift!'
rgùùu'b 'sucks'	bdùùu'b 'suck!'
rgùunny 'scratches'	blùunny 'scratch!'
rihah 'goes'	gweheh 'go!'
rzah 'walks'	bzah 'walk!'

Given only a habitual verb (from the first column) or an imperative verb (from the second column), it is not possible to predict if the other will have a suppletive root or not. However, the allomorph of the imperative prefix (*b*- or *gw*-) which will be used for a given verb is predictable from another part of the data. Segment the prefixes from the habitual and imperative forms above, look at the roots of these verbs (minus the *r*-, *b*-, and *gw*- prefixes), and find the generalization that explains which roots use the imperative allomorph *b*- and which use the imperative allomorph *gw*-.

EXERCISE 2.15 ANSWERS

Here are the verbs in (34), p. 53 of textbook, and the exercise with morpheme boundaries inserted:

r-zhihby 'gets scared'	b-zhihby! 'get scared!'
r-àa'izy 'hits'	gw-àa'izy! 'hit!'
r-a'ihsy 'sleeps'	b-ta'ihsy! 'sleep!'
r-e'ihpy 'tells'	gw-u'ahts! 'tell!'
r-àann 'looks'	gw-àann 'look!'
r-a'uh 'eats'	bda'uh 'eat!'
r-cwààa'ah 'throws'	b-cwààa'ah 'throw!'
r-de's 'lifts'	b-de's 'lift!'

r-gùùu'b 'sucks'   b-dùùu'b 'suck!'
r-gùunny 'scratches'   b-lùunny 'scratch!'
r-ihah 'goes'   gw-eheh 'go!'
r-zah 'walks'   b-zah 'walk!'

Consider the part of the verb following the prefix *r-* as the stem. If the stem begins with a vowel, the imperative prefix will be *gw-*. If the stem begins with a consonant, the imperative prefix will be *b-*. Note that when there is a suppletive stem in the imperative, it is the form of that stem rather than the habitual stem that determines the form of the prefix. ('Sleep' and 'eat', for example, have stems that start with vowels in the habitual but stems that start with consonants in the imperative; they use the imperative prefix *b-*.)

Draw trees to illustrate the structure of the following English words, labeling as many nodes in the trees as you can. If there are two possible ways to draw a tree, show the alternative trees and present an argument in favor of the one you choose, explaining why the constituency within the tree must be as you have represented it.

EXERCISE 2.16

greener, kissed, driver, buildings, cowardly, unkindness, replays, anti-Trotskyite.

---

greener

kissed

driver

EXERCISE 2.16 ANSWERS

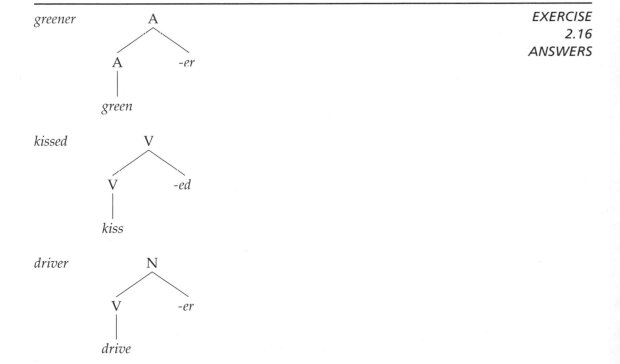

buildings

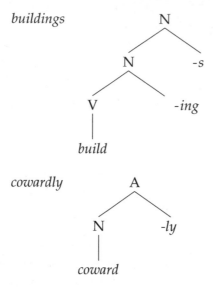

cowardly

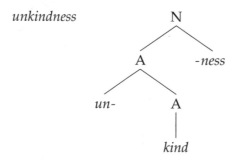

(*coward* is probably related to the verb *cow*, but this doesn't seem like a relationship reflecting current morphology.)

unkindness

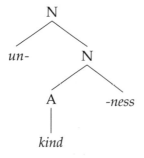

The discussion of trees (41) and (41'), p. 56 of textbook, explains why we would not want to propose the alternative tree:

Although this tree correctly reflects the derivation of *kindness*, it incorrectly shows that the prefix *un-* can attach to a noun.

replays

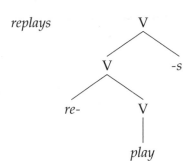

This tree is preferred to the following one, because derivational affixes like *re-* attach to words before inflectional affixes like *-s*:

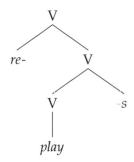

anti-Trotskyite. There seem to be two possible trees, reflecting an ambiguity of interpretation of the word. The usual interpretation of *anti-Trotskyite* is 'person who is opposed to a follower of Trotsky'; the tree for this interpretation is:

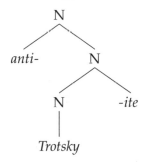

An alternative possible interpretation is 'follower of (an) opponent of Trotsky'; the tree for this interpretation is:

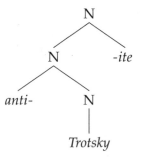

EXERCISE 2.17	Give labeled bracketings equivalent to the correct trees you drew for Exercise 2.16.

EXERCISE 2.17 ANSWERS		
	greener	[$_A$ [$_A$ *green*] *-er*]
	kissed	[$_V$ [$_V$ *kiss*] *-ed*
	driver	[$_N$ [$_V$ *drive*] *-er*]
	buildings	[$_N$ [$_N$ [$_V$ *build*] *-ing*] *-s*]
	cowardly	[$_A$ [$_N$ *coward*] *-ly*]
	unkindness	[$_N$ [$_A$ *un-* [$_A$ *kind*]] *-ness*]
	replays	[$_V$ [$_V$ *re-* [$_V$ *play*]] *-s*]
	anti-Trotskyite	[$_N$ *anti-* [$_N$ [$_N$ *Trotsky*] *-ite*]]
	or	[$_N$ [$_N$ *anti-* [$_N$ *Trotsky*]] *-ite*]

EXERCISE 2.18	Consider the following Tagalog verbs, which may occur in three forms, depending on which sentence role is 'focused' or emphasized, and answer the questions that follow. Each verb can be used in sentences with three nouns, such as 'The man brings rice to a woman'. AF (actor focus) verb forms are used when the actor (roughly, the subject) is focused; OF (object focus) verb forms have a focused object; and in DF (directional focus) verb forms the third noun is focused. In the example above, 'the man' is the actor, 'rice' is the object, and 'a woman' is the directional.

	AF	OF	DF
'accuse of'	magbintang	ibintang	pagbintangan
'base on'	magbatay	ibatay	pagbatayan
'borrow from'	humiram	hiramin	hiraman
'bring out of'	mag'alis	'alisin	'alisan
'bring to'	mag'akyat	i'akyat	'akyatan
'entrust with'	magbilin	ibilin	pagbilinan
'give to'	magbigay	ibigay	bigayan
'hand to'	mag'abot	i'abot	'abutan
'offer to'	mag'alok	i'alok	'alukin
'scrape from'	magkuskos	kuskusin	kuskusan
'sing to'	umawit	awitin	awitan
'throw at'	magbalibag	ibalibag	balibagin
'throw at'	magpukol	ipukol	pukulin
'write to'	sumulat	isulat	sulatan

(a)   What morphemes may indicate AF, OF, and DF? (Don't try to find a semantic (meaning) explanation of why one verb uses one, and another another.) Classify each as a prefix, suffix, or infix. (You may also be able to use the term **circumfix**, meaning an affix that surrounds a root.) One of the morphemes appears to be used in two different ways with different verbs.

(b)   What is the root of each verb? (For four verbs, the root has two alternating forms. List both of these.)

(c)   The variation in these alternating roots is conditioned, based on the overall distribution of sounds in these Tagalog verbs. Propose an explanation which accounts for the variation you observe. (There are several possible explanations based on the data presented above.)

(d)   What is the explanation for the two different uses of the affix *um* that you discovered in (a)?

EXERCISE
2.18
ANSWERS

(a)   AF – *mag-* (prefix), *-um-* (infix) / *um-* (prefix)
OF – *i-* (prefix), *-in* (suffix)
DF – *pag-* . . . *-an* (circumfix), *-an* (suffix)

(b)   'accuse of' bintang
'base on' batay
'borrow from' hiram
'bring out of' 'alis
'bring to' 'akyat
'entrust with' bilin
'give to' bigay
'hand to' 'abot / 'abut
'offer to' 'alok / 'aluk
'scrape from' kuskos / kuskus
'sing to' awit
'throw at' balibag
'throw at' pukol / pukul
'write to' sulat

(c)   In the four alternating roots, the last vowel is *o* when it is the last vowel in the root and *u* when it is not the last vowel. On the basis of the data presented, we could assume that the basic form of each verb has *o* for the last vowel, and that this *o* changes to *u* when something is affixed after the root. Another possibility would be to assume that the verbs have *u* as their last vowel, but that this *u* changes to *o* when no affix is added.

(d)   *Um* is used as an infix when it is added to a verb beginning with a consonant, like those in the text and most of those above. *Um-* seems to function as a prefix when added to a verb with no initial consonant, like 'sing to'.

	BASIC VERBS	INTENSIVE VERBS

EXERCISE 2.19

Below are some more Tagalog verbs. The verbs in the first column have derived reduplicated intensive verbs (translated with 'repeatedly' or 'thoroughly') in the second column.

	BASIC VERBS	INTENSIVE VERBS
'become kind'	buma'it	magpakaba'itba'it
'become rich'	yumaman	magpakayamanyaman
'cook'	magluto	magluluto
'cry'	'umiyak	mag'i'iyak
'get hungry'	maggutom	magpakagutumgutom
'get quiet'	magtahimik	magpakatahitahimik
'open'	buksan	pagbubuksan
'throw'	'itapon	'ipagtatapon
'travel'	maglakbay	maglalakbay
'walk'	lumakad	maglalakad

(a)   Segment the verbs above. (Many of the morphemes they contain are familiar from the text and Exercise 2.18. You also may observe the conditioned variation you identified in Exercise 2.18.) Identify each morpheme as a root, prefix, infix, suffix, or as a reduplicated element.

(b)   What part of the basic verb gets reduplicated? Illustrate the different possibilities with examples.

(c)   Two different types of reduplication are used in the derived verbs. Explain how these differ morphologically (in terms of how the reduplication processes operate). What differences, if any, can you see between the verbs in the two groups?

(d)   Now, go back to the grammatical morphemes you segmented in (a). Which of these elements are associated with basic verbs, and which with derived intensive verbs? Is the presence of any affix associated with the difference in reduplication type? What signals the intensive meaning in the derived verbs – reduplication or some other element? Explain your answer.

EXERCISE 2.19 ANSWERS

(a)   The morphemes in the segmented verbs are identified as root, prefix, infix, suffix, or reduplicated element (redup). Perhaps arbitrarily, all the reduplicated elements are assumed to occur before their roots. The analysis of the suffix is discussed below:

	BASIC VERBS	INTENSIVE VERBS
'become kind'	b,um,a'it	mag-paka-ba'it-ba'it
	root,infix,root	prefix-prefix-redup-root
'become rich'	y,um,aman	mag-paka-yaman-yaman
	root,infix,root	prefix-prefix-redup-root
'cook'	mag-luto	mag-lu-luto
	prefix-root	prefix-redup-root
'cry'	',um,iyak	mag-'i-'iyak
	root,infix,root	prefix-redup-root
'get hungry'	mag-gutom	mag-paka-gutum-gutom
	prefix-root	prefix-prefix-redup-root
'get quiet'	mag-tahi-mik	mag-paka-tahi-tahi-mik
	prefix-root-suffix	prefix-prefix-redup-root-suffix
'open'	buksan	pag-bu-buksan
	root	prefix-redup-root
'throw'	'i-tapon	'i-pag-ta-tapon
	prefix-root	prefix-prefix-redup-root
'travel'	mag-lakbay	mag-la-lakbay
	prefix-root	prefix-redup-root
'walk'	l,um,akad	mag-la-lakad
	root,infix,root	prefix-redup-root

(b)   In some verbs (e.g. *magpakaba'itba'it*) the whole root is reduplicated. In others (e.g. *magluluto*) only the first consonant and vowel of the root are reduplicated.

   The exception to this statement is *magpakatahitahimik*, in which it appears at first that the root is *tahimik*. If this is so, the first two consonant–vowel sequences are reduplicated, but not the whole root. One way to account for this is to assume that *-mik* is a suffix, and that suffixes are not reduplicated.

(c)   Here are the verbs organized according to these two different types of reduplication.

   1.   Whole root reduplication (whole root is reduplicated):

'become kind'	b,um,a'it	mag-paka-ba'it-ba'it
	root,infix,root	prefix-prefix-redup-root
'become rich'	y,um,aman	mag-paka-yaman-yaman
	root,infix,root	prefix-prefix-redup-root
'get hungry'	mag-gutom	mag-paka-gutum-gutom
	prefix-root	prefix-prefix-redup-root
'get quiet'	mag-tahi-mik	mag-paka-tahi-tahi-mik
	prefix-root-suffix	prefix-prefix-redup-root-suffix

   2.   Consonant–vowel reduplication (only the first consonant and vowel of the root are reduplicated):

'cook'	mag-luto	mag-lu-luto
	prefix-root	prefix-redup-root
'cry'	',um,iyak	mag-'i-'iyak
	root,infix,root	prefix-redup-root
'open'	buksan	pag-bu-buksan
	root	prefix-redup-root
'throw'	'i-tapon	'i-pag-ta-tapon
	prefix-root	prefix-prefix-redup-root
'travel'	mag-lakbay	mag-la-lakbay
	prefix-root	prefix-redup-root
'walk'	l,um,akad	mag-la-lakad
	root,infix,root	prefix-redup-root

There seem to be few differences between the roots in the two groups. Both groups can include roots of the form CVCV (consonant–vowel–consonant–vowel) and CVCVC (consonant–vowel–consonant–vowel–consonant). However, longer roots, such as *buksan* and *lakbay*, occur only in the second group. (But note that *tahi-mik*, the suffixed root in the first group, is also longer than usual.)

(d)   *Um* and the lack of any affix (as in *buksan*) are associated with basic verbs.

Mag- and *'i-* are associated with both basic and derived verbs.

Paka- and *pag-* are associated only with derived verbs.

The whole verb reduplication (type 1) seems to occur only in the presence of the prefix *paka-*.

However, we cannot say that the intensive meaning is associated only with prefixes like *paka-* or *pag-*, since several verbs do not have one of these prefixes in the derived form (e.g. *mag'i'iyak*, *maglalakad*). It must be the reduplication itself which signals the intensive meaning, at least in the consonant–vowel reduplications (type 2). (It is possible that the prefix *paka-* is also associated with intensive meaning, since that prefix always occurs along with type 1 reduplication.)

EXERCISE 2.20   (49), p. 65 of textbook, presents four different types of English ablauted past tense verb forms – words in which the only morphological indication of the meaning change is a change in the stressed vowel of the word. Find at least five additional different types of past tense ablaut, classified according to the change in the verb's vowel. (You may have already identified these in your answer to Exercise 2.14.) Then try to find several more examples of each type of change you've identified. (This may not be possible for every example.) For each type of change that you discover, try to find a verb that sounds similar but forms its past form regularly (comparable to the noun plurals in (52), versus those in (50), both p. 65 of textbook).

Examples in (49), p. 65 of textbook:	Additional examples:	*EXERCISE 2.20 ANSWERS*

swear —— swore   wear —— wore, tear —— tore, bear —— bore

see —— saw

run —— ran

fight —— fought   find —— found, wind —— wound, grind —— ground

Additional examples (based on American English pronunciation):

sit —— sat   begin —— began

know —— knew   blow —— blew, throw —— threw, grow —— grew

write —— wrote   rise —— rose, drive —— drove

wake —— woke   break —— broke

speak —— spoke   weave —— wove, freeze —— froze

Verbs with regular past tenses like those above:

swear type: bare —— bared

see type: free —— freed

run type: gun —— gunned

fight type: blight —— blighted

sit type: knit —— knitted

know type: sow —— sowed

write type: knight —— knighted (or blight —— blighted above)

wake type: bake —— baked

speak type: reek —— reeked

(*Note*: although all the words in this list have regular past tenses, they are not all completely regular verbs: some of them have irregular past participles at least for some speakers (e.g. sow —— sown).)

Consider the following English N–N–N compounds and compound phrases. Some of them would typically receive only one of their logically possible interpretations, while others could be interpreted in more than one way. For all those with more than one plausible interpretation, give all these structures, and explain (with a paraphrase) what each means. For those which have only one sensible interpretation, give that structure, and then explain what any interpretation or interpretations that you did not represent would mean. Describe any difficulties you encounter. **EXERCISE 2.21**

apartment plumbing contractor, art appreciation course, baby buggy bumper, ballpoint pen, hair care product, Korean English dictionary, linguistics department secretary, metal filing cabinet, mother seagull, rubber ducky lover, Shakespeare sonnet meter, World Trade Center.

apartment plumbing contractor
Both of the following seem plausible:

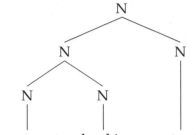

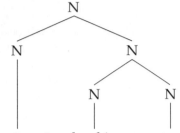

apartment   plumbing   contractor   apartment   plumbing   contractor
(contractor for apartment plumbing)   (plumbing contractor for apartments)

art appreciation course
Both of the following seem possible, but the first is probably more likely:

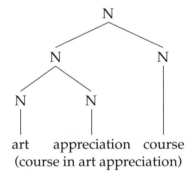

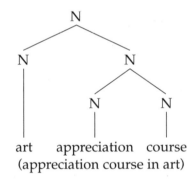

art   appreciation   course   art   appreciation   course
(course in art appreciation)   (appreciation course in art)

baby buggy bumper
Both of the following are possible, but the first is probably the likely
interpretation:

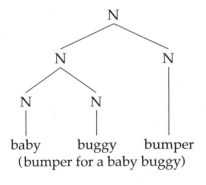

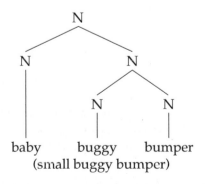

baby   buggy   bumper   baby   buggy   bumper
(bumper for a baby buggy)   (small buggy bumper)

ballpoint pen
Only the interpretation below seems likely:

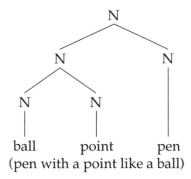

(pen with a point like a ball)

The alternative interpretation would mean something like 'pointed pen with a ball' (?).

The spelling of the compound *ballpoint* is a clue here.

hair care product
Only the interpretation below seems likely:

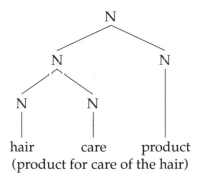

(product for care of the hair)

The alternative interpretation would be something like 'product for caring applied to hair'.

Korean English dictionary
Both of the following structures are plausible:

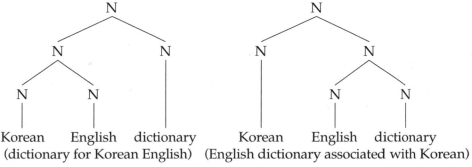

(dictionary for Korean English)   (English dictionary associated with Korean)

The first structure refers to a dictionary of English as used by Koreans (*Korean English*). The second could refer to a dictionary of English with definitions in Korean, or a dictionary of English published for Koreans.

A problem here is that *Korean* is both a noun ('person from Korea', 'language of Korea') and an adjective ('associated with Korea'). Similarly, *English* is both a noun ('language of England, the United States, etc.') and an adjective ('associated with England'). Since the structures above are identified as N–N–N compounds, we should rule out any interpretation in which *Korean* or *English* is an adjective.

linguistics department secretary
In principle, perhaps both interpretations below are possible, but the first seems more likely:

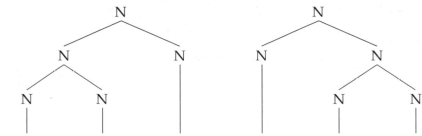

linguistics department   secretary   linguistics department   secretary
(secretary of the linguistics deparment)   (department secretary for linguistics)

metal filing cabinet
While both interpretations below might be possible, only the second seems likely:

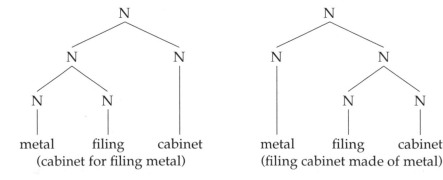

metal   filing   cabinet   metal   filing   cabinet
(cabinet for filing metal)   (filing cabinet made of metal)

mother seagull
Only the following interpretation is plausible:

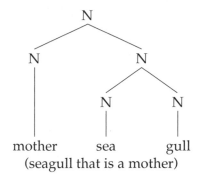

(seagull that is a mother)

The alternative interpretation would be something like 'gull associated with the mother sea'. As with *ballpoint pen*, the spelling of the compound *seagull* is a clue to the standard interpretation (in this case with a different structure).

rubber ducky lover
Either interpretation below is possible, but given the popularity of the phrase *rubber ducky* (as in *Ernie loves rubber duckies*), the first structure presents a more likely interpretation:

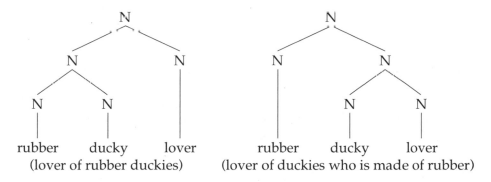

(lover of rubber duckies)   (lover of duckies who is made of rubber)

Shakespeare sonnet meter
Both interpretations seem almost equally likely.

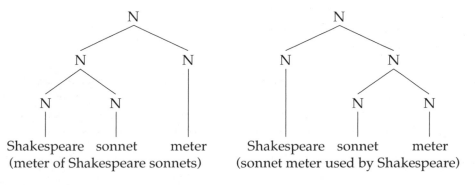

(meter of Shakespeare sonnets)   (sonnet meter used by Shakespeare)

(This assumes that *meter* refers to the prosodic form of the sonnet. If *meter* is assumed to refer to a device for measuring, additional interpretations are possible, though less likely.)

World Trade Center
Both interpretations below seem possible:

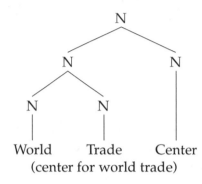

(center for world trade)

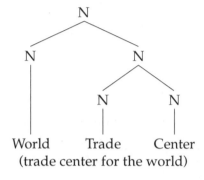

(trade center for the world)

EXERCISE 2.22

As noted on pp. 69–73 of the textbook, English contractions like *'s* (for *is* or *has*) are clitics, just as genitive *'s* is. How many other English contractions can you think of? Choose one of them and construct examples like those in Sidebar 2.10, pp. 72–3 of textbook, to show that it may follow words of different lexical classes.

EXERCISE 2.22 ANSWERS

Other contractions: *'ll* (for *will*), *'d* (for *had* or *would*), *'ve* (for *have*), *'re* (for *are* or *were*), *n't* (for *not*).

It is not equally easy to construct examples to show that all of these are clitics. (In particular, this is difficult with *n't*.) But for most of them, examples just like those in Sidebar 2.9, p. 71 of textbook, are possible in casual speech.

For example, *'ll* can follow:

- pronouns (*He'll go there tomorrow*)
- nouns (*The king'll go there tomorrow*)
- prepositions (*The king we spoke of'll go there tomorrow*)
- verbs (*The king who abdicated'll go there tomorrow*)
- adverbs (*The king who sings slowly'll go there tomorrow*)

In each of these cases, *'ll* follows the end of a complete subject phrase, no matter what the class of its last word. Words that generally don't come at the end of a noun phrase, such as determiners, are harder to construct examples with, but even these might be possible in contrived contexts, such as:

The king who wrote the word the'll go there tomorrow.

Consider the following Tolkapaya and Chickasaw imperative sentences, using verbs you have seen earlier in this chapter of the textbook.

EXERCISE 2.23

Tolkapaya	*Mchthúli!*	'Wash it!'
	Mvyámi!	'Run!'
	Mthíi!	'Drink it!'
Chickasaw	*Isso!*	'Hit it!'
	Afama!	'Meet him!'
	Hilha!	'Dance!'

First, analyze these sentences into morphemes, with a complete gloss for each sentence (if necessary, review the Tolkapaya and Chickasaw data presented earlier in the textbook).

(a) See if you can construct an additional argument concerning the question of whether these languages have third-person zero subject prefixes, based on this data.

(b) Given the 'want' sentences and the imperatives that you have seen, which language, Tolkapaya or Chickasaw, is more like English? Explain why.

Morphological analysis:

EXERCISE 2.23 ANSWERS

Tolkapaya	*M-chthúl-i!*	'Wash it!'
	2-wash-abs	
	M-vyám-i!	'Run!'
	2-run-abs	
	M-thíi!	'Drink it!'
	2-drink	

(See Exercise 2.9 and the accompanying text in the textbook for the analysis of absolutive (abs) -*i* and its form after a verb ending in a vowel.)

Chickasaw	*Isso!*	'Hit it!'
	hit	
	Afama!	'Meet him!'
	meet	
	Hilha!	'Dance!'
	dance	

(a) As the discussion of the 'want' sentences on pp. 77–8 of the textbook showed, Chickasaw sentences without subject markers are interpreted differently in different contexts. In Chickasaw, imperatives have no prefix, but (as with imperatives in many languages) they are interpreted to refer to actions to be performed by the person being addressed. Crucially, although the Chickasaw imperative verbs above have the same form as verbs with third-person subjects, in the context where imperatives would be used, they will not be interpreted as referring to third persons.

In contrast, the Tolkapaya verbs have second-person subject prefixes, because Tolkapaya verbs are always marked to indicate their subjects. The data presented in this chapter of the textbook show that a prefixless Tolkapaya verb is always interpreted as having a third-person subject. So if there was no prefix on these imperatives, they could not be interpreted as referring to actions to be performed by the person addressed.

The imperative data provide more support for the idea that Tolkapaya has zero third-person subject prefixes, but that Chickasaw does not.

(b) On the basis of the 'want' sentences and the imperatives, Chickasaw seems to be more like English than Tolkapaya. In Chickasaw, verbs used with 'want' and imperatives have no subject, but the rules of the language tell us what the intended subject of these verbs is. Thus, in English,

I want to dance

and Chickasaw

Hilha sa-banna

there is no subject with the verbs *dance* or *hilha*, but in each case we know that the subject must be 'I'. (In contrast, in Tolkapaya 'I want' sentences the verb used with 'want' must be marked for an 'I' subject.) Similarly, the imperatives

Dance!

and

Hilha!

do not have any subject indicated, but we know by the rules of the language that these imperatives have a 'you' subject. (In contrast, though, Tolkapaya imperatives like those above must have a 'you' subject indicated.)

Thus, English and Chickasaw share some types of rule for interpreting verbs without subjects that Tolkapaya does not have.

The parallelism between the order of subject, object, and verb morphemes in a complex word and the order of these elements in a sentence is not always as complete as in Chickasaw and SLQ Zapotec. For example, Tolkapaya has SOV word order, and Swahili has SVO word order. What order do the subject, object, and verb elements of polysynthetic words in these languages come in? (Look back at the templates you devised in Exercise 2.8.) Are these cases parallel?

**EXERCISE
2.24**

Neither Tolkapaya nor Swahili exhibits a parallelism between the order of subject, object, and verb morphemes in polysynthetic verbs and the order of these elements in independent sentences.

*EXERCISE
2.24
ANSWERS*

Tolkapaya sentences have SOV word order, but the order of these elements in polysynthetic verbs according to the template:

(*paa*) - (OBJECT) - (SUBJECT) - VERB - (*n*) - (*ch*) - TENSE

(Exercise 2.8) is OSV.

Swahili sentences have SVO word order, but the order of these elements in polysynthetic verbs according to the template:

SUBJECT - TENSE - (OBJECT) - VERB

(Exercise 2.8) is SOV.

Thus, there is not always a parallelism between the order of elements in polysynthetic words and independent sentences. (Explaining such apparent anomalies has been one of the important concerns of recent syntactic theory.)

· ·

Consider the following sentences from Shakespeare. Segment each one into morphemes, and then identify each morpheme as a prefix, suffix, clitic, or root and as a grammatical or lexical morpheme. Underline each root (independent word) that you would consider a grammatical morpheme. Identify each grammatical prefix or suffix as inflectional or derivational, give another word containing the same morpheme, and do your best to identify the meaning of the morpheme. Discuss each word with an irregular pronunciation and each clitic that you identify. Note any compounds. Tell what (expected) component morphemes you would expect to find in any morphemes you can identify as portmanteau.

**EXERCISE
2.25**

They have been at a great feast of languages, and stolen the scraps.
(*Love's Labour's Lost*, V, i, 39)

All the world's a stage, and all the men and women merely players.
(*As You Like It*, II, vii, 139)

As the old hermit of Prague, that never saw pen and ink, very wittily said
to a niece of King Gorboduc, 'That that is, is.'

(Twelfth Night, IV, ii, 14)

How silver-sweet sound lovers' tongues by night, Like softest music to
attending ears!   *(Romeo and Juliet*, II, ii, 165)

I have done a thousand dreadful things, As willingly as one would kill
a fly.   *(Titus Andronicus*, V, i, 141)

Kindness in women, not their beauteous looks, Shall win my love.

(The Taming of the Shrew, IV, ii, 41)

Let's choose executors and talk of wills.   *(Richard II*, III, ii, 144)

Love, first learned in a lady's eyes, Lives not alone immured in the brain.

(Love's Labour's Lost, IV, iii, 327)

EXERCISE
2.25
ANSWERS

There might be some disagreement about some of these identifications!
And many answers will vary:

They have bee-n at a great feast of language-s,
root root root-suffix root root root root root root-suffix
and stol-en the scrap-s.
root root-suffix root root-suffix
been, stolen: *-en, -n* (inflectional) forms past participles from 'irregular' verbs:
see-n
languages, scraps: *-s* (inflectional) forms plural nouns from singular nouns:
house-s

The auxiliary *have* (used in the present perfect *have been, (have) stolen*)
and other auxiliaries are considered grammatical morphemes in this
exercise.

All the world-'s a stage, and all the men and women mere-ly play-er-s.
root root root-clitic root root root root root root root-suffix root-suffix-
suffix
merely: *-ly* (derivational) forms adverbs from adjectives: *slow-ly*
players: *-er* (derivational) forms nouns from verbs: *sing-er*
players: *-s* (as above, *languages*)
world's: The clitic *'s* is a form of *is*.

Men is a portmanteau of *man* + plural: expected *mans*.
Women is a portmanteau of *woman* + plural: expected *womans*.

As the old hermit of Prague, that never saw pen and ink, very witt-i-ly
root root root root root root root root root root root root root root-suffix-
suffix
sai-d to a niece of King Gorboduc, 'That that is, is.'
root-suffix root root root root root root root root root root
wittily: *-y* (*-i*) (derivational) forms adjectives from nouns: *sleep-y*
wittily: *-ly* (as above, *merely*)
said: *-ed* (*-d*) (inflectional) forms past tense of verbs: *kiss-ed* (Note that
sai-d is irregular: we would expect this word to be pronounced like
play-ed.)

Saw is a portmanteau of *see* + past: expected *seed*.

How silver-sweet sound lov-er-s-' tongue-s by night,
root root-root root root-suffix-suffix-clitic root-suffix root root
Like soft-est music to attend-ing ear-s!
root root-suffix root root root-suffix root-suffix
lovers': *-er* (as above, *player*)
lovers', tongues, ears: *-s* (as above, *languages*)
softest: *-est* (inflectional) forms superlatives of adjectives: *old-est*
attending: *-ing* (inflectional) forms present participles from verbs: *play-ing*
(here, *attending* is used as an adjective)
lovers': The clitic ' (standing for *'s*; no *'s* is pronounced in *lovers'*) is the
genitive clitic.

Silver-sweet is a compound.
Attend can also be segmented; although *tend* is a regular English word, the
meaning of *at-* is hard to generalize without more extensive study.

I have do-ne a thousand dread-ful thing-s
root root root-suffix root root root-suffix root-suffix
As will-ing-ly as one woul-d kill a fly.
root root-suffix-suffix root root root-suffix root root root
done: *-ne* – same as *-en* (as above, *been*) (Note that *done* is not pronounced as
expected; we would expect this word to be pronounced like *dune*.)
dreadful: *-ful* (derivational) forms adjectives from nouns: *wonder-ful*
things: *-s* (as above, *languages*)
willingly: *-ing* (as above, *attending*)
willingly: *-ly* (as above, *merely*)

would: -*ed* (as above, *said*) (Note that *would* is not pronounced as expected: we would expect *will-ed*.) *Would* is (originally) a past form of *will*, though not all speakers would see this as a regular grammatical relationship.

Kind-ness <u>in</u> women, <u>not</u> <u>their</u> beaute-ous look-s, <u>Shall</u> win <u>my</u> love.
root-suffix root root root root root-suffix root-suffix root root root root
kindness: -*ness* forms nouns from adjectives: *good-ness*
beauteous: -*ous* forms adjectives from nouns: *victori-ous*
looks: -*s* (as above, *languages*)
women: (portmanteau, see above)

Their is a portmanteau for *they* + '*s*; we would expect *they's* (?).
My is a portmanteau for *I* + '*s*; we would expect *I's*.
Shall is a modal, and as such is considered a grammatical morpheme here. Some analysts might want to segment *beauty* as *beau-ty*, but the connection with *beau* doesn't seem fully clear.

Let-'s choose execut-or-s <u>and</u> talk <u>of</u> will-s.
root-clitic root root-suffix-suffix root root root root-suffix
executors: -*or* (same as -*er*, above, *player*)
executors, wills: -*s* (as above, *languages*)
Let's: '*s* is a clitic form of *us*.

Love, first learn-ed <u>in</u> a lady-'s eye-s, live-s *not* a-lone
root root root-suffix root root root-clitic root-suffix root-suffix root
prefix-root
immur-ed <u>in</u> *the* brain.
root-suffix root root root
learned, immured: -*ed* (inflectional) forms past participles of 'regular' verbs (when these are not formed with the allomorph -*en*, as above, *been*): *liv-ed*
lady's: '*s* (as above, *lovers'*)
eyes: -*s* (as above, *languages*)
lives: -*s* (inflectional) forms third-person singular present forms of verbs: *play-s*
alone: *a*- (derivational) forms adverbs and adjectives: *a-sleep*, *a-back*, *a-fire* (This is not a common prefix, and words formed with it have a number of odd distributional properties.)

(The *im*- of *immure* is also a derivational prefix. But since -*mure* (related to words meaning 'wall') is not an English root, we don't consider *im-mure* to be segmentable here.)

. . . .

Unlike most of the languages illustrated in this chapter of the textbook, Spanish grammar identifies every noun phrase as either masculine or feminine.

EXERCISE 2.26

(a) Segment each word of each Spanish noun phrase below into morphemes, and identify the meaning (or function) of each morpheme by writing a gloss underneath each phrase. (You can regard 'some' as the plural of 'a'/'an'.) Remember that the number of morphemes, hyphens, and spaces in your segmented data and your gloss must match exactly.

el perro negro	'the black (male) dog'
el palo nuevo	'the new stick'
la casa blanca	'the white house'
las mesas negras	'the black tables'
las perras rojas	'the red (female) dogs'
los libros viejos	'the old books'
un libro nuevo	'an old book'
una mesa blanca	'a white table'
una perra vieja	'an old (female) dog'
unas casas rojas	'some red houses'
unos palos negros	'some black sticks'
unos perros blancos	'some white (male) dogs'

(b) The general pattern of masculine versus feminine morphemes is very regular, but there are irregularities. Discuss them.

(c) Notice that the order of adjectives and nouns differs between English and Spanish. Translate the following into Spanish: 'the red sticks', 'an old house', 'some white (female) dogs', 'the white book', 'a red (male) dog'.

Note: Lack of knowledge of Spanish is no disadvantage! If you speak Spanish, you will probably find this exercise easiest if you try to approach it as you would completely new data (perhaps from Swahili or Zapotec).

. . . .

(a) Abbreviations used: m = masculine, f = feminine, pl = plural. As explained in the chapter of the textbook, a period is used to separate elements of a portmanteau gloss.

EXERCISE 2.26 ANSWERS

el perr-o negr-o	'the black (male) dog'
the.m dog-m black-m	
el pal-o nuev-o	'the new stick'
the.m stick-m new-m	
l-a cas-a blanc-a	'the white house'
the-f house-f white-f	
l-a-s mes-a-s negr-a-s	'the black tables'
the-f-pl table-f-pl black-f-pl	
l-a-s perr-a-s roj-a-s	'the red (female) dogs'
the-f-pl dog-f-pl red-f-pl	
l-o-s libr-o-s viej-o-s	'the old books'
the-m-pl book-m-pl old-m-pl	
un libr-o nuev-o	'an old book'
a.m book-m new-m	
un-a mes-a blanc-a	'a white table'
a-f table-f white-f	
un-a perr-a viej-a	'an old (female) dog'
a-f dog-f old-f	
un-a-s cas-a-s roj-a-s	'some red houses'
a-f-pl house-f-pl red-f-pl	
un-o-s pal-o-s negr-o-s	'some black sticks'
a-m-pl stick-m-pl black-m-pl	
un-o-s perr-o-s blanc-o-s	'some white (male) dogs'
a-m-pl dog-m-pl white-m-pl	

(b) 1. The irregularities occur in the masculine singular articles: on the basis of the data, we would expect masculine singular 'the' to be *lo*, not *el*, and masculine singular 'a' to be *uno*, not *un*. (Readers familiar with Spanish know that *lo* and *uno* are used elsewhere in the language – but the point is that the non-occurrence of these morphemes in these data represents a slight irregularity in this otherwise very regular system.) *El* and *un* are portmanteaus.

2. Some analysts might question the segmentation of *pal-o*, *mes-a*, *libr-o*, and *cas-a*, since there are no parallel nouns *pal-a*, *mes-o*, *libr-a*, or *cas-o* in the data. But the evidence of *perr-o* / *perr-a* shows that even on nouns the *-a* and *-o* morphemes are functional.

(c) 'the red sticks': *los palos rojos*
'an old house': *una casa vieja*
'some white (female) dogs': *unas perras blancas*
'the white book': *el libro blanco*
'a red (male) dog': *un perro rojo*

· ·

Consider the following examples of Chickasaw verbs with and without   **EXERCISE**
'me', 'you', and 'us' objects, and then answer the questions that follow.   **2.27**

pisa 'see'   *sapisa* 'he sees me'
                           chipisa 'he sees you'
                           popisa 'he sees us'
ithána 'know'   *sathána* 'he knows me'
                           chithána 'he knows you'
                           pothána 'he knows us'
lohmi 'hide'   *salohmi* 'he hides me'
                           chilohmi 'he hides you'
                           polohmi 'he hides us'
afama 'meet'   *asafama* 'he meets me'
                           achifama 'he meets you'
                           apofama 'he meets us'
chokfiyammi 'tickle'   *sachokfiyammi* 'he tickles me'
                           chichokfiyammi 'he tickles you'
isso 'hit'   *chisso* 'he hits you'
                           posso 'he hits us'
anokfilli 'think about' *asanokfilli* 'he thinks about me'
                           aponokfilli 'he thinks about us'

(a) Segment each Chickasaw word by putting hyphens between the morphemes. (You may change your mind about some of the segmentations as you work through the problem.)

(b) What are the Chickasaw first-person singular and plural and second-person object affixes?

(c) What is the Chickasaw for 'he tickles us', 'he hits me', and 'he thinks about you'?

(d) *Ipita* means 'feed' in Chickasaw. How would you say 'he feeds me', 'he feeds you', and 'he feeds us'? Give as general an explanation as you can of what happens when the prefixes are attached to these words.

(e) *Apila* means 'help' in Chickasaw. How would you say 'he helps me', 'he helps you', and 'he helps us'? Give as general an explanation as you can of what happens when the prefixes are attached to these words.

(f) Someone proposes that in the formation of a word like *Chisso*, 'He hits you', from *chi-*+*isso*, the *i* of the *chi* prefix is deleted. This account makes sense for this word, but is not consistent with the rest of the data. Present an argument against it.

(g) Someone proposes that in the formation of a word like *Asafama*, 'He meets me', from *sa-*+*afama*, the *s* and *a* of the prefix are transposed (undergoing **metathesis**), becoming *as*. This account makes sense for this word, but is not consistent with the rest of the data. Present an argument against it.

· ·

(a) *pisa* 'see'   *sa-pisa* 'he sees me'
    chi-pisa 'he sees you'
    po-pisa 'he sees us'

ithána 'know'   *sa-thána* 'he knows me'
    chi-thána 'he knows you'
    po-thána 'he knows us'

lohmi 'hide'   *sa-lohmi* 'he hides me'
    chi-lohmi 'he hides you'
    po-lohmi 'he hides us'

afama 'meet'   *a,sa,fama* 'he meets me'
    a,chi,fama 'he meets you'
    a,po,fama 'he meets us'

chokfiyammi 'tickle'   *sa-chokfiyammi* 'he tickles me'
    chi-chokfiyammi 'he tickles you'

isso 'hit'   *chi-sso* 'he hits you'
    po-sso 'he hits us'

anokfilli 'think about'   *a,sa,nokfilli* 'he thinks about me'
    a,po,nokfilli 'he thinks about us'

(b) *sa-* (first-person singular object), *po-* (first-person plural object), *chi-* (second-person object)

(c) 'he tickles us': *pochokfiyammi*
'he hits me': *sasso*
'he thinks about you': *achinokfilli*

(d) 'he feeds me': *sapita*
'he feeds you': *chipita*
'he feeds us': *popita*

When the prefixes are attached to *ipita* (or *isso* or *ithána*), the *i* at the beginning of the verb drops following the vowel of the prefix. Thus, *sa* + *ipita* > *sa-pita*.

(e) 'he helps me': *asapila*
'he helps you': *achipila*
'he helps us': *apopila*

When the prefixes are attached to *apila* (or *afama* or *anokfilli*), they are infixed after the *a* at the beginning of the verb. Thus, *a,sa,pila*.

(f) This proposal works for *chisso* (*chi* + *isso* > *ch-isso*), but does not work for verbs starting with *i* with the prefixes *sa-* and *po-*. If it were true that the vowel of the prefix was deleted, we would expect that 'he hits us' would be *pisso*, 'he knows me' would be *sithẚna*, and 'he knows us' would be *pithẚna*. The data above show this is not correct. The forms given can be produced only if we assume that it is the first vowel of the verb (*i*) that is deleted, not the vowel of the prefix.

(g) This proposal works for *asafama*, but does not work for verbs starting with *a* with the prefixes *chi-* and *po-*. If it were true that the consonant and vowel of the prefix were metathesized (transposed) before verbs starting with *a*, we would expect that 'he meets you' would be *ichafama* (*chi + afama* > *ich-afama*), 'he meets us' would be *opafama* (*po + afama* > *op-afama*), and 'he thinks about us' would be *opanokfilli* (*po + anokfilli* > *op-anokfilli*). The data above show that this is not correct. The forms given can be produced only if we assume that the prefix is infixed after the first vowel (*a*) of the verb.

Note that these Chickasaw data show that morphology may be crucially sensitive to the form of a root (whether it begins with *i* or *a*, for example).

· ·

Consider the following sentences from Ineseño Chumash, a language of the Chumash family formerly spoken north of Santa Barbara, California. (In the Chumash orthography used here, a consonant followed by ' represents a single consonant sound. *Ĭ* represents a vowel sound that does not occur in English.)

EXERCISE 2.28

Stelmemen.	'He touches it.'
Noktelmemen.	'I will touch it.'
Nosiytelmemen.	'They will touch it.'
Nokc'imutelew.	'I will bite it.'
Kiyc'imutelew.	'We bite it.'
Sxiliwayan.	'It floats.'
Nokiyxiliwayan.	'We will float.'

(a) Begin by segmenting the morphemes that appear in the data above. Identify the Ineseño lexical and grammatical morphemes used here. How many morphemes can occur in a single Ineseño word? Make a template (as in (20), p. 44 of textbook, and Exercise 2.8) to show what order they occur in. Put parentheses around the elements in the template that are not required parts of such Ineseño words.

(b) Translate the following Ineseño sentences into English:

Ktelmemen; Sc'imutelew; Nosiyc'imutelew; Kiyxiliwayan; Nokxiliwayan.

Here are some examples of Ineseño sentences in which reduplication is used:

Nosiyteltelmemen.	'They will grope around for it.'
Kteltelmemen.	'I grope around for it.'
Sc'imc'imutelew.	'He nibbles it.'
Nokxilxiliwayan.	'I will float around.'

(c)   What is the semantic effect of reduplication in Ineseño? Is Ineseño reduplication partial or complete? Is it regular or irregular? Describe the Ineseño reduplication process, making reference to the template you developed in (a).

(d)   *Kxuniyïw* means 'I look for it'. How would you translate 'They look all over for it'? *Sk'ilitap* means 'He comes in'. How would you translate 'We will push in all over (We will intrude)'?

Now consider these additional sentences:

Salimexkeken.	'He stretches it out.'
Nokalkalimexkeken.	'I will stretch it out all over.'
Seqwel.	'He does it.'
Keqkeqwel.	'I do it all around.'
Nosiysiyeqwel.	'They will do it all around.'

(e)   Translate these sentences into Ineseño: 'I do it'; 'He will do it all around'; 'We do it all around'; 'He stretches it out all over'; 'We will stretch it out'; 'We stretch it out all over'.

(f)   The new data may require you to modify the description of Ineseño reduplication you developed in (c) above. Explain any changes you need to make.

· ·

EXERCISE 2.28 ANSWERS

(a)

S-telmemen.	'He touches it.'
No-k-telmemen.	'I will touch it.'
No-s-iy-telmemen.	'They will touch it.'
No-k-c'imutelew.	'I will bite it.'
K-iy-c'imutelew.	'We bite it.'
S-xiliwayan.	'It floats.'
No-k-iy-xiliwayan.	'We will float.'

Morphemes:

s-	third-person subject
no-	future
k-	first-person subject
iy-	plural
telmemen	touch
c'imutelew	bite
xiliwayan	float

According to these data, there can be four morphemes in a word. Template:

(FUTURE -)   PERSON -   (PLURAL -)   VERB

There appears to be no morpheme to mark a third-person 'it' object.

(b)   *Ktelmemen*: 'I touch it.'
Sc'imutelew: 'He bites it.'
Nosiyc'imutelew: 'They will bite it.'
Kiyxiliwayan: 'We float.'
Nokxiliwayan: 'I will float.'

(c)   Ineseño reduplication changes verbs so that they refer to actions done tentatively or 'around'. (Later examples suggest 'all over' in addition to 'around'.)
  Ineseño reduplication is partial, since the whole stem is not reduplicated: for example, instead of *c'imutelaw*, we see *c'imc'imutelaw*.
  These examples look regular. The first consonant–vowel–consonant sequence of the VERB stem of the template in (a) is reduplicated in each case.

(d)   'They look all over for it': *Siyxunxuniyiw*.
'We will push in all over (We will intrude)': *Nokiyk'ilk'ilitap*.

(e)   'I do it': *Keqwel*.
'He will do it all around': *Noseqseqwel*.
'We do it all around': *Kiykiyeqwel*.
'He stretches it out all over': *Salsalimexkeken*.
'We will stretch it out': *Nokiyalimexkeken*.
'We stretch it out all over': *Kiykiyalimexkeken*.

(f)   The new data show that with verb stems that do not start with a consonant (such as 'do' (*eqwel*) and 'stretch out' (*alimexkeken*)) reduplication does not affect the beginning of the verb. Rather, reduplation affects the first consonant–vowel–consonant starting with the person prefix. This means that sometimes the consonant–vowel–consonant that is reduplicated is the person prefix plus the first vowel and consonant of the verb stem (as in *keqkeqwel* or *nokalkalimexkeken*), and sometimes it is the person prefix plus the plural morpheme *iy* (as in *nosiysiyeqwel*).

  Consider again the template in (a):

(FUTURE -)   PERSON -   (PLURAL -)   VERB

The reduplication process described in (c) affects the first consonant–vowel–consonant of the underlined portion of this template:

(FUTURE -)   PERSON -   (PLURAL -)   <u>VERB</u>

But the reduplication process described in (f) – used with VERBs that start with vowels – affects the first consonant–vowel–consonant of the underlined portion of this template:

(FUTURE -)   PERSON -   (PLURAL -)   VERB

(It is not enough to say that reduplication always affects the first consonant–vowel–consonant of the underlined portion here for all verbs. That would correctly predict the result for the reduplications in (c) with consonant-initial verbs with singular prefixes, because there the underlined sequence would begin with two consonants. But verbs containing plural subject *k-iy-* or *s-iy-* do not reduplicate those sequences unless a verb beginning with a vowel follows.)

. . . .

EXERCISE 2.29   Read Sidebar 2.12, p. 80 of textbook, and then consider the following additional Egyptian Arabic verbs.

daxal 'he entered'   *sakan* 'he lived in'
badxul 'I enter'   *baskun* 'I live in'
udxul! 'enter!'   *uskun!* 'live in!'
daaxil 'enterer'   *saakin* 'liver in'
madxuul 'entered'   *maskuum* 'lived in'

(a)   Verbs like these represent a different class of verbs from the ones illustrated in Sidebar 2.12. Explain how they are different, in terms of specific contrasts in their patterns of grammatical morphemes.

(b)   *Na'ash* means 'he carved' (*sh* represents a single consonant sound, like the *sh* of English *she*), and *nashar* means 'he sewed'. These verbs work like the two verbs given earlier in this exercise. Tell how to say 'I carve', 'carve!', 'carver', and 'carved'; 'I sew', 'sew!', 'sewer' ('one who sews'), and 'sewn'.

(c)   The normal form of an Arabic verb that is listed in dictionaries and cited by grammarians is the third-person singular masculine perfective (the first verb in each column of verbs above and in Sidebar 2.12). Is this the most basic form, of those listed, from which (given knowledge of possible patterns of grammatical morphemes) all other forms can be predicted? (If you think it is the most basic form, show how the other forms can be predicted from it; if you think that it is not, nominate another form that is more basic.)

(d)   *Biyiktib* means 'he writes', *biyudxul* means 'he enters'. Give the equivalent third-person singular masculine imperfective form for each of the six other verbs given here and in Sidebar 2.12.

. . . .

(a)   1.   The imperfective first-person singular forms contain *ba* —— —— *u* ——, rather than *be* —— —— *i* ——, like those in Sidebar 2.12, p. 80 of textbook.

      2.   The imperatives in the new verbs contain *u* —— —— *u* ——, rather than *i* —— —— *i* ——, like those in Sidebar 2.12.

(b)   'I carve': *ban'ush*   'I sew': *banshur*
      'carve!': *un'ush!*   'sew!': *unshur!*
      'carver': *naa'ish*   'sewer': *naashir*
      'carved': *man'uush*   'sewn': *manshuur*

(c)   The third-person singular masculine perfective is not the most basic form of these verbs, since verbs of both types (like those above and like those in Sidebar 2.12) use the pattern —— *a* —— *a* ——, so this form does not contain information that will allow the dictionary user to know how to form the imperfective first-person singular or the imperative (the forms whose patterns differ between the two groups). On the basis of the data presented, either of these two forms would be a better candidate to list in the dictionary, from which all the forms given here could be predicted.

(d)   *biyidrib*: 'he studies'
      biyiʕmil: 'he does'
      biyin'il: 'he copies'
      biyuskun: 'he lives in'
      biyun'ush: 'he carves'
      biyunshur: 'he sews'

3

Syntax I: Argument Structure and Phrase Structure

EXERCISE 3.1

(a) Construct five additional sentences conforming to the template in (4a), p. 97 of textbook. Select the words for these sentences from the list of words belonging to each lexical category in (3), p. 95 of textbook. Are these sentences grammatical? If you are a native speaker of English, use your own intuitions to decide this. If not, try to consult a native speaker of English; if no native speaker is available, make a guess based on your knowledge of English as a second language.

(b) The templates in (4), p. 97 of textbook, give three possible arrangements of the five lexical categories *Auxiliary*, *Determiner*, *Name*, *Noun*, and *Verb* within a sentence; one of these is grammatical, while the other two are ungrammatical. However, there are actually 120 possible arrangements of these five lexical categories. Construct five additional templates by rearranging these lexical categories in various ways. Use each template as the basis for forming an actual sentence by choosing words from the list in (3), p. 95 of textbook. Try to find at least one additional template for grammatical sentences in this way.

(c) Translate sentences (1a) and (1b), p. 90 of textbook, into a language other than English; we will refer to this language as X. (If you are a native speaker of a language other than English, use it as Language X; if not, consult a friend who is a native speaker of another language, or use a language that you have studied.) Do these sentences in Language X contain the same number of words as (1a) and (1b)? If not, explain why. For each sentence, construct a template similar to those in (4), p. 97 of textbook. Are these two templates the same? If not, explain why. Construct two additional sentences in Language X that conform to the same template(s), using different words. (If you are unsure which lexical categories these words belong to, just make a guess.)

(a) There are hundreds of possible answers to this. Note that not all of the sentences formed in this way will be grammatical, since they may violate selectional requirements of the verb, verbal agreement, etc. Ungrammmatical sentences are preceded by *.

1. *Kate has kill that happiness.
2. Duncan should attack this sword.
3. *Ophelia is appear a king.
4. Bianca did carry that girl.
5. *Desdemona were fall a friend.

(b) Once again, the list of possible answers is vast. Here are five examples:

1.	*Name	Determiner	Verb	Noun	Auxiliary
	*Duncan	the	marry	witch	must
2.	*Determiner	Auxiliary	Verb	Noun	Name
	*That	did	kiss	sword	Othello
3.	Auxiliary	Determiner	Noun	Verb	Name
	Must	the	king	kiss	Macbeth?
4.	*Auxiliary	Verb	Name	Determiner	Noun
	*had	attack	Kate	this	lover
5.	*Verb	Name	Auxiliary	Noun	Determiner
	*fall	Duncan	should	witch	an

(c) The answer of course depends on the language chosen. Students should be instructed to provide examples with both a morpheme-by-morpheme gloss and an idiomatic translation. The translations may differ from the English sentences in various ways; for example, the translation for 'marry' may not be a transitive verb; it may require a preposition or another element (such as a reflexive clitic). The language may not have overt articles. Future tense may be realized as a verbal affix rather than by an auxiliary verb (or it may be null); there may be no exact counterpart to the English present perfect, and so on. These differences will be reflected both in the actual sentences provided and in the templates based on them.

(a) For each of the following example sentences, make a list of every name and DP occurring in the sentence. Remember that some DPs contain other DPs or names within them, in the nominal specifier position. Beside each name or DP in your list, indicate the name of the θ-role assigned to it, based on the list of θ-roles given in (16), p. 106 of textbook.

(i)   Henry's wife hated Falstaff.
(ii)   Iago attacked Othello.
(iii)   Falstaff drank the wine.
(iv)   Caesar's power frightened Brutus.
(v)   Bassanio handed the ring to Portia.
(vi)   Claudius gave Hamlet's father some poison.

(b)   For each name and DP on your list, indicate the name of the syntactic position that it occupies (subject, object, indirect object, or nominal specifier position).

EXERCISE 3.2 ANSWERS

(a)   In cases where a DP occurs in the nominal specifier position of another DP, students may either omit or include the possessive (genitive) enclitic -s on the smaller DP. For example, in (i) the first DP may be either *Henry* or *Henry's*. Also allow some flexibility in terms of other terminology; for example the direct object position in (b) may simply be called the object position; the indirect object position in the prepositional dative construction may be referred to as the object of the preposition *to*, etc.

(i)	Henry	Possessor
	Henry's wife	Experiencer
	Falstaff	Theme
(ii)	Iago	Agent
	Othello	Patient
(iii)	Falstaff	Agent
	the wine	Patient
(iv)	Caesar	Possessor
	Caesar's power	Theme
	Brutus	Experiencer
(v)	Bassanio	Agent
	the ring	Theme or Patient
	Portia	Goal
(vi)	Claudius	Agent
	Hamlet	Possessor
	Hamlet's father	Goal
	some poison	Theme or Patient

(b)	(i)	Henry	Nominal Specifier
		Henry's wife	Subject
		Falstaff	(Direct) Object
	(ii)	Iago	Subject
		Othello	(Direct) Object

(iii)	Falstaff	Subject
	the wine	(Direct) Object
(iv)	Caesar	Nominal Specifier
	Caesar's power	Subject
	Brutus	(Direct) Object
(v)	Bassanio	Subject
	the ring	(Direct) Object
	Portia	Indirect Object (or object of *to*)
(vi)	Claudius	Subject
	Hamlet	Nominal Specifier
	Hamlet's father	First DP in double object construction, or (direct) Object
	some poison	Second DP in double object construction

Examine the following sentences in Tibetan. In three of these sentences, the verb is followed by a perfective 'evidential' particle, glossed simply as 'Perf'. You can ignore the differences between these evidential particles in your answer; you should simply assume that each of them functions like an auxiliary verb in English.

EXERCISE 3.3

(i)   ngas dkaryol chags - song.
       I-Erg cup   break + Perf
       'I broke the cup.'

(ii)   khos   nga-la dep   sprad - byung.
       he-Erg I-Dat book give + perf
       'He gave me a book.'

(iii) khos   cookie bzas - duk.
       he-Erg cookie eat + perf
       'He has eaten the cookies.'

(iv)   tengsang   kho khyang-pa rgyab - gi - red.
       these days he   house   build + Habitual
       'These days, he builds houses.'

(a) Make an organized list of all the words occurring in these sentences, and indicate the English translation for each word. Group together words belonging to the same lexical category (verb, adverb, noun, etc.).
(b) Based on these data, determine the basic constituent order for Tibetan sentences. You should state this in terms of a single formula, analogous to the English formula *Subject–(Auxiliary Verb)–Verb–(Object)–(Indirect Object)*, where parentheses are placed around constituents

that occur in some sentences but not in others. Be sure to indicate the positions of the verb, the (evidential) auxiliary, the subject, the object, the indirect object, and the time adverbs.

EXERCISE 3.3 ANSWERS

(a) The lexicons for Tibetan should be organized into groups of lexical categories (pronouns, verbs, nouns, etc.).

Pronouns

kho	he
khos	he-Erg
ngas	I-Erg
nga-la	I-Dat

Nouns

cookie	cookie
dep	book
dkaryol	cup
khyang-pa	house

Verbs

bzas-	eat
chags-	break
rgyab-	build
sprad-	give

Evidential particles

byung	perf
duk	perf
gi - red	Habitual
song	Perf

Adverbial

tengsang	these days

(b) It does not matter whether students analyze the evidential particles as auxiliary verbs, as verbal affixes, or simply as 'evidential particles'. Likewise, the time adverbs may be called Adverbials. Such terminological details are not essential. All of the examples given include a subject, (direct) object, verb, and evidential particle, so all of these elements are obligatory in the template. Adverbials and indirect objects only occur in one sentence each, so they should be listed as optional.

(Adverbial)–Subject–(Indirect Object)–Direct Object–Verb–Auxiliary Verb

Examine the following sentences in Japanese. Many of the words in these sentences have case suffixes on them, which we have glossed simply as 'CM' (for case marking).

(i) gakusei-ga sake-o nonda.
     student-CM sake-CM drank
     'The student drank sake.'

(ii) Taro-ga sensei-no hon-o suteta.
      Taro-CM teacher-CM book threw-away
      'Taro threw away the teacher's book.'

(iii) Sensei-ga Mari-ni gakusei-no hon-o watasita.
      teacher-CM Mari-CM student-CM book-CM passed
      'The teacher passed the student's book to Mari.'

(iv) gakusei-ga sensei-ni hanasi-ta.
      student-CM sensei-CM talked
      'The student talked to the teacher.'

(a) Make an organized list of the Japanese words occurring in these sentences, and give the English translation of each word. Ignore the case-marking suffixes in answering this question.
(b) Based on these sentences, state the basic constituent order of Japanese sentences, mentioning the position of the verb, the subject, the object, and the indirect object.
(c) Now make a list of the different case suffixes. Based on our discussion in the textbook of case marking in languages such as Russian, identify each of the case suffixes in these sentences, including Nominative, Accusative, Genitive, and Dative.

(a) It does not matter whether students leave the case affixes on the nouns and names in their lexicons; thus the entry for 'student' may simply be *gakusei* (as below), or it may be listed with both case-marked forms (*gakusei-ga* and *gakusei-no*).

Nouns
gakusei   student
hon   book
sake   sake
sensei   teacher

Names
Mari   Mari (name)
Taro   Taro (name)

Verbs

hanasita	talked
nonda	drank
suteta	threw away
watasita	passed

(b) Students may be confused by the fact that some of these DPs contain another (genitive) DP within them. Note that both the direct object and indirect object are listed as optional below, since there is no indirect object in (i) and (ii), and there is no direct object in (iv).

Subject–(Indirect Object)–(Direct Object)–Verb

(c) -ga   Nominative
-o   Accusative
-no   Genitive
-ni   Dative

EXERCISE 3.5

(a) In the following example sentences, indicate whether the verb is transitive, intransitive, or ditransitive. Note that some verbs can be used either as transitive or as intransitive verbs; you should state how each verb is being used in the sentence you are discussing.

(i)   Romeo sang to Juliet.
(ii) Henry's invasion of France terrified the Dauphin.
(iii) Petruccio resided in Italy.
(iv) The soothsayer gave Caesar a warning.
(v)   Othello was distrustful of his wife.

(b) Make a list of the predicates occurring in the sentences above, and for each predicate, indicate how many arguments it has, identify the arguments, and indicate the θ-role assigned to each argument.
(c) For each verb, noun, preposition, and adjective occurring in these sentences, indicate whether it is followed by a complement, and identify the complement.

EXERCISE 3.5 ANSWERS

(a) There is a possibility for misunderstanding the use of the term 'ditransitive', in terms of whether a verb should be called 'ditransitive' when it occurs in the prepositional dative construction (as opposed to the double object construction). Here we follow the textbook in using the term 'ditranstive' only for verbs occurring in the double object construction, though some flexibility should be permitted here. Also, verbs may be cited either in their past tense forms, or in their bare root forms (as below). Note that students may confused about whether the verb in (v) should be simply the copula (*be*, as below) or the complex predicate *be-distrustful*; in either case, it is intransitive.

(i)	sing	Intransitive
(ii)	terrify	Transitive
(iii)	reside	Intransitive
(iv)	give	Ditransitive
(v)	be	Intransitive

(b) It does not matter whether students include the preposition *to* in listing the indirect object (goal) argument. Note that, in (v), if the students have listed the verb as *be-distrustful* rather than simply as *be*, then they will have an additional argument (*his wife*, assigned the theme θ-role). There also may be some confustion about the θ-role assigned to the subject (Othello). If students pay attention to the meaning of the adjective *distrustful*, they will recognize that *Othello* receives the experiencer θ-role, just like the subject of the psychological verb *distrust*; however, if they simply pay attention to the verb *be*, and if they assume that the AP *distrustful of his wife* simply denotes a property attributed to the subject, they may treat Othello as a theme rather than as an experiencer.

(i)	sing	2 arguments	
		Romeo	Agent
		Juliet	Goal
(ii)	terrify	2 arguments	
		Henry's invasion of France	Theme (or Inanimate Cause)
		the Dauphin	Experiencer
(iii)	reside	2 arguments	
		Petruccio	Theme (or possibly Agent)
		in Italy	Location
(iv)	give	3 arguments	
		The soothsayer	Agent
		Caesar	Goal
		a warning	Theme (or Patient)
(v)	be	1 argument	
		Othello	Experiencer (or Theme; see discussion)

or
be-distrusful   2 arguments
              Othello   Experiencer
              his wife   Theme

(c)   The status of case-marking prepositions such as *to* and *of* allows for more than one possible answer here; for example, in (i), students may say that *sing* selects a PP complement, or alternatively they may say that it selects a DP complement bearing dative case (if *to* is analyzed as a case marker). If they analyze *to* and *of* as case markers, rather than as true prepositions, then they may decide to omit them from the list of heads that select complements. Some students may be confused in terms of whether they should identify the complements in terms of their grammatical relations (direct object, indirect object, etc.) or in terms of the category of the complement (DP, PP, AP, etc.). They may need to be told explicitly to name the category of the complement. Note that complements should be identified as phrases (e.g. DP, not D).

(i)	sing	yes	PP (or dative-marked DP) (*to Juliet*)
	to	yes	DP (*Juliet*)
(ii)	invasion	yes	PP (or genitive-marked DP) (*of France*)
	of	yes	DP (*France*)
	terrify	yes	DP (*the Dauphin*)
	Dauphin	no	
(iii)	reside	yes	PP (*in Italy*)
	in	yes	DP (*Italy*)
(iv)	soothsayer	no	
	give	yes (2)	DP (*Caesar*) and DP (*a warning*)
	warning	no	
(v)	be	yes	AP
	distrustful	yes	PP (or genitive-marked DP) (*of his wife*)
	of	yes	DP (*his wife*)
	wife	no	

EXERCISE 3.6   Each of the following pairs of examples contains one grammatical sentence and one ungrammatical sentence. In each case, the ungrammatical example involves a violation of the θ-Criterion, either because an obligatory θ-role cannot be assigned to a referential expression or because a referential expression cannot be assigned a θ-role. For each grammatical sentence, identify the θ-role assigned to each argument by the verb. For each ungrammatical sentence, identify the θ-role or argument that leads to the ungrammaticality of the example, comparing it with the grammatical sentence preceding it.

(i)   (a)   Shylock handed the money to Antonio.
      (b)   *Shylock handed to Antonio.
(ii) (a)   The king's troops entered the city.
      (b)   *The king's troops entered the city to Shylock.
(iii) (a)   Henry laughed at Falstaff.
      (b)   *Henry laughed the book at Falstaff.
(iv) (a)   Juliet died a sad death.
      (b)   *Died a sad death.

There may be some uncertainty about the θ-roles assigned in some cases; for this reason, some flexibility should be allowed, as indicated below. For example, students may be uncertain whether the subject of a verb of motion such as *enter* should be identified as an agent (if they interpret the action as volitional) or as a theme (since the referent of the DP undergoes a change of location).

*EXERCISE
3.6
ANSWERS*

(i)   (a)   Shylock   Agent
            the money   Theme (or Patient)
            Antonio   Goal

      (b)   *Shylock handed to Antonio.
            The object θ-role (Theme or Patient) is not assigned.

(ii) (a)   the king   Possessor
            the king's troops   Agent (or Theme)
            the city   Location (or Goal)

      (b)   *The king's troops entered the city to Shylock.
            There is no θ-role assigned to the indirect object *(to) Shylock*.

(iii) (a)   Henry   Agent
            Falstaff   Theme

      (b)   *Henry laughed the book at Falstaff.
            There is no θ-role assigned to the DP *the book*.

(iv) (a)   Juliet   Theme (or Agent)
            a sad death.   Event

      (b)   *Died a sad death.
            The subject θ-role (Theme or Agent) is not assigned.

EXERCISE 3.7

Each of the following sentences is ungrammatical (or semantically anomalous) because it violates one or more selectional properties of the verb. In each case, state the relevant semantic selectional restriction(s) or categorial selectional property that the sentence violates, and provide a grammatical and semantically natural sentence using the same verb.

(i)   *The witches stirred the tree.
(ii)   *Shylock died Bassanio.
(iii)   *Portia ate that mercy is admirable.
(iv)   *Antony informed to Cleopatra that she was beautiful.
(v)   *Kate should angry at Petruccio.
(vi)   *The lords made.

EXERCISE 3.7 ANSWERS

It may be useful to advise students, in composing their alternative sentences, to make the minimal change(s) necessary in order to eliminate the violation. In all cases, there are two possible ways of resolving the violation: either by changing or eliminating the complement, or by changing the verb. You may wish to advise students to do both.

(i)   *The witches stirred the tree.

The verb *stir* selects a DP that refers to a substance that is liquid or malleable.
    Either the DP complement should be changed to satisfy the verb's selectional restriction, or else the verb should be changed so that it allows this kind of DP complement.

The witches stirred the soup

or

The witches saw the tree.

(ii)   *Shylock died Bassanio.*

The verb *die* is intransitive; it does not select a DP complement in addition to the subject. Moreover, the verb *die* has no additional θ-role to assign to this DP.
    The sentence should be changed, either by eliminating the DP complement, or by substituting a transitive verb (such as *kill*), which allows a DP complement.

Shylock died

or

Shylock killed Bassanio.

(iii)   *Portia ate that mercy is admirable.

The verb *eat* does not select a CP complement; it may occur with a DP complement or without any overt complement (in which case there is an implict argument corresponding to the missing DP).

 The sentence should be changed, either by eliminating the CP (and replacing it with either a DP or nothing at all), or by substituting a verb that selects a CP complement.

Portia ate (the apple)

or

Portia said that mercy is admirable.

(iv)   *Antony informed to Cleopatra that she was beautiful.

The verb *inform* selects an (accusative or direct object) DP complement, rather than a PP (or dative or indirect object DP) complement.

 The sentence should be changed, either by replacing the PP *to Cleopatra* with an accusative direct object DP, or else by substituting a verb such as *say*, which allows an indirect object PP (or dative DP).

Antony informed Cleopatra that she was beautiful

or

Antony said to Cleopatra that she was beautiful.

(v)   *Kate should angry at Petruccio.

The modal verb *should* selects a VP complement, not an AP complement.

 The sentence should be changed, either by replacing the AP with a VP (by replacing the adjective *angry* with a verb that allows an at-PP complement, such as *look*, or by inserting the copular verb *be*), or by replacing *should* with a different verb (such as *be*).

Kate should look at Petruccio

or

Kate should be angry at Petruccio

or

Kate was angry at Petruccio.

(vi)   *The lords made.

> The verb *make* selects a DP complement.
>   The sentence should be changed, either by adding a DP complement, or by replacing the verb *make* with a verb that does not require any complement (such as *arrive*).

> The lords made an apple pie

> or

> The lords arrived.

EXERCISE 3.8

(a)   Draw phrase structure trees for each of the following sentences, based on the rules in (73), pp. 138–9 of textbook, and the trees given in this section of the textbook. In sentence (ii), analyze *Law* as a (proper) name.

(i)   The Dauphin will give the old balls to the king.
(ii)   The Doge believed that Portia was a doctor of Law.
(iii)   The soothsayer told Caesar that he should stay in this house.

(b)   How many nonterminal nodes are there in the tree for sentence (i)? How many nodes does the VP node dominating the verb *give* in (i) immediately dominate? How many binary-branching nodes occur in the tree for sentence (ii)? How many sisters does the determiner *the* have in sentence (ii)? How many nodes does the CP node in sentence (iii) dominate? What are the immediate constituents of the PP node in sentence (iii)?

(c)   Now represent the same constituent structures for sentences (i–iii) in the labeled bracketing notation.

EXERCISE 3.8 ANSWERS

(a)   For the purposes of drawing trees, it may be appropriate to advise students to make the following simplifying assumptions: auxiliary verbs should be analyzed simply as verbs (V, functioning as the head of VP) rather than as members of a special category Aux(iliary); all prepositions (including *to* and *of*) should be treated as prepositions (P, functioning as the head of PP) rather than as case markers (which students may not know how to represent on a tree); tensed verbs should be treated in the same way as root forms of the verb (i.e. they should be analyzed as V, the head of VP). To save space, single-letter abbreviations of category names should be used (A, C, D, N, P, V), except for the categories *Name* and *Pronoun*. Some students may analyze proper names as nouns (N) and pronouns as determiners (D), following the discussion in section 3.3.4 of textbook; this should be allowed.
    Special note: We have not yet discussed bare nouns such as *law*. Students should be advised that they should treat *Law* as a proper name in sentence (i).

(i)

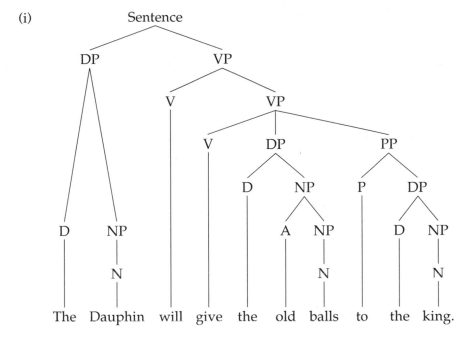

(ii)

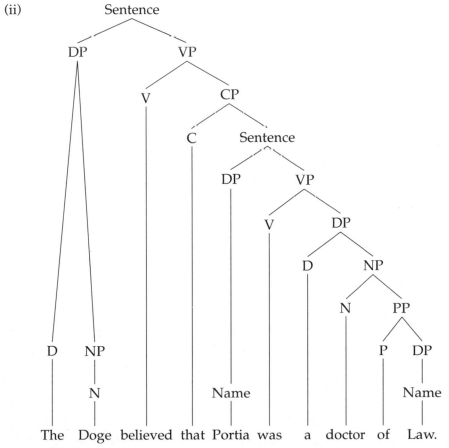

(iii)

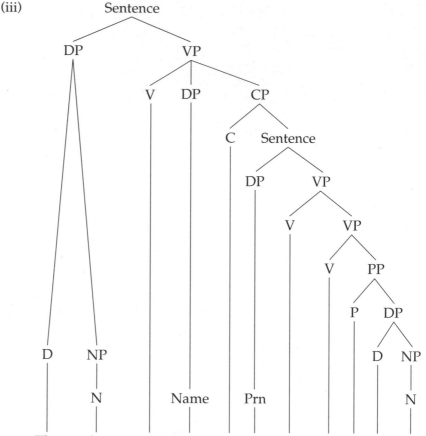

The soothsayer told Caesar that he should stay in this house.

(b)   The answers to the following questions assume that the students have correctly followed the rules for forming phrase structure trees in (73), pp. 138–9 of textbook. However, they may have made some mistakes in part (a), or there may be alternative analyses possible that we have overlooked. In any event, their answers to part (b) should be consistent with their answers to part (a); thus, if their tree for sentence (i) has fewer nonterminal nodes in it, then this should be reflected in their answer to the first question of this part of the exercise.

There are twelve (12) nonterminal nodes in the tree for sentence (i).

The VP node dominating the verb *give* in (i) immediately dominates three (3) nodes.

Nine (9) binary-branching nodes occur in the tree for sentence (ii).

The determiner *the* in sentence (ii) has one (1) sister (the NP node above *soothsayer*).

The CP node in sentence (iii) dominates fourteen (14) nodes, counting both terminal and nonterminal nodes, including nonbranching nodes such as the NP node above the noun *house*.

The immediate constituents of the PP node in sentence (iii) are P (dominating the preposition *in*) and DP (dominating *this house*).

(c) Again, the structures assigned in the labeled bracketing structures should match the structures in the tree diagrams in the answers to part (a). Particular care should be taken to check that each left bracket is paired with a right bracket in the appropriate location.

(i) [SENTENCE [DP [D The] [NP [N Dauphin]]] [VP [V will] [VP [V give] [DP [D the] [NP [A old] [NP [N balls]]]] [PP [P to] [DP [D the] [NP [N king]]]]]]]]

(ii) [SENTENCE [DP [D The] [NP [N Doge]]] [VP [V believed] [CP [C that] [SENTENCE [DP [NAME Portia]] [VP [V was] [DP [D a] [NP [N doctor] [PP [P of] [DP [NAME Law]]]]]]]]]]

(iii) [SENTENCE [DP [D The] [NP [N soothsayer]]] [VP [V told] [DP [NAME Caesar]] [CP [C that] [SENTENCE [DP [PRN he]] [VP [V should] [VP [V stay] [PP [P in] [DP [D this] [NP [N house]]]]]]]]]]

In the following sentence, the adjective *alone* occurs at the end of the sentence:

(i) Falstaff must drink his beer alone.

This sentence contains two VP nodes: one VP node immediately dominates the verb *must*, and the other VP node immediately dominates the verb *drink*. Since the adjective occurs at the end of the sentence, it is not obvious which VP node immediately dominates it.

(a) Draw two tree diagrams for this sentence; in one tree, the adjective should be an immediate constituent of the higher VP node, and in the other tree, it should be dominated by the lower VP node.

(b) The following data provide evidence bearing on the constituent structure of Sentence (i). The data involve movement, VP-deletion, and pro-forms. Use these data to decide which of the tree structures given above is correct. For each example, explain how the constituency test works, and construct an argument for one structure or the other.

(ii) The king stated that Shylock must drink his beer alone, and drink his beer alone Shylock must.

(iii) *The king stated that Shylock must drink his beer alone, and drink his beer Shylock must alone.

(iv) Shylock must drink his beer alone, and Henry must too.
(This sentence implies that Henry must drink his beer alone.)

(v)   *Shylock must drink his beer alone, and Henry must with Pistol.

(vi)   Shylock must drink his beer alone, and so must Henry.
            (This sentence implies that Henry must drink his beer alone.)

EXERCISE
3.9
ANSWERS

(a)

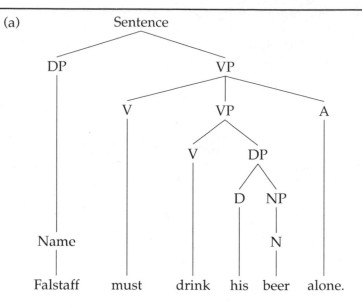

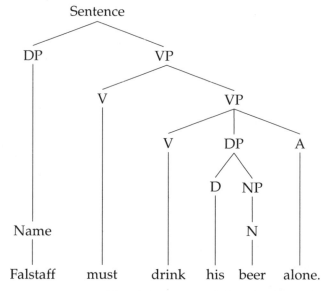

(b)   Sentences (ii) and (iii) involve the test of movement; the smaller VP
        is moved to the Topic position at the beginning of the second of the
        two conjoined sentences; the higher (modal) verb *must* is left behind,
        indicating that the larger VP does not move. If the adjective can move

along with the smaller VP, then it must be a subconstituent of that VP; if not (i.e. if it is immediately dominated by the higher VP node), then it should be left behind. In (ii), the smaller VP headed by the verb *drink* undergoes movement; since the adjective moves along with it, it must be part of the smaller VP. Sentence (iii), where the adjective is left behind, is ungrammatical. Since the placement of the adjective is the only difference between (ii) and (iii), this must be the cause of the ungrammaticality. Therefore, the movement test provides evidence that the adjective must be a subconstituent of the lower VP headed by the verb *drink*.

Sentences (iv) and (v) involve the deletion test (specifically, VP deletion). In each case, the smaller VP (headed by *drink*) is deleted. If the adjective is deleted along with this VP, then it is a subconstituent of the lower VP; if not, then it must be outside this VP, presumably immediately dominated by the higher VP headed by *must*. In (iv), the adjective is deleted along with the rest of the smaller VP, and the result is grammatical, indicating that the adjective may be analyzed as a subconstituent of the lower VP. In (v), the adjective is not deleted, and the result is ungrammatical, indicating again that the adjective must be treated as a subconstituent of the lower VP.

Sentence (vi) involves the pro-form test, where the antecedent of the pro-form *so* is a VP; the VP in question must be the lower VP of the first conjoined clause (since a modal verb may not function as the head of a bare VP complement to another modal verb). In (vi), the pro-form *so* is interpreted as if the adjective *alone* is part of the antecedent VP, thus providing evidence that the adjective is a subconstituent of the lower VP. (Students may have difficulty in filling in all the steps of the argument based on this example, so this question should be graded leniently.)

EXERCISE 3.10

The phrase structure rules for NP and DP in (123), (124), and (126), pp. 164–5 of textbook, do not account for the structure of DPs containing numbers, or nominal specifiers. Based on the following data, propose revisions in either or both of these rules to account for the facts. In answering this question, you will need to decide whether these elements are immediately dominated by NP, DP, or some additional phrase. There is more than one possible answer to this question, so do not be too concerned if you have difficulty in deciding which structure is correct; however, you should explain how your rules account for the data.

(i)   Macbeth's unpardonable murder of Duncan shocked the lords.
(ii)   Lear adored his three beautiful daughters.
(iii) The three old witches lived in the dark, mysterious forest.

Bear in mind that there are many possible answers to the questions in this assignment. It will be necessary to evaluate each student's answer in order to determine whether it solves the problem at hand. Bear in mind that the students may not be aware of all the subtleties involved in the reasoning given in the sample answers below.

To account for sentence (i), we need to introduce a position for the nominal specifier, either in the rule for NP or in the rule for DP. Since the nominal specifier may occur only if there is no overt determiner in the DP, one possibility is that the nominal specifier and the determiner occupy the same position. To accommodate this, we could make use of curly brackets, revising the top line of (124), p. 165 of textbook, as follows:

$$
DP \rightarrow \left\{ \begin{array}{l} \overset{\displaystyle DP}{\underset{\displaystyle \begin{array}{cc} D & NP \end{array}}{[+GEN]}} \\[1ex] Name \\ Pronoun \end{array} \right\}
$$

To account for sentence (ii), we need to introduce a position for the number. Since this can occur in DPs containing common nouns, but not in DPs consisting of pronouns or proper names, it should be included in the top line of the revised version of (124), given immediately above. The position for the number should be before the NP, since it precedes all adjectives. Given the data provided, it is not clear whether the number should be analyzed as a sister of both D (or the genitive DP in the nominal specifier position) and NP, or whether it should be included in some other kind of phrase (e.g. a phrase containing the number and the NP but not the determiner or nominal specifier). For the sake of simplicity, we will assume the former analysis. Note that the number must be optional, since it does not occur in all DPs:

$$
DP \rightarrow \left\{ \begin{array}{l} \overset{\displaystyle DP}{\underset{\displaystyle \begin{array}{ccc} D & (Num) & NP \end{array}}{[+GEN]}} \\[1ex] Name \\ Pronoun \end{array} \right\}
$$

Given the revised rule, sentence (iii) can be accommodated straightforwardly; the number occurs between the determiner and the NP, consistent with our assumption that the determiner and the nominal specifier occupy the same position.

· ·

Malagasy

Consider the following data from Malagasy, an Austronesian language spoken throughout Madagascar. In these examples, the glosses for some words have been simplified, omitting translations of some morphemes.

(i) namangy anay ny ankizy
     visited   us   the children
     'The children visited us.'

(ii) mihinana ahitra ny omby
      eat   grass the cow
      'Cows eat grass.'

(iii) matory ny mpamboly
       sleep   the farmer
       'The farmer(s) is/are sleeping.'

(iv) tonga   taorian' ny rahalahi -ko ny mpampianatra antitra
      arrived after   the brother -my the teacher   old
      'The old teacher arrived after my brother.'

(v) namono ny akoho   tamin' ny antsy ny vehivavy
     killed   the chicken with   the knife the woman
     'The woman killed the chicken(s) with the knife.'

(vi) nandroso vary ny ankizy   tamin' ny lovia vaovao i – Noro
      served   rice the children on   the dish new   Noro
      'Noro served the children rice on the new dishes.'

(vii) nanascho sari-n'   i-Noro ny lehilahy ny reni-n'   ny zaza
       showed   picture-of Noro   the man   the mother-of the child
       'The child's mother showed the man a picture of Noro.'

(a) What is the basic order of major constituents (subject, object, indirect object, verb, PP) in Malagasy?
(b) Construct a lexicon for Malagasy based on the words occurring in these sentences. For each Malagasy verb, state how many arguments it selects, and what θ-roles it assigns to them. Organize your lexicon by grouping together words belonging to the same lexical category.
(c) Construct phrase structure rules for PP, DP, VP, and TP (Sentence) in Malagasy.
(d) Draw tree diagrams for Sentences (i), (iv), and (vii) that are consistent with your phrase structure rules.

. . . .

EXERCISE   (a)   The basic constituent order is as follows:
3.11
ANSWERS   Verb–(Direct Object)–(Indirect Object)–(PP)–Subject

Note that indirect objects, like direct objects, consist of bare DPs, without any overt preposition such as English *to*. We do not have clear evidence as to the precise location of the temporal PP in (iii). For simplicity, we assume that it is located in the same position (after the direct and indirect objects) as the PPs in Sentences (v–vii).

(b)   Malagasy lexicon based on these data:

Verbs

matory	sleep
mihinana	eat
namangy	visited
namono	killed
nanaseho	showed
nandroso	served
tonga	arrived

Nouns

ahitra	grass
akoho	chicken
ankizy	children
antsy	knife
lehilahy	man
lovia	dish
mpamboly	farmer
mpampianatra	teacher
omby	cow
rahalahi	brother
reni-n'	mother-of
sari-n'	picture-of
vary	rice
vehivavy	woman
zaza	child

Names
i-Noro

Pronouns

anay	us
-ko	my

Determiner
ny   the

*Preposition*s
tamin'   with or on
taorian'   after

*Adjective*s
antitra   old
vaovao   new

(c)   PP   →   P   DP

DP   → $\begin{Bmatrix} \text{D} & \text{NP} \\ \text{Name} \end{Bmatrix}$

NP   →   N   (-n'   DP)   (A)
                   [+GEN]

VP   →   V   (DP)   (DP)   (PP)

TP   →   VP   DP

Comments: The PP rule is straightforward.

The DP rule allows for either a proper name or a D taking an NP complement. This is captured by means of curly brackets. (Based on the discussion in section 3.3.4 of textbook, it would be possible to eliminate the curly brackets, by assuming that names originate in the same position as common nouns. The particle *i-* preceding the proper name *Noro* might be analyzed as a determiner; alternatively, we would assume a null determiner here.)

The NP rule requires a noun, followed by two optional constituents – a postnominal genitive DP (corresponding to the English nominal specifier position) and a postnominal adjective. We have no evidence that they are ordered as in this rule, since they never co-occur in the data given; they might actually occur in the opposite order. More data would be needed to clarify this. Also, our rule only allows for one adjective, since this is all we see in our data. Other data might show that additional adjectives are allowed, in which case we might adopt a rule similar to (but the mirror image of) (126), p. 165 of textbook, adjoining A to NP.

The VP rule allows for three complement positions: two for DP and one for PP. In all likelihood, further data would motivate a more complex set of possibilities.

The TP rule is the mirror image of its English counterpart.

(i)

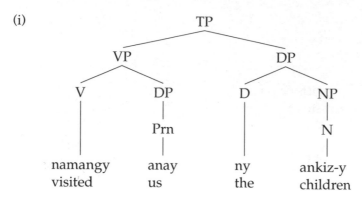

(iv)

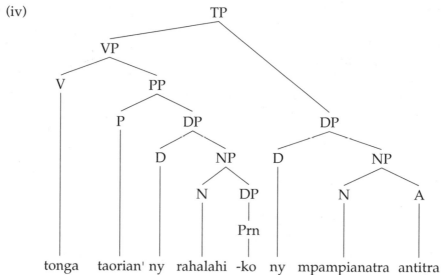

(vii)

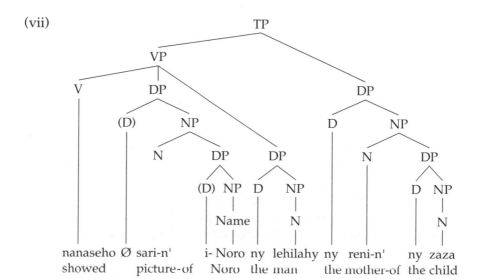

. . . .

SLQ Zapotec

Consider the following data from SLQ Zapotec, a Zapotecan language spoken in Mexico.

(i) Y-tàa'az Gyeeihlly Li'eb
     Irr-beat Mike   Felipe
     'Mike will beat Felipe.'

(ii) B-gu'ty-a'   bzihny
      Perf-kill-1sg mouse
      'I killed the mouse.'

(iii) Y-tòo'oh Gyeeihlly ca'rr
       Irr-sell Mike   car
       'Mike will sell the car.'

(iv) N-àa-'ng   banguual
      Neut-be-3sg old
      'He is old.' or 'She is old.'

(v) B-da'uh-zhya' Gyeeihlly bx:àady
     Perf-eat-might Mike   grasshopper
     'Mike might have eaten grasshoppers.'

(vi) Gw-ùa'il-rëng li'ebr
      Irr-read-3pl books
      'They will read the books.'

(vii) B-dèèi'dy Gyeeihlly bx:àady   Li'eb
       Perf-give Mike   grasshopper Felipe
       'Mike gave the grasshoppers to Felipe.'

(viii) W-nnàa'az Gyeeihlly bx:àady   cuahnn gyìi'x
        Perf-catch Mike   grasshopper with   net
        'Mike caught grasshoppers with the net.'

(ix) N-àa   Li'eb banguual
      Neut-be Felipe old
      'Felipe is old.'

(x) R-càa'z-a'   y-gu'ty-a' bzihny
     Hab-want-1sg Irr-kill-I   mouse
     'I want to kill the mouse.'

(xi)　B-inydyahg Li'eb　y-tòo'oh Gyeeihlly ca'rr
　　　Perf-hear　Felipe Irr-sell　Mike　　car
　　　'Felipe heard that Mike will sell the car.'

(xii)　R-e'ihpy Lia Pa'amm làa'-rëng　gw-ùa'll-rëng li'ebr
　　　Hab-tell　　Ms.　　Pam them Irr-read-they　book
　　　'Pam told them to read the books.'

(a)　Construct a lexicon for SLQ Zapotec based on the words occurring in these sentences. For words containing more than one morpheme, try to identify the meaning of each morpheme and add a lexical entry for each of these morphemes. Group together words belonging to the same lexical category.

(b)　What is the basic order of major constituents (subject, verb, object, etc.) in SLQ Zapotec?

(c)　Comment on two differences between English and SLQ Zapotec involving (i) definite articles, and (ii) singular and plural nouns.

(d)　In SLQ Zapotec, the morphemes occurring at the end of the verbs in Sentences (ii), (iv), (vi), and (x) are glossed with features for person and number. There are two possible analyses for these morphemes: they might be pronominal subject clitics, analogous to the pronominal object clitics in French and Spanish in (21), p. 109 of textbook, or they might be subject agreement markers, analogous to the subject agreement affixes in Italian and Spanish in (51), p. 123 of textbook. Which of these analyses would require us to assume that SLQ Zapotec allows null pronouns to occur in the subject position? Explain your reasoning. Now compare the verbs in sentences (iv) and (ix), and explain why the form of the verb in (ix) supports the pronominal clitic analysis.

(e)　In SLQ Zapotec, the order of the subject and verb relative to each other is different from what we find in English. Propose two alternative theories to account for this.

　　(I)　The first theory should account for the word order in the example sentences above using only phrase structure rules. Formulate a set of phrase structure rules to account for all the data above and draw tree diagrams based on these rules to account for sentences (vii) and (xi). Note that SLQ Zapotec does not have an overt complementizer such as English *that*; assume that embedded sentences in this language are simply TPs, without any CP node.

　　(II)　The second theory should assume that the SLQ Zapotec phrase structure rules for VP and TP resemble those of English, with a verb position located inside VP, and the subject DP position located outside of VP (to the left of it). This implies that the word order in the data above must result from the application of a transformational movement rule, similar to the rule that derives Subject–Auxiliary Inversion constructions in English. Formulate phrase structure rules for VP and TP in SLQ Zapotec that are consistent with this assumption, and explain how the transformational movement rule would change the word order produced by these rules. Draw a tree diagram based on these phrase structure rules for sentence (xi), showing the word order before the transformational movement rule has been applied.

· ·

(a)   Zapotec Lexicon

Verbs

àa	be
càa'z	want
dèèi'dy	give
da'uh	eat
e'ihpy	tell
gu'ty	kill
inydyahg	hear
nnàa'a	catch
tàa'az	beat
tòo'oh	sell
ùa'll	read

Verbal Aspect prefixes

b-, w-	Perf(ect)
n-	Neut(ral)
r-	Habitual
y-, gw-	Irr(ealis)

Verbal suffixes

-a'	1sg
-'ng	3sg
-rëng	3pl
-zhya'	might

Nouns

bx:àady	grasshopper
bzihny	mouse
ca'rr	car
gyìi'x	net
li'ebr	book

Names
Gyeeihlly   Mike
Lia Pa'amm   Pam
Li'eb   Felipe

Adjective
banguual   old

Preposition
cuahnn   with

Pronoun
làa'-rëng   them

(b)   The basic order of major constituents in SLQ Zapotec is as follows:

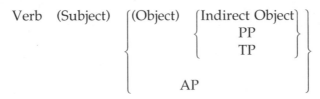

In this formula, we have treated indirect object DPs, PPs, and subordinate clause TPs as if they all occupied the same position; further data might provide evidence against this. We have also treated predicate adjectives as full APs, and we have used curly brackets to represent the fact that, at least in these data, they function as the sole complements of the verb in the sentences where they appear. Finally, the subject position (like all other positions, except for the verb) is listed here as optional; this effectively treats null subjects as if they were structurally absent, which is arguably the wrong analysis.

(c)   (i)   In SLQ Zapotec, unlike English, the definite article is null.

      (ii)   No overt plural marking occurs on the noun; thus, the bare form of the noun is used for both singular and plural meanings.

(d)   The agreement analysis, unlike the clitic analysis, requires there to be a null pronoun in the subject position so that there is a DP with which the inflected verb can agree.

    Example (ix) supports the clitic analysis because the suffix appears on the verb only when there is no overt subject. This contrasts with finite verb agreement in null-subject languages like Italian and Spanish in the sense that we get agreement regardless of whether a third-person subject is null or overt. On the other hand, if the suffix is actually a pronominal clitic that originates in the subject position and cliticizes onto the verb, then we expect it to show up on the verb only when the subject position is empty.

(e)   (1)   The first theory relies only on phrase structure rules to account for the differences in word order between SLQ Zapotec and English.

Since the subject occurs in between the verb and the object, this implies that there is no constituent containing both the verb and the object but not the subject. Thus, either the subject, like the object, occurs inside the VP, or, alternatively, there is no VP in Zapotec and the subject, verb, and object are all immediately dominated by the highest node of the tree (the Sentence or TP node). For concreteness, let us assume the latter; we would then have a very simple rule for VP (containing only the verb) but a more complex rule for TP, such as the following:

$$TP \rightarrow V \; (DP) \; (DP) \; \begin{matrix} DP \\ \{ \; PP \; \} \\ \{ \quad TP \quad \} \\ AP \end{matrix}$$

Trees for Sentences (vii) and (xi) according to this theory would be as follows:

(vii)

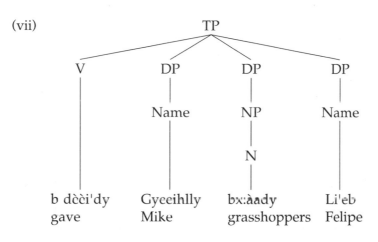

(xi)

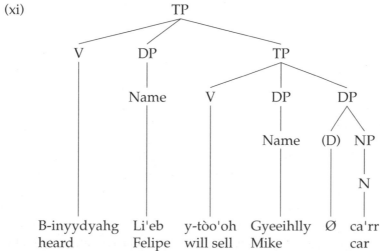

(II)   The second theory assumes an underlying phrase structure similar to that of English, and allows for the possibility of movement, similar to English Subject–Auxiliary Inversion. The simplest version of this would be to assume that the verb originates within VP (in the same position as in English) and then undergoes movement out of VP to a position before the subject DP. We could then assume the following phrase structure rules for TP and VP, with Sentence (xi) having the underlying structure of the tree below:

$$\begin{aligned}
\text{TP} &\rightarrow \text{DP } \text{TP} \\
\text{VP} &\rightarrow \text{V} \quad \left\{ (\text{DP}) \quad \begin{cases} (\text{DP}) \\ (\text{PP}) \\ (\text{TP}) \end{cases} \right\} \\
& \qquad\qquad \text{AP}
\end{aligned}$$

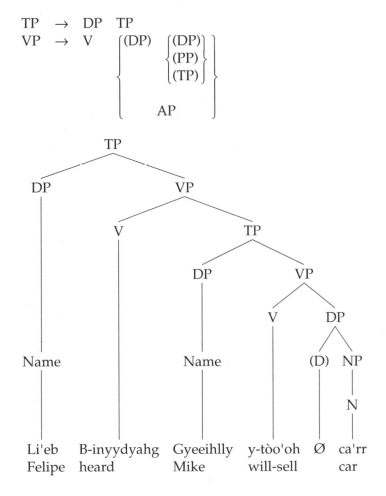

. . . .

EXERCISE
3.13

English Quantifiers

Recall that a finite (tensed) verb in English agrees in person and number features with the DP occurring in the subject position of the sentence in which it occurs, and that this agreement is represented overtly (as the suffix *-s* on the verb) only if the subject DP is third-person singular. Assume that this agreement relation is enforced by a constraint requiring the subject DP and the finite verb to have the same person and number features.

Now consider the data in (i–x) involving the quantifiers *all*, *many*, *some*, *each*, and *every*. These data show that English has another agreement constraint involving quantifiers and nouns (or NPs). In this respect, quantifiers resemble the demonstrative determiners *this*, *that*, *these*, and *those*.

(i)   All lords respect Duncan.
(ii)   Many young lords respect Duncan.
(iii)   Some kings of Scotland admire Macbeth.
(iv)   Each Scottish lord owns a castle.
(v)   Every murder of a king offends his lords.
(vi)   *All/Many (young) lord respect(s) Duncan.
(vii)   *Each/Every Scottish lords own(s) a castle.
(viii) Some lord admires Macbeth.
(ix)   *Some lords admires Macbeth.
(x)   *Each/Every Scottish lord own a castle.

Now answer these questions:
(a)   Assume that each quantifier is specified in the lexicon as being either [+Plural], [–Plural] (singular), or ambiguous (allowing either feature value for number). Construct a lexical entry for the quantifiers *all*, *many*, *some*, *each*, and *every*, stating the feature specification for each of them, and propose an agreement constraint that accounts for the data in (i–v) in comparison with the data in (vi–viii). In answering this question, assume that an NP counts as [+Plural] if the noun occupying the head N position in the NP is [+Plural].
(b)   Explain why (vi) and (vii) are ungrammatical, with or without the third-person agreement suffix *-s* on the verb. Also explain why (iii) and (viii) are both grammatical.
(c)   Explain why (ix) and (x) are ungrammatical.
(d)   Assume that quantifiers are determiners. Based on the data in (i–v), what kind of category does each of these quantifiers c-select as its complement?
(e)   Draw a tree diagram for sentence (ii), following the constraints of the X-bar theory of phrase structure discussed in section 3.3.4 of textbook.
(f)   Would it be possible to eliminate the agreement constraint that you proposed in your answer to (a) by assuming that the lexical entry of each quantifier can select the number feature of the quantifier's complement? Explain, making explicit reference to how this theory would (or would not) account for the ungrammaticality of (vi) and (vii).
(g)   Now consider these additional data:

      (xi)   All/Many/Some of the lords respect Duncan.
      (xii)   *All/Many/Some of the lords respects Duncan.
      (xiii) *All/Many/Some of the lord respect(s) Duncan.
      (xiv)   Each of the lords owns a castle.

(xv)   *Each of the lord own(s) a castle.
(xvi)   *Every of the lord(s) own(s) a castle.

Revise your answers to questions (d) and (f) in whatever ways are necessary in order to account for these additional data. Assume that the preposition *of* occurring in these examples is a genitive case particle indicating the genitive case feature of the DP that immediately follows it, rather than a true preposition; thus, the sequence *of the lords* should be analyzed as a [+Genitive] DP, rather than as a PP. Explain why each revision is necessary by making explicit reference to the examples given; note that each example provides a crucial piece of information, so a complete answer will mention every example. Draw a tree for Sentence (xiv).

(h)   Now consider these additional data, involving the **Quantifier Float (Q-float)** construction, in which a quantifier occurs after the noun phrase, rather than before it.

(xvii)   The (Scottish) lords all/each own a castle.
(xviii)   *The (Scottish) lords many/some own a castle.
(xix)   *The (Scottish) lord(s) every own a castle.
(xx)   *The lords all/each owns a castle.

Before attempting to understand the structure of these sentences, draw some generalizations about the Q-float construction based on these examples. Each sentence provides at least one important clue about Q-float; in each case, state what the example shows. For example, (xvii) shows that the quantifiers *all* and *every* can occur in the Q-float construction, and also that the DP in the subject position of the sentence can be [+Plural], as indicated by the agreement affix on the finite verb.

(i)   Now consider these data:

(xxi)   They all support Duncan.
(xxii)   All of them support Duncan.

Assume that Q-float constructions are formed by a transformational movement rule which moves a DP from a position in which it would normally be assigned Genitive case into the subject position of the sentence, where it is assigned Nominative case. Explain how this analysis would account for the derivation of sentences (xxi) and (xxii). How might the ungrammaticality of (xix) be explained in terms of the ungrammaticality of (xvi)?

(j)   Now consider the constituent structure of the Q-float construction: the quantifier might be contained within the same DP as the determiner and NP preceding it, or it might be part of the VP that follows this DP, or in some other position. Use the following data to answer this question:

(xxiii)   The lords should all respect Duncan.
(xxiv)   The lords may each own a castle.
(xxv)   The lords should all respect Duncan, and all respect Duncan they will!
(xxvi)   *The lords should all respect Duncan, and respect Duncan they will all!
(xxvii)   The lords all should respect Duncan, and respect Duncan they all will!

(k) Based on your answers to questions (i) and (j), it is possible to propose an analysis of the Q-float construction based on the VP-internal subject hypothesis discussed in section 3.3.4 of textbook, according to which the subject DP originates in the Specifier position of VP and is moved to the Specifier position of TP by a transformational movement rule. Explain how this analysis would work, using a tree diagram for Sentence (xxii) to illustrate your answer. If possible, also explain why the VP-internal subject hypothesis plays a crucial role in explaining where the quantifier may occur in Q-float constructions, and how it is possible to move the pronoun in (xxi) into a position where Nominative case is assigned. (Hint: assume that Nominative case is assigned only to the subject position, and that it is only possible to move a DP into a position that is not already occupied by another DP.)

. . . .

(a)   all   [+PL]   EXERCISE
        many [+PL]   3.13
        some [+PL]   (actually [±PL] but the data given here only show   ANSWERS
                             plural *some*)

        each   [–PL]
        every [–PL]

        The agreement constraint is as follows: if Q immediately precedes NP in a DP, then Q and NP must have the same value for [±PL] (i.e. they must agree).

(b)   Sentence (vi) is ungrammatical because it violates the agreement constraint in (a); a plural quantifier immediately precedes a singular ([–PL]) NP. Sentence (vii) is ungrammatical for a similar reason: a singular Q is immediately followed by a plural NP, so the agreement constraint is again violated.

(c)   Sentences (ix) and (x) are ungrammatical because the subject DP fails to agree for [±PL] with the finite verb. In (ix) the subject DP is plural but the finite verb shows agreement for a third-person singular subject; in (x) the subject DP is singular but the finite verb fails to bear singular agreement.

(d)   All of the quantifiers occurring in these data select an NP complement.

(e)

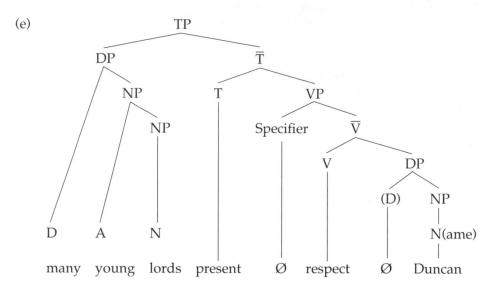

(f)   Yes; we could say that the quantifiers (determiners) *all*, *many*, and *some* select an NP complement with the feature [+PL], whereas the quantifiers (determiners) *each* and *every* select an NP complement with the feature [–PL].

(g)   The answer to this question depends on how we analyze the sequence *of*-DP following the quantifiers in (xi–xvi). If we analyze it as a PP headed by the preposition *of*, then we must say that the quantifiers *all*, *many*, *some*, and *each* also select a PP headed by *of*, and that this preposition in turn selects a DP complement bearing the feature [+PL]. On the other hand, if we analyze the *of*-DP sequences as genitive DPs, i.e. if we analyze *of* as a genitive case marker, then we would assume that the quantifiers *all*, *many*, *some*, and *each* can select a DP complement bearing genitive case and the feature value [+PL]. In either case, we must allow for the quantifier *each*, which is itself singular ([–PL]) to select a plural *of*-DP. In (xi), both the quantifier and the *of*-DP are plural, and the finite verb bears plural agreement. In (xii), the finite verb bears agreement features for a third-person singular subject, but the subject DP is plural, headed by a plural quantifier/determiner. Sentence (xiii) is ungrammatical because the selectional requirement discussed above is violated: the *of*-DP should be [+PL]. In (xiv), the quantifier *each* and the DP it heads are singular, even though the *of*-DP is [+PL]. This indicates that when the complement of *each* is an *of*-DP, as opposed to an NP, the quantifier does not agree in plurality with its complement. Sentence (xv) is ungrammatical because the quantifier's selectional requirement is violated: the *of*-DP should be [+PL]. The ungrammaticality of (xvi), regardless of the plurality of the *of*-DP, and regardless of the agreement feature on the finite verb, indicates that the quantifier *every* does not select an *of*-DP complement; its complement must be a singular NP, as in (v).

(h) Sentence (xvii) shows that the quantifiers *all* and *each* can occur in the Q-float construction, whereas sentence (xviii) shows that the quantifiers *some* and *many* may not. Sentence (xix) shows that the quantifier *every* also may not occur in the Q-float construction, regardless of whether the definite DP is singular or plural. Sentences (xvii) and (xx) indicate that in the Q-float construction, the finite verb agrees in number with the definite DP preceding the floated quantifier, rather than with the floated quantifier itself; this is shown by the fact that even when the singular quantifier *each* occurs, the finite verb shows plural agreement.

(i) Assuming that *they* is nominative in (xxi) and that *of them* is genitive in (xxii), the analysis is that the third-person plural pronominal DP in (xxi) has undergone movement from the position after the quantifier *all* to the subject position, where it is assigned nominative case. This suggests that the DP headed by the quantifier *all*, out of which the pronoun in (xxi) moves, must be located in some other position. (This position is probably within the lower VP, as in the answer to part (k) below.) In (xxii), the pronoun fails to undergo movement and is assigned genitive case. The entire DP headed by the quantifier *all* presumably occupies the matrix subject position; if so, then this DP must undergo movement in (xxii) from whatever position it occupies in (xxi) to the subject position. The ungrammaticality of (xix) can be related to the ungrammaticality of (xvi) by virtue of the fact that the two sentences share the same underlying structure; the fact that both sentences are ungrammatical suggests that the quantifier *every* obligatorily selects a singular NP complement, and does not allow a plural DP complement.

(j) Sentences (xxiii) and (xxiv) show that the floated Q may follow the modal verb; therefore it could be located within the VP headed by the verbs *respect* or *own*, or perhaps in a position between the modal verb and this VP, but it could not be located in the same DP as the subject DP *the lords*. Sentence (xxv) provides evidence from VP movement supporting the analysis that the floated quantifier is located within the VP headed by *respect*, since it moves along with this VP to the front of the sentence. Sentence (xxvi) shows that the floated QP must be within this VP, since it cannot be left behind when the VP is fronted. Surprisingly, however, Sentence (xxvii) shows that the floated quantifier may occur in another position as well: in front of the modal verb. This suggests that the floated Q may occur at the front of either VP: the VP headed by the modal, or the VP headed by the main verb (*respect*).

(k)   According to this analysis, the DP occupying the subject position in (xxiii), (xxiv), (xxv), and (xxvii) originates in the Specifier position of the lower VP. We may further assume, as in part (i) above, that this DP originates in the position where genitive case is normally assigned, within the DP headed by the quantifier, as in (xxii). Putting these two observations together, the entire DP headed by the quantifier originates in the Specifier position of the lower VP in (xxi–xxv). This DP may move to the Specifier position in TP; this derives (xxii), as illustrated in the tree below.

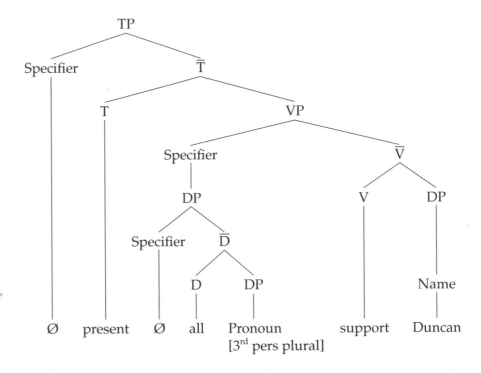

Alternatively, the smaller DP may move into the main clause subject position, leaving behind the remnant of the larger DP (consisting of just the quantifier) in the Specifier of VP position; this derives the structure of (xxiii) and (xxiv).

The contrast between (xxv) and (xxvi) follows as in (j). Because the remnant DP headed by the quantifier is left behind in the Specifier position of the lower VP when the smaller DP moves to the subject position (the Specifier of TP), the remnant DP must move along with the rest of the lower VP in (xxv); (xxiv) is excluded because there is no way to move the lower VP leftward without also moving the remnant DP within it.

As noted in the answer to (j), the grammaticality of (xxvii) suggests that the quantifier (or rather, the remnant DP headed by the quantifier) may occur outside the lower VP, provided that it precedes the modal verb. The fact that it must precede the modal verb suggests that it is occupying the Specifier position of the VP headed by the modal. This would follow if (a) the DP headed by the quantifier may originate in the Specifier position of either one of the two VPs, or (b) the DP headed by the quantifier always originates in the lower VP, as assumed above, and this DP has the option of moving to the Specifier position of the higher VP headed by the modal verb, instead of moving directly to the Specifier of TP position. If the entire DP moves to the Specifier of TP position, then (xxii) is derived; but if the smaller DP moves to the Specifier of TP position, then the remnant of the DP headed by the quantifier (consisting of just the quantifier) is left behind in the Specifier position of the VP headed by the modal verb, correctly deriving the word order in (xxvii).

. . . .

The Phrase Structure of Language X   EXERCISE
                                                                             3.14

This exercise is intended to give you a taste of the experience of working on a language other than English. If this textbook is being used in a class in which there are native speakers of several languages other than English, it may be appropriate for small groups of students to work together on a particular language, with one of the members of the group serving as the native speaker, whose acceptability judgments will serve as the source of data for the group. (Depending on the wishes of the instructor, the assignment may be written up either by the group as a whole, or by individual members of the group working independently after discussing the issues with each other.)

If the textbook is being used in a class where there are very few speakers of a language other than English, it may be appropriate for the instructor to provide judgment data that are distributed to the entire class, so that each student can work independently. Alternatively, it may be appropriate for students to work individually or in groups with a native speaker of a foreign language.

If the textbook is being used in a class in which all or most of the students are native speakers of the same language (for example, if the class is being used in a non-English-speaking country), then it may be appropriate for each student to work independently, relying on his or her own intuitions.

Ask your native speaker to produce some simple sentences, involving translations of the following English sentences (or similar sentences; e.g. feel free to use different names but preserve the gender). Since your native speaker is one of you, you can rely on his/her ability to segment the sentences into words and to supply glosses for each word (and morphemes within the word). For each sentence, give a morpheme-by-morpheme gloss followed by an idiomatic gloss. Feel free to construct additional examples, especially if you have problems with these examples for an unforeseen reason.

(a)   Provide translations for the following sentences into Language X. Each example sentence in Language X should have an English gloss listed under each morpheme, in addition to the original English sentence.

1   The king found some books.
2   He read the books to his son.
3   The three soldiers stirred the soup.
4   They stirred it for three hours.
5   The soldier was old and ugly.
6   The castle is on a hill near a lake.
7   Antonio lives in Venice.
8   Duncan arrived at the castle yesterday.
9   Prospero's book will arrive next week.
10   The kind man gave a book to his daughter.
11   She will put the book on a chair.
12   Macbeth may find them in the forest. (Assume that the pronoun *them* refers to people.)
13   Falstaff drank a glass of beer.
14   Falstaff drank because he was thirsty.
15   Miranda knew that Prospero had many books.
16   Hamlet said that his mother was disloyal.
17   Portia told Shylock that he should be kind to Antonio.
18   Macbeth tried to kill the king.
19   Macbeth wanted to meet a witch.
20   Prospero has promised to give her the book.

(b)   Construct a lexicon for Language X, with English translations for each word. Organize the lexicon in terms of lexical categories, as in the previous exercises.

(c)   If you believe that some of the words in your lexicon contain more than one morpheme, try to identify the meaning of each morpheme and formulate morphological rules for combining the morphemes to form words.

(d)   Make a list of the different types of lexical categories (noun, verb, pronoun, preposition, etc.) in Language X. Indicate the lexical category for each word in your lexicon. If in doubt, assume that words in Language X belong to the same category as their English translations unless you have evidence suggesting otherwise.

(e)   Does Language X have pronouns like English *he/she/they/them/his/ her*? Can these pronouns be null (silent)? If so, in which syntactic positions (subject, object, indirect object, etc.)? You may need to consult your native speaker to determine whether certain pronouns are optional.

(f)   Does Language X have definite and/or indefinite articles like English *the* and *a(n)*? Illustrate.

(g)   Does Language X allow for tensed sentences to occur as embedded clauses? If so, what changes, if any, do you observe between a main clause and an embedded clause, in terms of complementizers, word order, special suffixes, etc.? Cite examples.

(h)   Does Language X have any auxiliary verbs, or does it just use affixes on the main verb? Illustrate.

(i)   Does Language X have any kind of case marking to indicate which DP is the subject, the object, the indirect object, etc.? Explain, citing examples.

(j)   Does Language X exhibit any kind of subject–verb agreement, of the type we find in English (*the boys are here* vs. *the boy is here*)? Give evidence one way or the other. What about object agreement – does the verb agree with its object? Is there any other kind of agreement, e.g. between a determiner or article and a noun?

(k)   Try to determine the basic constituent order for Language X, identifying the positions for the subject, object, indirect object, verb, etc. If you find that more than one ordering is possible, you may want to consult with your native speaker to find out if Language X allows more than one possible word order for the translations of each of these sentences.

(l)   Try to formulate phrase structure rules for each type of phrase that occurs in these data. Illustrate each rule with an example drawn from your data. Remember that the constituent order within each type of phrase may be different from English. In answering this question, you may come to the conclusion that certain constituents (such as verbs, pronouns, or other categories) may be affected by transformational movement rules; if so, you should feel free to posit the existence of one or more movement rules in addition to your phrase structure rules, but you should explain your reasoning, citing evidence from the data.

(m)   Draw tree diagrams for sentences 1, 2, 6, 9, 15, and 20. Make sure that your tree diagrams are consistent with your phrase structure rules.

(n)   Identify the c-selection properties of each verb in your lexicon for Language X.

(o)   Mention anything else that seems distinctive or interesting about the word order and basic grammar of Language X.

· ·

EXERCISE
3.14
ANSWERS

There is no single correct answer for this question; it depends on the language chosen. This means that if students all work on different languages, it can be very time-consuming and difficult to grade carefully. For this reason, it may be advisable to limit students in their choice of language, e.g. by organizing them into large groups all working on the same language, or by providing a set of data from a single language to the entire class.

(a)   Answers should contain all 20 sentences, with glosses conforming to the style used in the text for citing foreign language examples.

(b)   The lexicons should conform to the style of Exercises 3.11 (Malagasy) and 3.12 (Zapotec).

(c)   Answers should analyze morphologically complex words, if applicable. It may be advisable to look at the data provided and see if there is an obvious morphological analysis available for verb forms, and then to check whether this is reflected in the answer. It may be useful to compare Sentences (5) and (6) (for the contrast between present and past tense with the copula), and Sentences (8) and (9) (for past and future forms of the verb *arrive*). Determiners, adjectives, and nouns may also be inflected (e.g. with number or gender features).

(d)   This should be relatively simple to answer, given the lexicons in (b).

(e)   Answers should distinguish between different syntactic positions, since in some languages null subjects are allowed only in the subject position, while in other languages, they are also allowed in object position. Some languages allow null pronouns in other positions too, such as the object of a preposition or a possessor (the nominal specifier position). Crucial data involve those example sentences that contain pronouns in the English glosses, i.e. (2), (4), (10), (11), (12), (14), (16), (17), and (20), as well as biclausal sentences in which the English gloss has an infinitive with a null PRO subject, namely (18) and (19).

(f)   Answers should note the presence or absence of both definite and indefinite articles. In some languages, definiteness is marked by a morphological affix on the noun. In other languages, either the indefinite article or the definite article, or both, may be null. Crucial data involve example sentences with articles or quantifiers in the English glosses, as well as those containing names (which may also have articles in Language X).

(g)   Some languages use nominalizations instead of true embedded sentences, though in most cases full tensed clause embedding is possible. All biclausal sentences are potential candidates, including those whose English glosses involve infinitives (18–20), as well as those whose English glosses contain embedded tensed clauses (14–17).

(h)   Answers should identify any auxiliary verbs appearing in the data. Crucial examples involve not only those sentences containing auxiliaries (including modals) in the English data, but also (in some cases) examples containing present or past tense, since in some languages tense is marked by an auxiliary verb.

(i)   Answers should identify case-marking affixes where applicable. Crucial data involve cases where the same DP occurs in two different positions, e.g. the contrast between (4) and (12), with a third-person plural pronoun, the contrast between the forms of the two pronouns in (2), and the contrast between (1) and (18) with the DP *the king*, as well as the contrast between (9) and (20) with the name *Prospero*. Also, the three examples involving indirect objects, i.e. (2), (10), and (20), may provide evidence for a dative case marker in the data.

(j)   Possible candidates for identifying subject agreement morphology on the verb are limited in the data provided to cases involving number agreement, since none of the data provided involve first- or second-person subjects. If the language in question has noun classes (this is true of Bantu languages, for example), then there may be evidence for noun-class agreement on the verb provided by sentence (6), the only example involving a non-human subject. Evidence for number agreement may involve sentences with plural subjects, i.e. (3) and (4), though the data provided are not particularly helpful on this point, since there are no examples involving exactly the same verbs with singular subjects.

Likewise, evidence for object agreement may appear in examples with plural direct objects (i.e. (1), (2), and (12)), though the lack of examples involving singular direct objects with the same verbs poses the same kind of problem. Many languages show object agreement only with definite objects, so there may be a contrast between sentences with indefinite objects (i.e. (1), (10), (13), and (19)) and those with definite objects (i.e. (2), (3), (4), (11), (12), (18), and (20)).

Finally, evidence for agreement between determiners and nouns may come from the contrast between (3) and (5) with *the soldier(s)*, and other examples involving singular/plural contrasts with definite and indefinite DPs.

It may be advisable to encourage students to elicit additional data to answer some of the questions left open by the gaps in the data noted above.

(k)   Complete answers should indicate the positions for the subject, verb, direct object, and indirect object, as well as the positions for PPs, adverbs, adverbial clauses, and complement clauses. Distinctive positions for pronouns (versus other DP-types) should also be noted, if applicable.

(l)   The phrase structure rules provided should match the order of constituents in the data provided, unless the answers include an explicit
discussion of transformational movement displacing one or more
constituents from its original position. Answers that develop a movement analysis that works correctly should be encouraged, especially
if a coherent rationale for the movement analysis is given (e.g. if
more than one order occurs in the data, or if a movement analysis
is required in order to posit a VP constituent, as in the case of VSO
constituent order). Rules for categories such as TP, VP, PP, DP, and
NP should be provided (unless the language lacks evidence for them,
e.g. if it lacks overt prepositions or determiners).

(m)   Tree diagrams should be provided for the sentences in question. They
should conform to the phrase structure rules given in the answer to
part (l).

(n)   In most cases the c-selection properties will be the same as those of
the English verbs in the glosses, except in cases where Language X
uses a different category from English, e.g. if a DP in Language X is
used instead of a PP or CP, or if Language X has no determiners and
the analysis in (l) and (m) allows NP instead of DP as a direct object.

(o)   The range of possible answers here is vast; an ideal answer will note
at least a couple of salient distinguishing features of Language X, but
only the best students can be expected to provide answers that go
beyond the kind of observation that would be evident even to a non-
linguist lay speaker.

4

Syntax II: Syntactic Dependencies

Applying Addition #3, p. 212 of textbook

(1) Consider the following example:
The man John met yesterday stuttered.

    (i)   Identify the verbs.
    (ii)   For each verb, identify its subject.
    (iii)   How many clauses are there?
    (iv)   On the basis of your answers to the preceding questions, explain
           the ill-formedness of the following example:
           *The man John did not meet yesterday stuttered at all.

(2) Answer all the same questions for the following examples:

    (a)   *I resent at all that you did not come.
    (b)   *That Mary did not answer my letters bothers me at all.

(3) Can you construct a well-formed sentence containing *not* and *at all*
and violating Addition #3?

---

(1) (i)   The verbs are italicized here:

          The man John *met* yesterday *stuttered*.

    (ii)   Verb *met*, subject *John*
         Verb *stuttered*, subject *The man John met*
            Examples of tests for subjecthood:

           (I)   Put the verb in the present tense. The third-person subject
                will trigger verbal agreeement.

The man *John* meets, The man *they* meet

(II)   In a simple statement, the subject precedes an auxiliary verb like *will*; in the corresponding yes–no question the subject follows it:

The man John met yesterday will stutter.
Will *the man John met yesterday* stutter?

(iii)   There are two clauses:

the whole sentence, and *John met yesterday.*

(iv)   The clause *John did not meet yesterday* does not contain the NPI *at all.* This contradicts Addition #3, p. 212 of textbook, which states that the negative licenser and the negative polarity item must both belong to exactly the same CLAUSES.

(2)   (a)   The verbs are *resent* and *come.* Their subjects are *I* and *you* respectively. The clauses are *that you did not come* and the whole sentence. The sentence is excluded because the NPI belongs to a clause not containing the negation.

(b)   The verbs are *answer* and *bothers.* Their subjects are *Mary* and *That Mary did not answer my letters* respectively. The clauses are *That Mary did not answer my letters* and the whole sentence. The sentence is excluded because the NPI belongs to a clause not containing the negation.

(3)   Example:

I did not think that Mary liked me at all.

The embedded clause *that Mary liked me at all* does not contain the negation, yet the sentence is well formed.

EXERCISE 4.2   Using a Constituency Test

Consider the following sentence:

(i)   Juliet says that Romeo lies to his parents a lot.

(1)   Note that this sentence is ambiguous as to which verb the measure adverb *a lot* modifies. Paraphrase the two meanings.

(2)   Draw two tree structures for this sentence, each corresponding to one of its meanings.

(3)   Recall that VP-constituency can be established by using VP-**preposing**: A string that can be preposed by VP preposing qualifies as a VP (cf. previous chapter of textbook).

(a)   Explain why the following VP-preposed version of sentence (i) is not ambiguous:

(ii)   lie to his parents a lot, Juliet says that Romeo does

(b)   Explain why the following VP-preposed version of sentence (i) is still ambiguous the same way (i) was:

(iii)   lie to his parents, Juliet says that Romeo does a lot

---

(1)   Juliet says: 'Romeo lies to his parents a lot.'

Juliet says a lot: 'Romeo lies to his parents.'

(2)   The adverb *a lot* is either in the embedded clause (modifying the verb *lie*) as in structure (a), or in the main clause (modifying the verb *say*) as in structure (b):

(a)

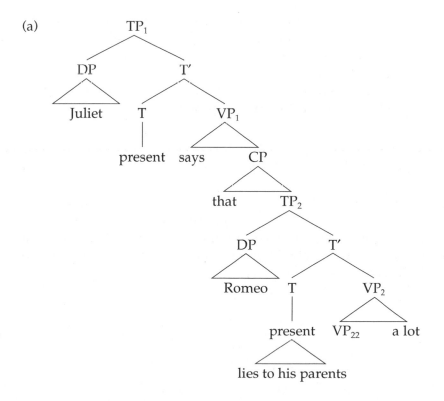

(b)

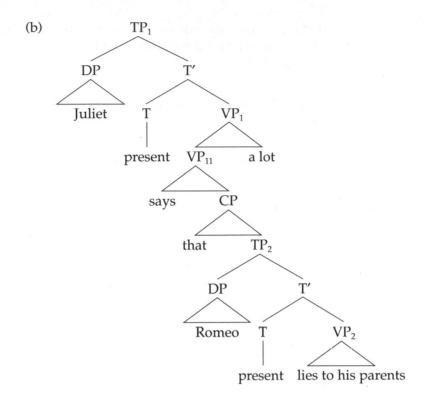

(3) (a) Since VP preposing has applied preposing *a lot*, it can only have applied in structure (a) above preposing VP₂. It can only have the meaning associated with structure (a) in which *a lot* modifies the VP *lie to his parents*.

(b) VP preposing could have applied to either structure (a), preposing VP₂₂, or to structure (b), preposing VP₁₁.

EXERCISE 4.3   Checking the NPI status of *any longer* and *anytime*

Construct examples showing that *any longer* and *anytime* are NPIs. In order to do this, you will have to produce for each of them a minimal pair of examples: one ill-formed example lacking an NPI licenser and one well-formed example only differing from the ill-formed one by containing an NPI licenser.

Examples:

John has slept/John will sleep.
*John has slept anywhere/*John will sleep any longer.
John has not slept anywhere/John will not sleep any longer.

The first example is well formed. The second, only differing from the first in the presence of *anywhere* (or *any longer*), is ill formed, showing that the presence of *anywhere* (or *any longer*) is creating a problem. The third is well formed, and minimally differs from the second in the presence of the NPI licenser *not*: this shows that *anywhere* (or *any longer*) is licensed by the presence of negation and thus that it is an NPI.

Check each sentence in (34) against Rule R5 modified by Addition #3, pp. 216, 207, and 212 of textbook. Do this by drawing a tree structure for each and deciding whether the modified rule is obeyed.

(a)

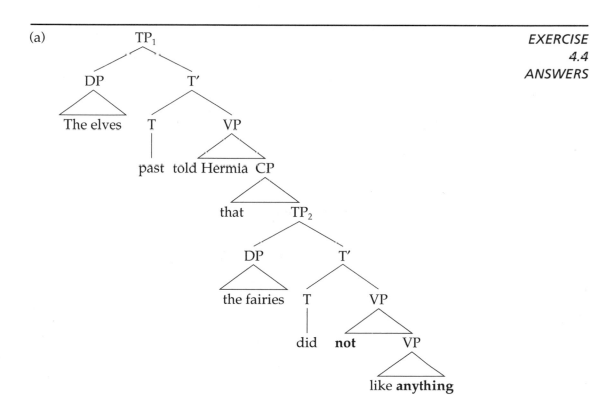

(b)

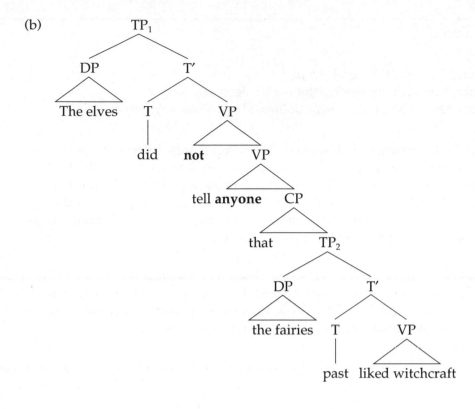

(c)

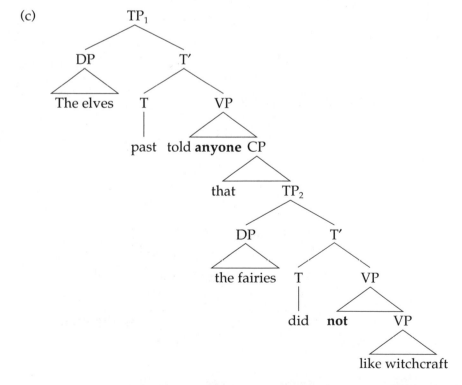

(d)

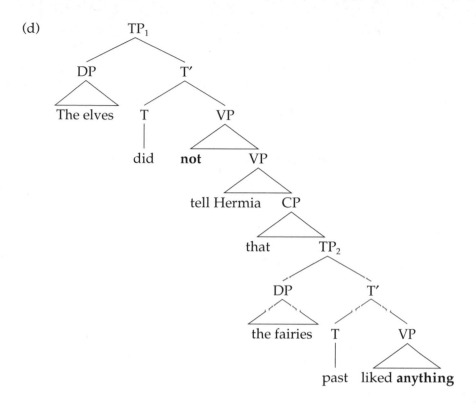

(e)

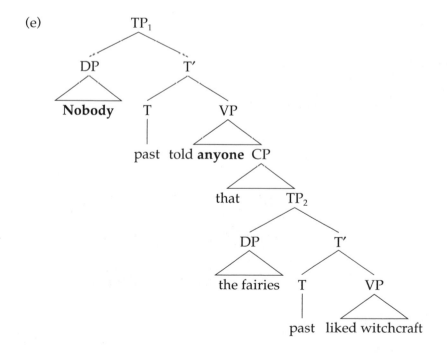

(f)

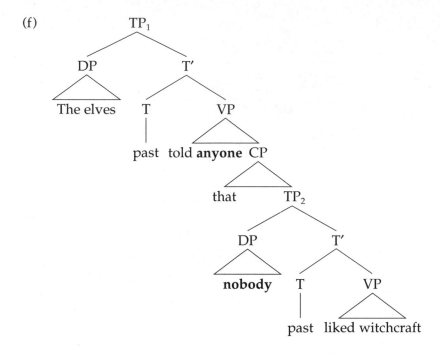

(g)

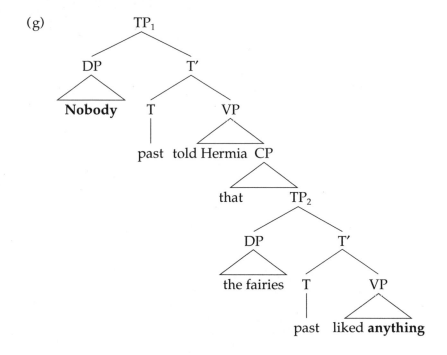

We now check whether the following rule (combining Rule 5 with Addition #3) is satisfied in each of the preceding structures:

Rule: If a negative polarity item appears in a sentence
  (i)   this sentence must also contain a negative element and
  (ii) the negative licenser and the NPI must both belong to exactly the same CLAUSES.

For each of the first three sentences of (48), p. 222 of textbook,   **EXERCISE 4.5**

(i)   Draw its constituent structure tree.
(ii) Verify and state exactly why it satisfies or fails to satisfy Rule R6, p. 220 of textbook.

(i)   (a)   *EXERCISE 4.5 ANSWERS*

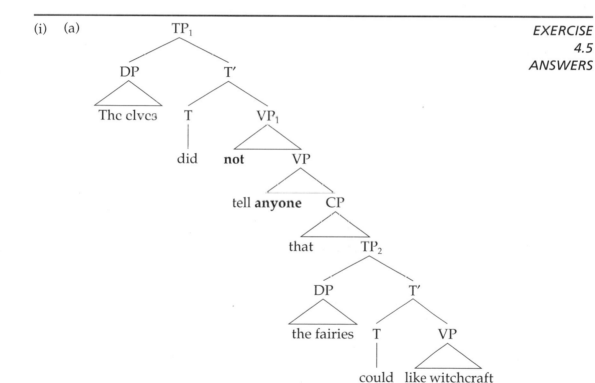

(b)

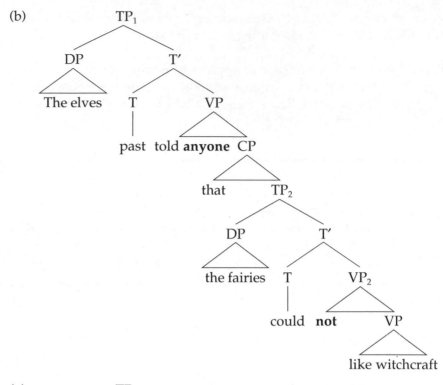

(c)

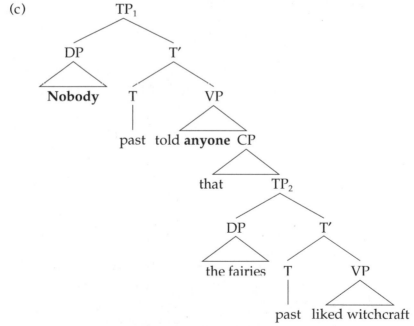

(ii)   We first need to state Rule R6:

R6: A negative polarity item must appear in a constituent that counts as negated.

To apply Rule R6 properly, we need to understand how to determine what counts as negated. This is given in the text, (45), p. 220, as follows:

APPROXIMATE RULE AS TO WHAT COUNTS AS NEGATED:
If a sentence contains a negative expression which is an XP (i.e. a DP, or an AdvP, etc.), what counts as negated is the smallest constituent containing XP.

Applying this rule to each of the trees, we see that in tree (a), the negated constituent is VP$_1$. Since the NPI *anyone* is contained in it, sentence (a) is correctly predicted to be well formed. In tree (b), the negated constituent is VP$_2$. Since the NPI *anyone* is not contained in it, sentence (b) is correctly predicted to be ill formed. Finally, in tree (c), the negated constituent is TP$_1$. Since the NPI *anyone* is contained in it, sentence (c) is correctly predicted to be well formed.

Consider the example given in (36), p. 217 of textbook, repeated below:

EXERCISE 4.6

(i)   *Anyone did not see Portia

1. (a)   To determine what counts as negated, use the procedure exemplified in (40), p. 218 of textbook, which replaces negation with *it is not the case that* . . .
    (b)   According to this procedure, is *anyone* part of the negated string?
    (c)   Is sentence (i) grammatical according to Addition #5, p. 220 of textbook?
2. (a)   Draw the tree structure for sentence (i).
    (b)   On the basis of this tree structure, determine what constituent is negated according to Rule (51), p. 223 of textbook.
    (c)   Is sentence (i) grammatical according to Rule (51)?
3. Which approach is superior: Rule R5, p. 207 of textbook, + Addition #5 or Rule (51)?

---

1. (a)   By the procedure given in the text, we can translate a sentence of the form 'X did not see Portia' as 'it is not the case that X saw Portia'. Applied to the present case, it gives us the result: 'it is not the case that anyone saw Portia'.

EXERCISE 4.6 ANSWERS

    (b)   This procedure leads us to believe that the negated string is: *anyone saw Portia*, and thus that the DP *anyone* is part of what is negated.
    (c)   According to the rule modified by Addition #5, p. 220 of textbook, a sentence is well formed if the negative polarity item appears in a constituent that counts as negated. Accordingly, sentence (i) is predicted to be well formed.

2.   (a)   The tree structure for sentence (i) is:

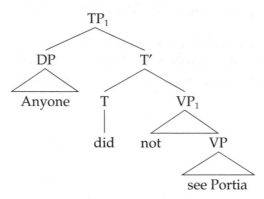

    (b)   The rule is as follows:

    (51) **Negative Polarity Items Licensing Rule**
    A sentence containing an NPI is well formed only if this NPI is in
    the c-command domain of a negative element.

    In other words, what counts as negated is the c-command domain
    of the negative item. In (i) the negative item is *not*, and its c-
    command domain, i.e. the smallest constituent containing it, is VP$_1$.
    (c)   Since the NPI *anyone* is not included in this VP$_1$, sentence (i) is
    correctly predicted to be ill formed.
3.   Clearly, the second approach is preferable.

EXERCISE 4.7   For each sentence, provide s-selection, c-selection and linking information
for the verb it contains and draw its tree.

    (i)   Macbeth left.
    (ii)   The soldiers put their weapons in the tower.
    (iii)   Petruccio thinks that Bianca left.

EXERCISE 4.7 ANSWERS

    (i)   leave (Xtheme)   (Note that the argument of the verb *leave* is taken to
                │   be a theme.)
            subject

    tree:

```
              TP
            /    \
         DP        T'
         /\       /  \
    Macbeth      T      VP
                 |      /\
                past   left
```

(ii)   Put (Xagent,   Xtheme,   Xlocation)

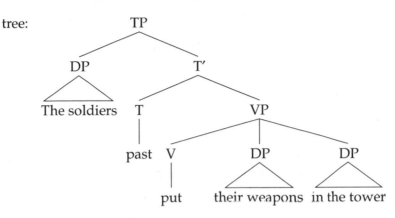

tree:

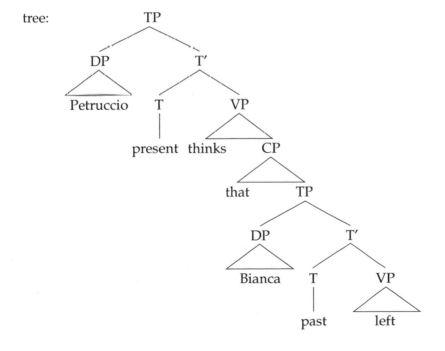

(iii)   think (Xagent,   Xtheme)

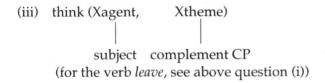

(for the verb *leave*, see above question (i))

tree:

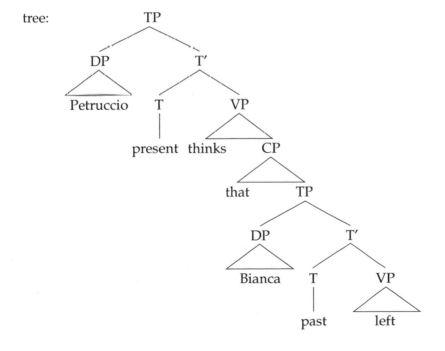

EXERCISE 4.8	The verbs *own* and *belong*

The two verbs *own* and *belong* establish a relation between a possessor and a possessed object. Consider the following sentences:

(i)   Bertram owns this castle.
(ii)   This castle belongs to Bertram.

1.   Draw the trees for each sentence.
2.   Answer the following questions for each of these two sentences:

   (a)   What DP refers to the possessor? Is this DP a subject or a complement? If it is a complement, what is it a complement of?
   (b)   What DP refers to the possessed object? Is this DP a subject or a complement? If it is a complement, what is it a complement of?

3.   For each of the verbs *own* and *belong*, write a representation of its linking properties as we did in (63), p. 228 of textbook, for the verb *describe* or in (67), p. 231 of textbook, for the verbs *wait* and *await* (use the labels Xpossessor and Xpossessee to identify the two arguments).
4.   What does the answer to the previous question show about the relation between the arguments of a predicate and their syntactic realization?

EXERCISE 4.8 ANSWERS   1.   (i)

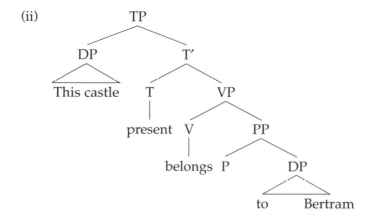

2. (a)   Sentence (i): Possessor: DP subject.
        Sentence (ii): Possessor: DP complement of the preposition *to*.
    (b)   Sentence (i): Possessed object: DP object of the Verb.
        Sentence (ii): Possessed object: DP subject.

3.   verb own: own   (Xpossessor,   Xpossessee)

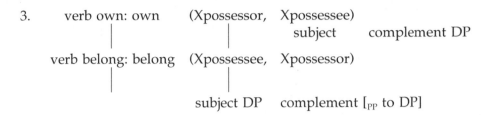

                                          subject   complement DP

         verb belong: belong   (Xpossessee,   Xpossessor)

                                     subject DP   complement [_PP to DP]

4. If the syntactic structures we have drawn for these sentences is
    correct, it means that we cannot predict the syntactic realization of
    arguments just by looking at their contribution to the meaning of the
    sentence.

Practice c-command   **EXERCISE**
                                                                   4.9

1. Draw the trees for each of the sentences (105a and b), p. 251 of textbook.
2. For each sentence, list the words c-commanded by the DP *Ophelia*.
3. Explain why these sentences are ill formed.
4. Explain why the second sentence below is ill formed:

    (i)   No one cut anyone.
    (ii) *Anyone cut no one.

Sentence (105)   a. * Herself cut Ophelia.   *EXERCISE*
Sentence (105)   b. * Ophelia's friends love herself.   *4.9*
                                                             ANSWERS

1. Sentence 105a:

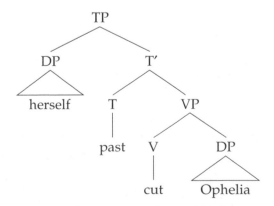

Sentence 105b:

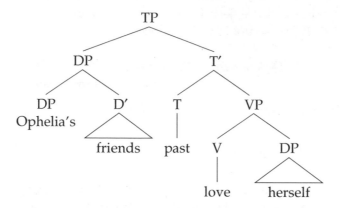

2. Recall that the c-command domain of a particular phrase (XP) is the smallest constituent containing XP. This XP is said to c-command everything in its c-command domain.

    Sentence 105a: the first XP containing the DP *Ophelia* is the VP. The c-commanded words are: *Ophelia* and *cut*.

    Sentence 105b: the first XP containing the DP *Ophelia* is the subject DP. The c-commanded words are: *Ophelia* and *friends*.

3. A reflexive must have an antecedent and the antecedent must c-command the reflexive. In neither of these sentences does the only available antecedent, *Ophelia*, c-command the reflexive.

4. The two sentences have similar structures:

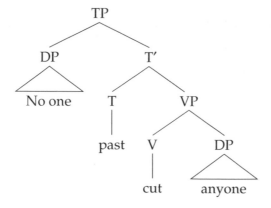

anyone is an NPI and it must be in the c-command domain of a negative element. In the NPI *anyone* is c-commanded by the negative DP *no one*. In the second sentence, the negative DP *no one* does not c-command the NPI *anyone*.

1.   Draw the tree for the following sentence:

(i)   Othello believes that the picture of Desdemona belongs to him.

2.   List all the DPs c-commanded by the DP *Desdemona*.
3.   List all the DPs c-commanded by the DP *Othello*.
4.   The following sentence is ill formed. Explain why.

(ii)   *Othello believes that the picture of Desdemona belongs to himself.

5.   Consider now the well-formedness of the following sentence:

(ii)   Nobody believes that the picture of Desdemona belongs to anyone.

Verify that it obeys the condition on NPI licensing.
Does NPI licensing obey the clausemate requirement?

1.

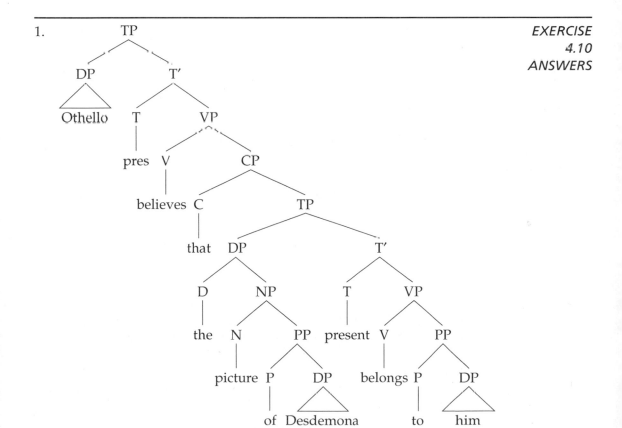

2.   The DP [Desdemona]. (The first XP containing the DP [Desdemona] is the PP [of Desdemona], which only contains only one DP: the DP [Desdemona].)
3.   The DPs [Othello], [the picture of Desdemona], [Desdemona], [him]. (The first XP containing the DP [Othello] is the matrix TP, which contains all the DPs in this sentence.)
4.   This sentence has the same structure as (i) above with *himself* replacing *him*. The only possible antecedent for the reflexive *himself* is [Othello], which belongs to a different clause than *himself*: the clausemate requirement is violated.
5.   This sentence has the same structure as (i) above, with *Nobody* replacing *Othello* and a*nyone* replacing *him*. The NPI *anyone* needs to be in a negated constituent. The constituent negated by *Nobody* is its c-command domain, which is the entire sentence. Therefore, *anyone* is within a negated constituent. The fact that this sentence is well formed shows that there is no clausemate requirement for NPI licensing.

· ·

EXERCISE
4.11

Principle B

We have seen in the text that the distribution of reflexive pronouns is constrained by the following two principles which we postulated as first approximation:

R1: The Clausemate Requirement: The reflexive and its antecedent must be in exactly the same clauses.
R2: The C-command Requirement: The antecedent DP must c-command the reflexive.

1.   Provide two (deviant) sentences containing a reflexive pronoun, each violating only one of these two principles.
2.   Remarkably, the distribution of (non-reflexive) pronouns is also constrained. This is illustrated by the following sentence:

*Othello likes him.

Although this sentence is well formed, it cannot be used to mean that Othello likes himself. In other words, the pronoun *him* cannot be coreferential with the DP *Othello*. In this problem, we investigate this distribution.
2.1   Consider the following sentences (where DPs sharing an index are supposed to be interpreted as referring to the same person):

(a)   *Othello$_j$ saw him$_j$.
(b)   Othello$_j$ said he$_j$ saw Portia$_k$.
(c)   Othello$_j$ said Portia$_k$ saw him$_j$.

  (i)   Draw the tree for each of these sentences.
  (ii)   Postulate a principle, let us call it P1, that separates the ill-formed (a) sentence from the well-formed (b) and (c) sentences. (Hint: this principle resembles the clausemate requirement R1, p. 200 of textbook: it will state some condition that a pronoun and its antecedent have to meet.)
  (iii) If properly formulated, your principle P1 should predict the ill-formedness of:

(d)   *Portia$_j$'s description of her$_j$ displeased Othello.

Draw the tree for (d) and verify that your principle handles it correctly. If not, revise it so that it does.

2.2   Consider now the following sentences:

(e)   Othello$_j$'s wife met him$_j$.
(f)   Portia's description of Othello$_j$ displeased him$_j$.

  (i)   Draw the tree for each of these sentences.
  (ii)   Postulate a principle, let us call it P2, modeled on the c-command requirement R2, p. 200 of textbook, that separates the well-formed (e) and (f) sentences from the ill-formed (a) sentence.

2.3   Comparing P1 and P2 with R1 and R2, can you formulate a general prediction regarding the distribution of pronouns as compared with that of reflexives?

2.4   Consider now the following sentence:

(g)   Othello$_j$ trusts his$_j$ wife.

Draw its tree. Do your principles P1 and P2 correctly predict the well-formedness of (g)? If not, amend P1 so that it correctly rules (g) in. (*Note*: In the syntactic literature, principles R1 and R2 are formulated as one principle called Principle A of the Binding Theory. Principles P1 and P2 are also formulated as one principle called Principle B of the Binding Theory.)

· ·

EXERCISE
4.11
ANSWERS

1. (i)   **Othello~j~ thinks that Desdemona lies to himself~j~*
    (ii) **Othello~j~'s picture belongs to himself~j~*

In the first sentence, the DP *Othello* c-commands the DP *himself* but belongs to a clause, the main clause, that *himself* does not belong to.

In the second sentence, *Othello* and *himself* belong to the same clauses (there is only one) but Othello does not c-command *himself*.

2.1 (i)   (a):

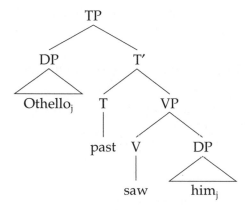

(b):

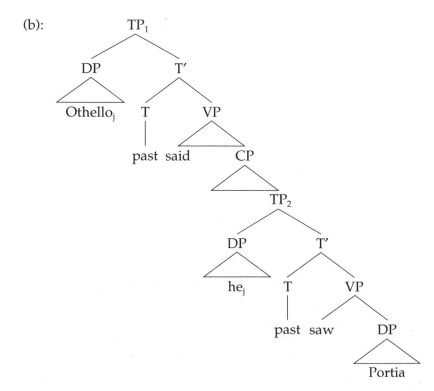

(c):

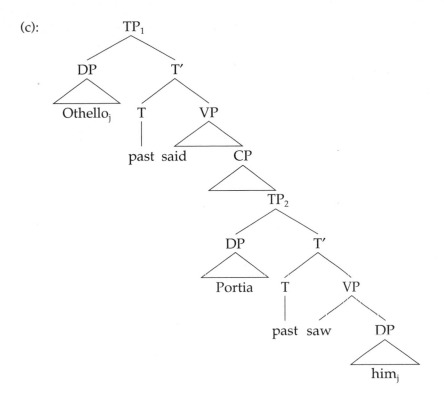

(ii) The sentences above suggest that:

P1: A pronoun and a DP coreferential with it cannot be clausemates.

(iii) (d):

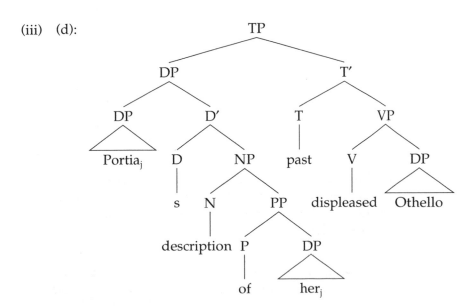

In this sentence, the pronoun *her* cannot be coreferential with the DP *Portia*. This is as predicted by R1, p. 200 of textbook, since these two elements are clausemates.

2.2　(i)　(e):

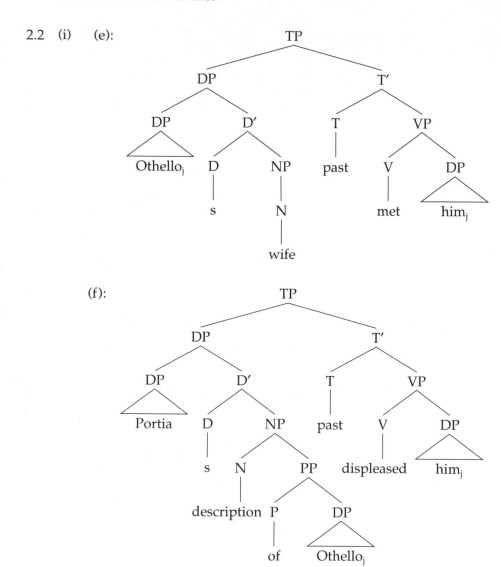

(ii)　In these sentences, the pronoun and its antecedent are clause-mates, yet the sentences are well formed. However, in neither of them is the pronoun c-commanded by its antecedent. This suggests P2:

P2: A pronoun may always be coreferential with an antecedent that does not c-command it.

2.3   Putting P1 and P2 together, we derive P:

P: A pronoun cannot be clausemate with an antecedent that c-commands it.

Putting R1 and R2 together, we derive R:

R: A reflexive must be clausemate with an antecedent that c-commands it.

    Suppose a DP is an antecedent of a reflexive. To satisfy R, this DP is clausemate and c-commands this reflexive. A pronoun could not appear in place of the reflexive with the same antecedent (this would violate P, since this pronoun would have a clausemate c-commanding antecedent).

    Suppose a DP is an antecedent of a pronoun. To satisfy P, this DP is either not clausemate with the pronoun, or does not c-command it. A reflexive could not appear in place of the pronoun with the same antecedent (this would violate R, since this pronoun would have a clausemate c-commanding antecedent).

    In other words, in a situation where a DP is antecedent of a pronoun, either this pronoun is a reflexive, or it is a non-reflexive pronoun. (This is sometimes described as the 'complementary distribution' of pronouns and reflexives.)

2.4

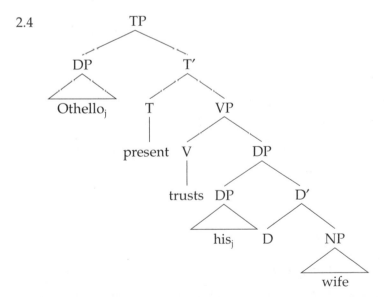

    P1 and P2 prohibit a pronoun from being clausemate with a c-commanding antecedent. Clearly, this is too strong, since (g) is well formed. We amend them so that a pronoun cannot be clausemate or DP-mate with a c-commanding antecedent.

. . . .

EXERCISE   **Principle C**
4.12
As the following examples show, a pronoun can have an antecedent preceding it in a different clause (where DPs sharing an index are supposed to be
interpreted as referring to the same person):

    (a)   Othello$_j$ said Portia$_k$ saw him$_j$.
    (b)   Othello$_j$ said he$_j$ saw Portia$_k$.

1. Consider the following sentences:

    (c)   *He$_j$ said that Othello$_j$ saw Portia.
    (d)   *He$_j$ said that Portia saw Othello$_j$.
    (e)   *He$_j$ said that Portia thinks that Othello$_j$ left.

    (i)   Draw the trees for sentences (a) and (c).
    (ii)   To separate the well-formed examples from the ill-formed ones,
          formulate a principle C1 stated in terms of the notion **precedence**
          and regulating the relation between a pronoun and its antecedent.
          Make sure that your principle correctly distinguishes between
          the examples (a) and (b) and the examples (c), (d), and (e).
    (iii) To separate the well-formed examples from the ill-formed ones,
          formulate a different principle – C2 – this time stated in terms of
          the notion **c-command** and regulating the relation between a pro-
          noun and its antecedent. Make sure that your principle correctly
          distinguishes between the examples (a) and (b) and the examples
          (c), (d), and (e).

2. Consider the following two sentences:

    (f)   His$_j$ wife says that Othello left.
    (g)   The rumor that he left pleased Othello$_j$'s wife.

    (i)   Draw the trees for these two sentences (for (g), assume that the
          CP [*that he left*] is a complement of the Noun *rumor*).
    (ii)   Compare the predictions made by C1 and C2 regarding sentences
          (f) and (g). What can be concluded?
    (iii) Is this conclusion compatible with the well-formedness of the
          following example?

    (h)   After he left, Othello fell.

(You may suppose that the string *he left* forms a TP constituent complement of the preposition *after* and that the PP headed by the P *after* is
adjoined to the matrix TP.)
(*Note*: In the syntactic literature, the principle responsible for account-
ing for the difference between a and b, and c, d, and e, is called Principle
C of the Binding Theory.)

1. (i)   (a):

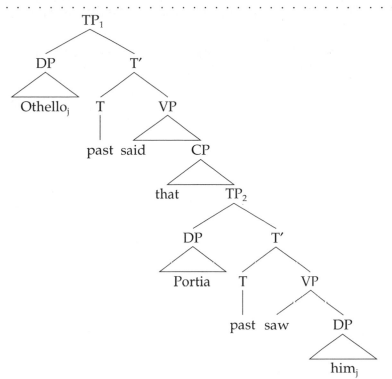

(c):

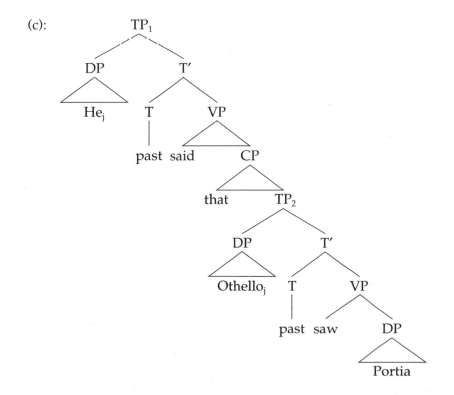

(ii)   C1: A name cannot be coindexed with a pronoun that precedes it.

(iii)   C2: A name cannot be coindexed with a pronoun that c-commands it.

2.   (i)   (f):

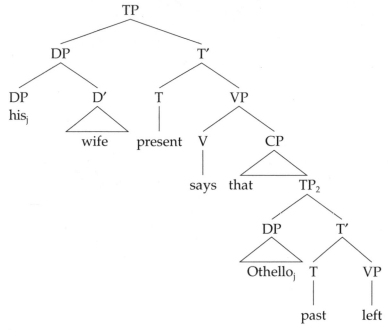

(g):

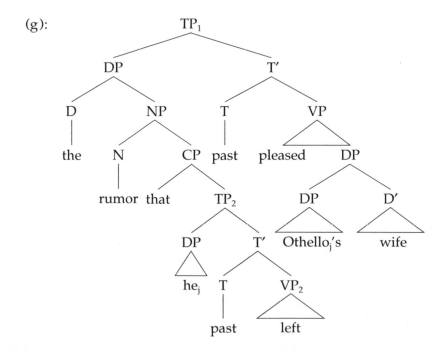

(ii) C1 predicts incorrectly that both (f) and (g) are ill formed, since the pronoun precedes the name it is coindexed with in both cases.

C2 correctly predicts that both (f) and (g) are well formed, since the pronoun does not c-command the name in either sentence.

Conclusion: so far C2 is to be preferred.

(iii) First let us draw the tree for sentence (h):

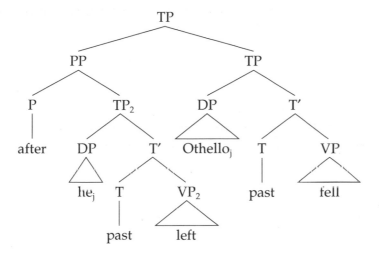

Since the pronoun *he* does not c-command (its c-command domain is TP_2) the name *Othello*, Principle C2 correctly predicts that sentence (h) is well formed.

·VP Preposing and Reflexive Pronouns   EXERCISE
                                                                           4.13

1. Construct the tree structure for the following example:

   (a) Ophelia thinks that Othello will survive the war.

2. Consider now the following example:

   (b) Ophelia thinks that survive the war, Othello will.

   Modeling on our treatment of wh-movement, propose a tree structure for (b) deriving it from (a) plus the application of a movement rule – VP preposing – which preposes a VP and adjoins it to TP. Show all the steps of the derivation.

3. The rule of VP preposing preposes a VP and adjoins it to TP. Provide a different sentence that could be derived from (a) by VP preposing and provide its tree structure.

4. State the two principles that the relationship between a reflexive pronoun and its antecedent must satisfy.
5. Draw the tree for the following sentence and verify that its structure satisfies these two principles:

    (c)   Ophelia expects that Macbeth$_j$ will hurt himself$_j$.

6. Draw the tree for the following sentence and verify that its structure does not satisfy any of these two principles:

    (d)   Hurt himself$_j$, Ophelia expects that Macbeth$_j$ will.

7. Propose an explanation for the fact that sentence (d) is well formed despite the fact that its structure does not satisfy the two principles in question. (Hint: reread the section, pp. 242–5 of textbook, on wh-movement and what was said about how basic dependencies are satisfied in wh-questions.)

- -

EXERCISE 4.13 ANSWERS

1. (a):

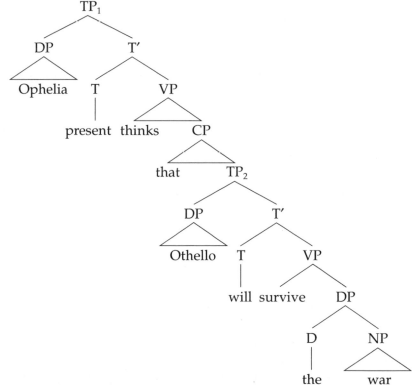

2. We can suppose that sentence (b) is derived from sentence (a) by a rule preposing the VP [survive the war] which adjoins it to TP, yielding the following tree for (b):

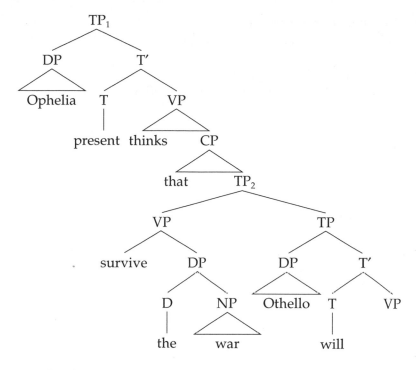

It is also fine to draw the tree without including the last VP node.

3. The rule of VP preposing could also prepose the VP [survive the war] and adjoin it to the matrix VP.

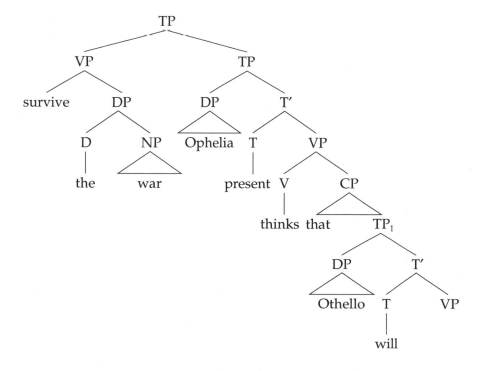

4. **The Clausemate requirement**
   The reflexive and its antecedent must be in exactly the same clauses.

   The C-command Requirement
   The antecedent DP must c-command the reflexive.

5. (c):

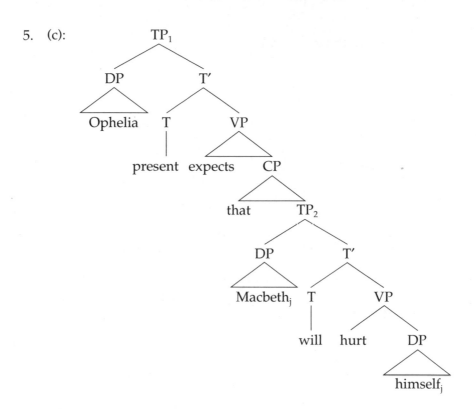

The DP *Macbeth* and the reflexive DP are in the same clause, namely TP$_2$. The c-command domain of the DP *Macbeth* is TP$_2$. This means that the DP *Macbeth* c-commands the reflexive.

6. Sentence (d) is the same as the (c) sentence to which VP preposing has applied. Its structure is:

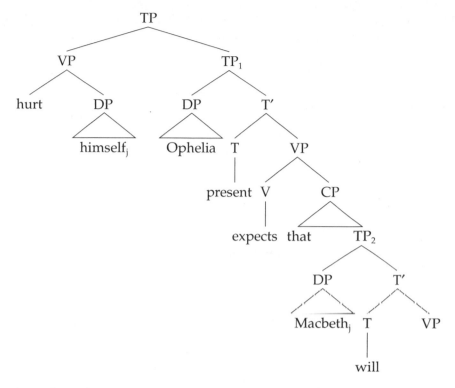

It is clear that neither of the two requirements is satisfied. First, the reflexive belongs to a clause, TP$_1$, that does not include the antecedent (i.e. the DP *Macbeth*). Secondly, the c-command domain of the DP *Macbeth* is TP$_2$. It does not c-command the reflexive.

7. One possibility would be to claim that these two requirements must be satisfied prior to the application of the rule of VP preposing, i.e. on the structure of (c). (This proposal works fine for the examples under discussion here, but is not tenable when a fuller array of data is considered.)

· ·

Indirect wh-questions and wh-islands   EXERCISE
                                                                            4.14

1.   Draw the tree for the following sentence:

     (a) The witches believed that Macbeth's armies would crush his
          enemies.

2.   Describe the s-selection, c-selection and linking properties of the verb
     crush. (Hint: reread section 4.2, pp. 224–51.)

3.1 In the following sentence, assume that the phrase *whose enemies* is the
     specifier of the embedded CP and draw its tree.

     (b) The witches wondered whose enemies Macbeth's armies would
          crush.

3.2   Underline the phrases selected by the verb *crush*. The structural positions of these phrases should not conform to the linking rules that you established for *crush* on the basis of sentence (a). Propose a syntactic analysis of this discrepancy. (Hint: reread section 4.2.3, pp. 238–45 of textbook, on wh-movement.)

4.1   Draw the trees for the following two sentences:

(c)   Oberon knew that Othello would kill Desdemona.
(d)   Oberon knew when Othello would kill Desdemona.

4.2   What is the determining structural factor explaining why wh-movement fails in (f) but not in (e)? (Hint: compare their underlying structures.)

(e)   Who did Oberon know that Othello would kill?
(f)   *Who did Oberon know when Othello would kill?

(*Note*: The construction exemplified by the (b) sentence is called an indirect question. The phenomenon exemplified in (f) is called a wh-island.)

EXERCISE
4.14
ANSWERS

1.   (a):

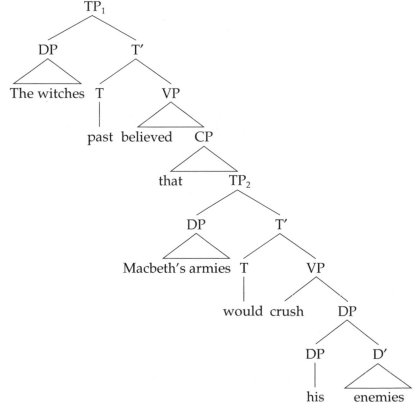

2.   verb crush: crush (Xagent,   Xtheme)

                             subject   complement DP

3.1   (b):

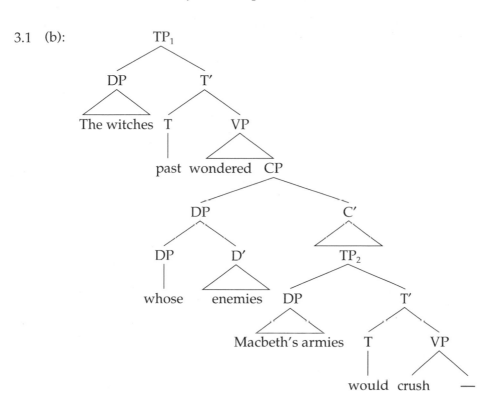

3.2   The DP selected by the verb *crush* is [whose enemies], which should appear as object of the verb *crush* but does not. To account for this discrepancy between sentence (a) and sentence (b), we postulate that the phrase [whose enemies] has been wh-moved from the object position of the verb *crush* after it has satisfied the various selectional restrictions of this verb.

4.1   (c):

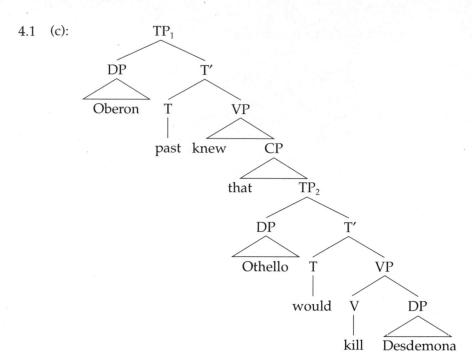

(d)   Here wh-movement has applied, moving the adverbial *when* to CP:

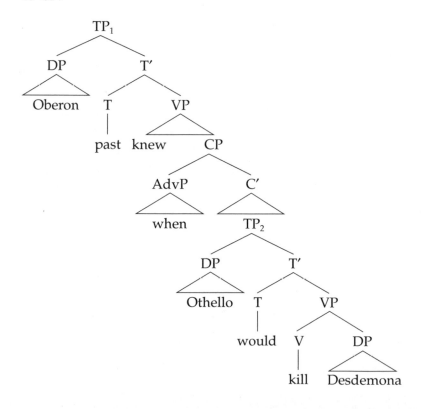

4.2   To derive (e) and (f), we can take (c) and (d), replace *Desdemona* by *who* in each, then apply wh-movement to this DP *who*, moving it to the beginning of the main clause. The only difference seems to be the presence of a preposed wh-phrase in the embedded clause of (d). The deviance of (f) can be attributed to the presence of this preposed wh-phrase. This could be formulated as:

A wh-phrase cannot be preposed across an already preposed wh-phrase.

5
Syntax III: The Distribution of Verbal Forms: A Case Study

EXERCISE 5.1 In the sentences below:

    (i)   Romeo seemed to have been kissed.
    (ii)   Writers try to adapt Romeo and Juliet to the big screen.
    (iii) They were told to go buy tomatoes.
    (iv) Do you believe that he has the nerves to go on stage?

1.   Circle all finite verb forms, underline past participles, double underline passive participles, wavy underline all infinitives.
2.   Give five examples of different types of embedded clauses.

EXERCISE 5.1 ANSWERS

1.   (i)   Romeo (seemed) to have been kissed.
       (ii)   Writers (try) to adapt Romeo and Juliet to the big screen.
       (iii) They (were) told to go buy tomatoes.
       (iv) (Do) you believe that he (has) the nerves to go on stage?

2.   Some examples of embedded clauses (non-exhaustive list):

    embedded tensed complement headed by *that*:
    I think [*that Romeo has been kissed*]
    embedded infinitival complement headed by *to*:
    Many students try [*to read Romeo and Juliet*]
    embedded *-ing* complement (gerund, present participle)
    Many students tried [*reading Romeo and Juliet*]
    embedded infinitival complement headed by *for*:
    I'd prefer [*for Bill to play Romeo*]

tensed indirect question:
I wonder [*if Bill will play Romeo*]
I wonder [*who will play Romeo*]
infinitival indirect question:
I wonder [*who to see*]
relative clause:
[The actor [*who plays Romeo*]] is called Bill

Constituent structure

In the text, the string *have read Hamlet* is assigned the constituent structure
in (16), p. 262 of textbook. In this exercise you are asked to show that this
is indeed the correct structure.

How do you test constituent structure? One of the tests to establish
constituent structure is **coordination**, as discussed in chapter 3 of textbook.
Only constituents that are alike can be coordinated by a coordination like
and or *but*. Coordination forms tree structures like (1), where X stands for
V, C, A, P, D, T, etc.:

1.

XP   and   XP

Now consider the following examples.

(i) (a)   Some of the students have read Hamlet and have seen King
           Lear.
     (b)   Some of the students have read Hamlet and seen King Lear.
     (c)   Some of the students have read Hamlet and King Lear.

A. Identify the syntactic category (VP, AP, TP, CP, DP, . . .) of the con-
    stituent following *and*:
    (a)   have seen King Lear   is a _____
    (b)   seen King Lear   is a _____
    (c)   King Lear   is a _____

B. Identify the first part of the coordination:
    (a)   _____ is coordinated with *have seen King Lear*
    (b)   _____ is coordinated with *seen King Lear*
    (c)   _____ is coordinated with *King Lear*

C.   Translate your findings in B into tree structures, using the format in (1) above.

(a)   The tree structure for B(a) is:

(b)   The tree structure for B(b) is:

(c)   The tree structure for B(c) is:

D.   State in one or two sentences how the structures in C support the constituent structure in (16). (XP is a constituent because. . . .)

E.   Chapter 3 discusses other constituent tests. List these, and try to apply these to each of the examples in (i) (applying means manipulating the string, and constructing relevant examples).

Discuss if these constituent tests work for the examples under discussion. If they do, what conclusions can you draw? If not, what conclusions can you draw?

EXERCISE 5.2 ANSWERS

A.   (a)   have seen King Lear   is a **TP (or VP)**
(b)   seen King Lear   is a **VP**
(c)   King Lear   is a **DP**

Comment on (a): Though TP is the correct answer, VP should be accepted as an answer as well. What is important at this point is the internal make-up of this constituent (the VP dominating *have* contains another VP).

Why is TP the correct answer? *Have* is a finite verb form: it will project a VP, because it is a V, and a TP, because it is a finite verb.

It is shown later in chapter 5 of textbook that finite *have* is in T, and therefore the label of the coordinated category is really TP. This means that the silent subject in the second conjunct needs to be accounted for. There are two ways to achieve this, both of which have been argued for in the literature; these can be found in students' attempts to solve this problem.

Either a deletion process deletes the subject from the second conjunct, a process called *coordination reduction*:

TP coordination analysis and coordination reduction:
. [$_{TP}$[$_{TP}$Some of the students have read Hamlet] and [$_{TP}$ some of the students have seen King Lear]]

or the subject is moved from both conjuncts, in an Across-the-Board manner (constituents can be extracted from a coordinated structure only if they are extracted from all conjuncts). The landing site of the subject is often called AgrSP (AgrS = agreement subject):

TP coordination and Across-the-Board movement of the subject:
[$_{AgrSP}$Some of the students$_i$ [$_{TP}$[$_{TP}$ [e]$_i$ have read Hamlet] and [$_{TP}$ [e]$_i$ have seen King Lear]]

B. (a) *have read Hamlet* is coordinated with *have seen King Lear*
    (b) *read Hamlet* is coordinated with *seen King Lear*
    (c) *Hamlet* is coordinated with *King Lear*

C. (a) The tree structure for B(a) is as follows:

     If TP was chosen:

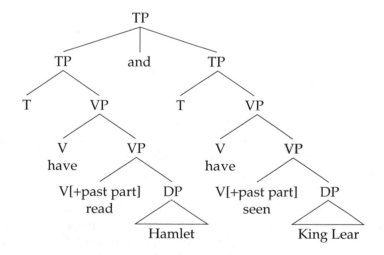

If VP was chosen:

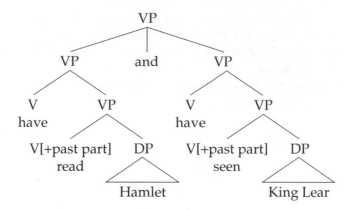

(b) The tree structure for B(b) is:

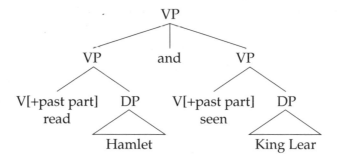

(c) The tree structure for B(c) is:

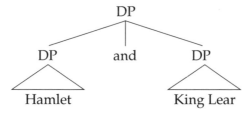

D. TP/VP (*have read Hamlet*) is a constituent because it can be coordinated with a constituent of the same type (*have seen King Lear*).

VP (*read Hamlet*) is a constituent because it can be coordinated with a constituent of the same type (*seen King Lear*).

DP (*King Lear*) is a constituent because it can be coordinated with a constituent of the same type (*Hamlet*).

Note: Applying constituent tests to particular strings is a very difficult task, especially if the resulting strings are impossible. In the case under question, applying the other constituent tests to (ia) is the most difficult. (ib) is intermediate in difficulty, and (ic) is easy.

(ia) Some of the students *have read Hamlet*
      VP preposing: * and *have read King Lear* some of the students
      VP deletion: Some of the students have read Hamlet and
                      some did not (have read Hamlet)
      movement (topicalization, wh-question, . . .)
                      *it is *have seen Hamlet* some of the students

(ib) Some of the students have read Hamlet and seen King Lear
      VP preposing: None of the students have seen King Lear, but
      read Hamlet they have!
      VP deletion: Have they read Hamlet? Yes, they have (read Hamlet)
      Displacement/movement (topicalization, wh-question, VP pre-
      posing: see above.)

(ic) Some of the students have read *Hamlet*
      VP preposing and VP deletion: not applicable
      DP (wh-movement):   *what play* did some of the student read
      replacement: They have read *it/the play Shakespeare
                          wrote/the newspaper.*

E. List of some other constituent tests:

    VP preposing, VP deletion, displacement/movement (topicalization,
    wh-question formation, relative clause formation), substitution

Note: Interpreting results of constituency tests is often a difficult matter,
particularly in cases where the tests do not yield uniform results.
   There is no problem interpreting the results in (ic). That VP preposing
and VP deletion do not work in this case is non-problematic, since, as
the labels of these processes show, these processes test for VP-hood, not
DP-hood. Often though, constituent tests do not give uniform results, as is
the case for (ib). In particular, the contrast between VP preposing and VP
deletion is difficult to interpret: if these processes test for VP-hood, why
do they not yield identical results? It is clear that some piece of the puzzle
is missing. The strategy to follow for such cases is to set up the paradigms
carefully, and to find some explanation for the paradigms in question. This
goes beyond the level of this textbook.
   Sometimes, only one constituency test shows some string is a constituent, as is the case for (ia) (only coordination works in this case). If we are
dealing with TP conjunction, this might simply be because VP preposing
and VP deletion test for VP-hood, but not for TP-hood.

Constructing trees

Give the tree structures for the italicized strings below:
(Do not forget to represent the internal arguments that V takes. Be careful,
DPs may have moved, so that they are pronounced in a different position
from where they are interpreted.)

**EXERCISE
5.3**

(i)   Dogberry will *be arresting Don John*
(ii)   Don John will *have been arrested*
(iii)   She will *have eaten*
(iv)   I will *be going to the theater*

EXERCISE
5.3
ANSWERS

(i)

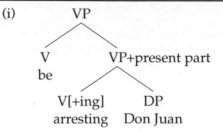

(ii)

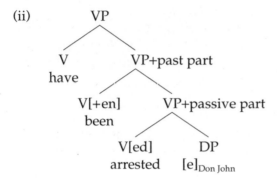

(iii)

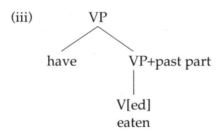

(iv)

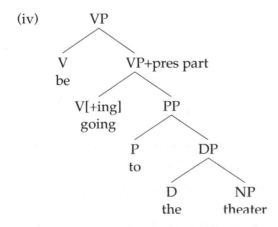

Classify the verbs in the following sentences as main verbs, modals, or auxiliaries. Construct an example for each of the sentences to support your classification.

For example:

(i)   They should go to the garden.   Should is a modal verb.

Support: It precedes the subject in yes/no questions: should they go to the garden?

(ii)   John seems to be sick.   seems is a _____
       Support:

(iii) John has a problem.   has is a _____
       Support:

(iv)   Juliet has left.   has is a _____
       Support:

(v)   Frank had his donkey saddled.   had is a _____
       Support:

(vi)   They go see their advisers every week. go is a _____
       Support:

(vii) They want to be left alone.   want is a _____
       Support:

(viii) They are happy.   are is a _____
       Support:

(ix)   They appear happy.   appear is a _____
       Support:

(x)   They need to act.   need is a _____
       Support:

Note: The classification of verbs into modals, auxiliaries, and main verbs is purely done on the basis of distributional criteria.

(ii)   John seems to be sick.   seems is a main verb

Support: *Seems* behaves as other main verbs, and cannot precede the subject in yes/no questions, or in negative sentences:

*Seems John to be sick

or

* John seemn't to be sick.

(iii)   John has a problem.   has is a main verb
                                                               (in American English)
Support: *Has* cannot precede the subject:

*Has John a problem

versus

Does John have a problem

Has cannot precede negation:

*John hasn't a problem

versus

John doesn't have a problem.

Note: *Have* distributes differently in English dialects. In some dialects, *have* has a much more auxiliary-like behavior, and it can precede the subject or negation. In these dialects *Has John a problem* and *John hasn't a problem* are fine.

(iv)   Juliet has left.   has is an auxiliary

Support: *Has* precedes the subject in yes–no questions:

Has Juliet left?

It agrees with the subject (unlike modals, like *will*, *must*, which do not)

(v)   Frank had his donkey saddled.   had is a main verb

Support: *Had* cannot precede the subject in yes–no questions:

*Had Frank his donkey saddled?

Note: This is true even in dialects that accept *Has John a problem*.

(vi)   They go see their advisers every week.   go is a main verb

Support: *Go* cannot precede the subject in yes–no questions or in wh-questions:

*When go they see their advisors

(vii)   They want to be left alone.   want is a main verb

Support: *Want* cannot precede the subject in questions:

*Why want they to be left alone?

(viii)   They are happy.   are is an auxiliary

Support: Yes–no questions:

Are they happy?

(ix)   They appear happy.   appear is a main verb

Support: Yes–no questions:

*appear they happy?

(x)   They need to act.   need is a main verb

Support: Yes–no questions:

* need they to act?

Construct parallel trees for the pair of English, Turkish sentences in (i) and English, Japanese in (ii). Use the same format as on pp. 303–304 of textbook, and build up the trees starting with the most deeply embedded constituent.   **EXERCISE 5.5**

(i)   (a)   Juliet went to the theater   (English)
     (b)   Juliet tiyatro-ya git-ti   (Turkish)
           Juliet theater-to go-past

For the examples in (ii), treat the Japanese *kiss do* as equivalent to the English *give a kiss to*. For the purposes of this exercise you may ignore the case markers, and treat the DP followed by the topic marker (top) as a regular subject.

(ii)   (a)   I think that Juliet gave a kiss to Romeo
       (b)   watashi wa Jurietto ga Romio ni kisu shita to   omo-u
             I   top Juliet nom Romeo to kiss did   that think-nonpast

Examine your trees. In which ways do the English–Turkish, English–Japanese, and Turkish–English trees differ?

EXERCISE 5.5 ANSWERS   (i)   (a):

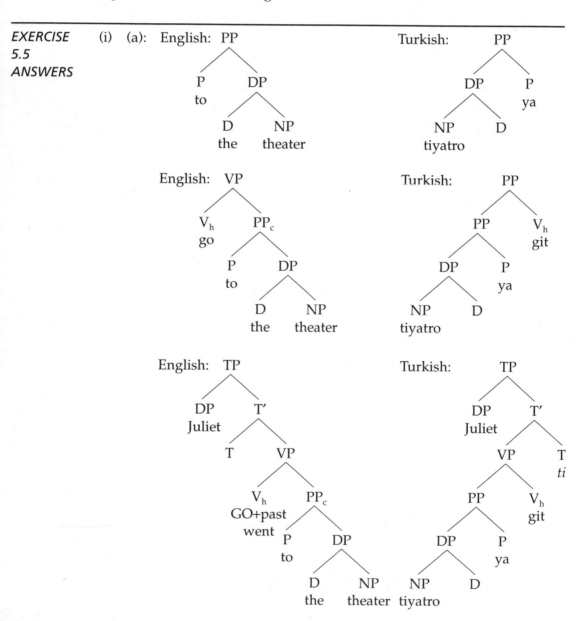

(ii)   English:

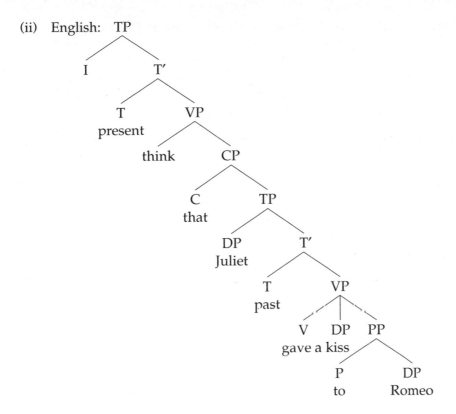

Japanese:

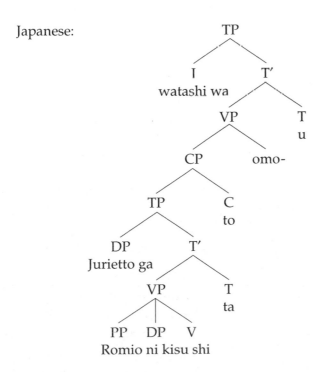

All three languages are Spec initial. Japanese and Turkish order complements before the heads.

It is unclear from the examples if there is head movement in Turkish or Japanese. Base generating the morphemes in their respective projections yields the correct linear order. Putting the V in T (by head movement) in Japanese is supported by the data in Exercise 5.6.

EXERCISE 5.6

Consider the following question and answer pair from Japanese.

(i)   Romio wa tamanegi o   kai ni kodomotachi o   maaketto ni
     Romeo top onion   acc buy to children   acc market   to
     ik-ase-ta   ka
     go-causative-past Q
     'Did Romeo send (= make go) children to the market to buy onions?'

(ii) Hai, ik-ase-ta
     yes, go-caus-past (lit: yes, send)
     'Yes, he did' (meaning: he sent the children to the market to buy onions)

Discuss in one paragraph what these data show about the position of the verb in Japanese. You may treat *ik-ase* as English *send*.

EXERCISE 5.6 ANSWERS

This exercise is supposed to lead students to the same point for Japanese as the text makes for Irish, Swahili, and Korean.

The elliptical sentence (ii) in Japanese:

(ii) Hai, ik-ase-ta
     yes, go-caus-past (lit: yes, send)
     'Yes, he did' (meaning: he sent the children to the market to buy onions)

only consists of the verb and the tense marker in T. VP material and the *in order to* adjunct are silent, but understood. This pattern is exactly the same as the one in English VP ellipsis. We can account for this pattern by assuming that Japanese has VP ellipsis, just like English, but differs from English in that the V obligatorily raises to T in Japanese.

. . . .

EXERCISE 5.7

The status of *to*

Suppose that you are one of several field linguists working together on English, and that English is a language that has no written tradition. As a field linguist, your task is to determine the status of the infinitival marker *to*. What syntactic category does *to* belong to?

The first problem you encounter is that there are several *to*s, which all sound alike, even though they are spelled differently, (*to, two, too*).

(i) (a) She wants *to* read *two* books.
     (b) These *two* books were fun *to* read.
     (c) He gave it *to* Cordelia.
     (d) He wants *to* read *too*.

A. Basing your answer on the meaning of each of the *to*s in (i), make a list of the different *to*s in English.

B. (1) Which of the *to*s are easy to distinguish? Why?
    (2) Which are difficult to distinguish? Why?

C. In your group of field linguists there is disagreement on how to treat *to* in (ia) and (ic). Some propose to treat *to* in (ia) and (ic) as the same element, i.e. as a preposition (P). Some propose to treat the two *to*s as different elements, the one in (ia) as an 'infinitival marker', of the same category as tense and modals, the one in (ic) as a P. You are asked to argue on the basis of the set of following examples which proposal you want to adopt.
    The first set to consider concerns properties of the P *to* (ii):

(ii) (a) she went to the market
      (b) she went to it
      (c) she went right to it
      (d) *she went to not the market

D. Based on the examples in (ii), state what the P *to* co-occurs with. (You may assume that *right* only co-occurs with Ps.)
    The second set considers *to* followed by an infinitive:

(iii) (a) She wants to read
       (b) *She wants read
       (c) *She wants to reading
       (d) I wonder what to read
       (e) *I wonder what read
       (f) *I wonder what reading

E. State in one line what infinitival *to* in (iii) co-occurs with.
    For the following examples, contrast the set in (iv) with the set in (ii):

(iv) (a) She does not want to not read
      (b) *She wants to it
      (c) *she wants right to read it

F.   In what ways does infinitival *to* differ from the P *to* in (ii)?
     On the basis of these sets of data, argue if *to* in (iii) is a P or not, and
     state exactly how you came to this conclusion.

G.   Some people argue that *to* is not a P, but basically an element that
     occupies the T node, just like modals and finite auxiliaries. Construct
     an argument for this position based on the paradigm in (v):

(v)   (a)   Will you come here? Yes I will.
      (b)   Do you want to do this? No, I don't want to.

H.   Write one page on the argumentation and present your conclusion.

- -

EXERCISE   A. Based on the interpretation, we distinguish different *tos*:
5.7   • *to* (co-occurring with an infinitival, no clear meaning);
ANSWERS   • *two* (co-occurring with the plural N, *books*; indicating the quantity
                       of books is *two*);
                    • *to* (co-occurring with a DP; meaning: recipient, goal);
                    • *too* (co-occurring with the subject (*He too wants to read*) or the VP *he*
                       wants to [_{VP}read] too (in addition to watching TV).

B. (1) It is easy to tease apart *two/too* from the other *tos*. They co-occur
             with different categories: *two* precedes plural nouns, and *too* fol-
             lows some constituent that it co-occurs with. They have quite
             different meanings.
        (2) Infinitival *to* and prepositional *to* are difficult to distinguish from
             each other. Both precede the category they co-occur with; it is
             unclear if *to* itself yields the meaning; it rather looks like this
             is done in conjunction with a particular predicate (*give, present,*
             go . . .).

D. The data set in (ii) shows that *to* behaves like other Ps. It is followed
        by a DP, which can be pronominalized; it can be preceded by *right*,
        which can only co-occur with Ps; and it cannot be followed by *not*, in
        contrast to the infinitival marker *to*.

E. The data set in (iii) shows that *to* co-occurs with an infinitive. It cannot
        co-occur with a gerund (iiic), and it is obligatory in certain clause
        types (infinitival wh-questions).

F. Infinitival *to* differs from P *to*: it cannot be followed by a DP, it cannot
        co-occur with *right*, and it can be followed by *not*.

G. The paradigm in (v) shows that, just like modals and finite auxiliaries,
        to can be stranded in T under VP ellipsis.

H. In conclusion, other than the form, the infinitival *to* and the P *to* have
        no distributional properties in common. The infinitival *to* has properties
        in common with modal and tensed auxiliaries (it can be followed by

not, or adverbs, and it can be stranded under VP ellipsis). Treating it as belonging to the same type of category as modals or tensed auxiliaries (i.e. as some kind of tense marker) captures this parallel distribution, and accounts for the difference between Ps and Modal/tensed auxaries and the infinitival marker.

. . . .

to: free morpheme or bound morpheme?

EXERCISE
5.8

Argue on the basis of the following data if *to* in (i) should be considered a free morpheme (an independent word) or a bound morpheme (part of the infinitive).

(i) (a) Cordelia wants to read.
     (b) (Does Cordelia want to read?) No, she does not want to.
     (c) He wants me to carefully turn the pages.

. . . .

to should be considered a free morpheme, since it can be separated from the infinitive, and either remain after VP ellipsis (ib), or be separated from the infinitive by free-standing adverbs (ic).

EXERCISE
5.8
ANSWERS

. . . .

Zero heads

EXERCISE
5.9

English has two types of compounds. In the first type (called endocentric compounds) the interpretation is determined by the righthand member of the compound: a *tree trunk* is a kind of a trunk, a *girlfriend* is a kind of a friend, etc. In the second type (exocentric compounds) this is not the case: *sabertooth* is not a type of tooth, but a type of tiger. If heads can be silent (zero heads), the second type of compound can be represented as having a silent head (basically meaning tiger), which determines the properties of the compound as a whole.

(a)

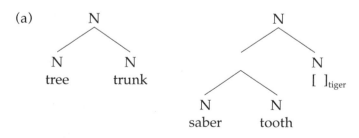

Now consider the following examples of compounds. (Remember that the head of the compound determines the properties of the compound as a whole.)

sabertooth	freeze-dry
beanie baby	poorhouse
tree trunk	pickpocket
redneck	Walkman
in-crowd	

A.   Classify each compound as Type 1 (endocentric), or Type 2 (exocentric).

B.   Give structural representations of *pickpocket*, *beanie baby* and *Walkman*.

· ·

EXERCISE
5.9
ANSWERS

A.

sabertooth	2
beanie baby	2
tree trunk	1
redneck	2
in-crowd	1
freeze-dry	1
poorhouse	1
pickpocket	2
Walkman	2

B.

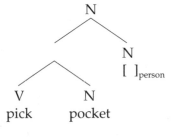

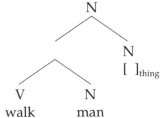

· ·

EXERCISE
5.10

Constructing trees

This is a simple exercise that asks for nothing else than constructing tree representations, and indicating if necessary which movement processes or insertion processes have taken place.

Give the tree representations for the following examples:

(i)   Cordelia did not insult Shylock.
(ii)   For Portia to confront Shylock, took courage.
(iii)   Mary should not have been playing Cordelia.
(iv)   Can anyone tell me what to do next?
(v)   Did you carefully read this book about linguistics?
(vi)   I did! (vi is an answer to v.)
(vii)   They are constantly wondering if they are constructing a nice set.

. . . .

(i)

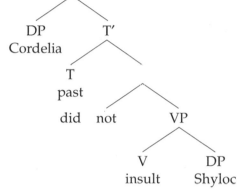

did is inserted in T[+Past] (do-support)

   Note: In chapter 5 of textbook, the label of the node dominating *not* is left unspecified. In the literature, it is assumed to be either VP (in which case *not* is treated as an adverb) or NegP (a projection of Negation which indicates that the clause is negative).

(ii)

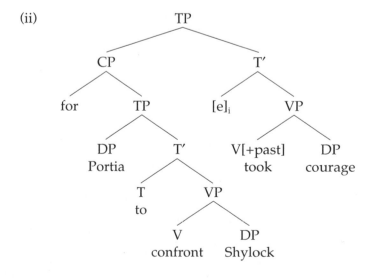

took gets inflected via affix hopping.

Note: Some students will assign a cascading structure of the type in (i). In such a structure, there is no way to indicate that *for Portia to confront Shylock* acts as the subject of the predicate *took courage*.

(iii)

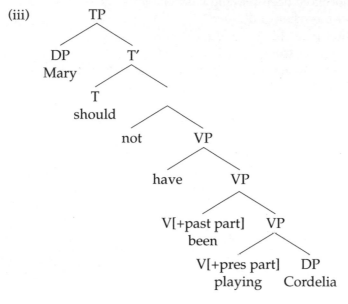

(iv)

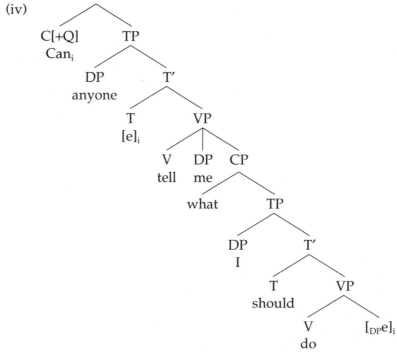

can moves to C[+Q]
what moves to CP

(v)

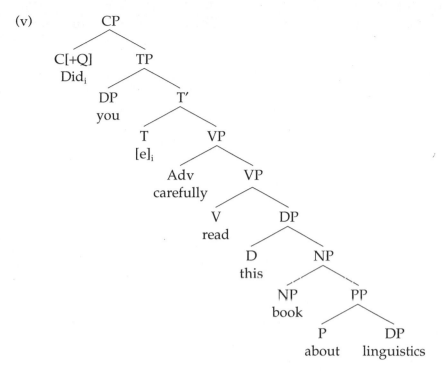

T to C[+Q] followed by do-support.

   Note: *this book about linguistics*: *about linguistics* is an adjunct, hence structurally represented very much like adverbs or relative clauses. Since chapter 5 of textbook does not go into this issue, it is also OK if students treat the *about* phrase as a sister to N, dominated by N′ (which in turn is dominated by NP).

(vi)

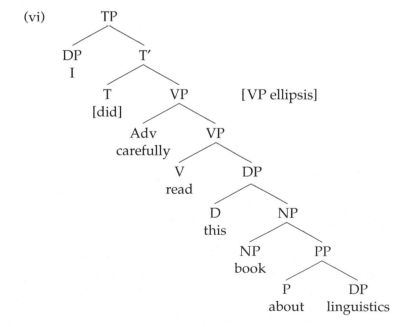

do-support (VP ellipsis silences the verbal base to which the affix should attach)
VP ellipsis

(vii)

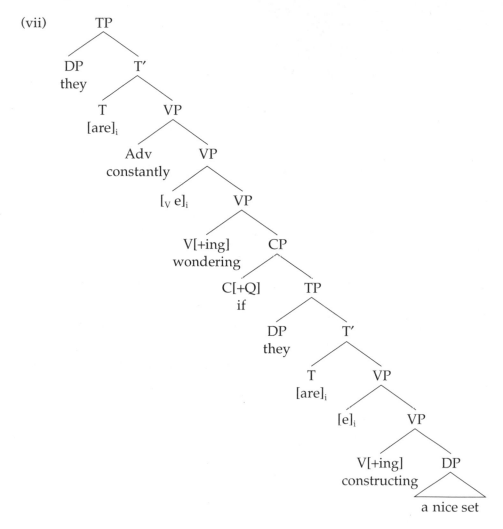

are from VP to T in main clause
are from VP to T in if-clause

. . . .

Imperatives (Nawdem)

While analyzing other languages, always keep the structure of the languages as similar as possible.

In Nawdem, a Niger-Congo Gur language spoken in Togo, declarative sentences with finite verbs have the following shape, regardless of whether they are matrix or embedded:

(i) (a) (...) a dʒun   deːte
              he eat+imperf food
              (...) he is eating
     (b) ne   dʒun   deːte
          you(pl) eat-imperf food
          'you are eating food'

A. Construct a tree representation for the sentence in (ia). What can you
    say about the position that the subject pronoun occupies?
        The following set of examples contains (second-)person plural
    imperatives in Nawdem. (Second-person singular pronouns are zero
    morphemes in tensed sentences and in imperatives, and thus cannot
    be used to show anything about order.)

(ii) (a) de   ne   deːte
           eat+imp you (pl) food
           'Eat food!' (addressed to 2nd person plural)
      (b) lo   ne   wadgaː kan
           put(+imp) you(pl) book-the there
           'Put the book there!'

B. What do you observe in these imperatives? Propose an analysis for
    imperative sentences, and state how you came to this analysis.

. . . .

A.   TP

    DP   T'
    a
        T   VP
        imp
        dʒun V   DP
             [e]   deːte

EXERCISE
5.11
ANSWERS

Since the subject precedes T/V, it can safely been concluded that the subject is in Spec, TP.
    Note: There is no information to decide if V is in T, as in French, or in the
VP, as in English. Given imperatives with overt subjects (i.e. the (ii) problem set), V to C is possible. Hence it is likely that the intermediate step V to
T is possible as well.

B. In imperatives, the verb has imperative morphology, and precedes the
    subject pronoun. The subject pronoun in turn precedes material inside
    the VP.

Since subject pronouns are in Spec, TP, we can analyze the imperative V as occurring in C. Nawdem imperatives are therefore CPs. The C heading the imperative clause in Nawdem has the same property as English C in questions: it needs to be associated with overt material. This causes V to move to C.

7

Semantics I: Compositionality

Explain why all of the following claims are true:

(i) The sentence *Viola has yellow stockings* entails the sentence *Viola has stockings*.

(ii) The sentence *Viola has stockings* does not entail the sentence *Viola has yellow stockings*.

(iii) The sentence *Viola has stockings* entails the sentence *Either Viola has stockings or 2 is an even number*.

(iv) The sentence *Viola has stockings* entails the sentence *Either two is an odd number or two is not an odd number*.

(v) The sentence *Two is an odd number* entails *Viola has stockings*.

(i) is true because in all possible situations, if Viola has yellow stockings, she has stockings.

(ii) is true because Viola could have stockings (blue ones), but not yellow stockings.

(iii) is true because whenever Viola has stockings, the second sentence must also be true.

(iv) is true because whenever the first sentence is true, the second is always true, because the second sentence is true in every possible situation.

(v) is true because there is no possible situation in which the first sentence is true but the second is false, because the first sentence is never true. In this, admittedly odd but conventional sense, the second sentence is true whenever the first is.

What does the following sentence assert and what does it presuppose?
The maid who was singing was singing.

What is the peculiarity of this sentence?

To determine what a sentence S1 asserts and what it presupposes, we negate S1 and compare the entailments of S1 and not-S1.

S1: *The maid who was singing was singing.*
not-S1: *The maid who was singing was not singing.*

Because the subject is a definite DP, both S1 and not-S1 entail S2:

S2: *There was a (uniquely identifiable) maid who was singing,*

hence they both presuppose S2.
    S2 entails S3, by virtue of the compositionality of the relative clause:

S3: *A (uniquely identifiable) maid was singing.*

So, what does S1 assert? If we ignore, for a second, what we learned from the subject DP, S1 seems to assert S4, because S1 entails S4 and not-S1 does not:

S4: *'Subject' was singing.*

But given what we already know about 'subject', S4 is already entailed by S1.
    A sentence asserts whatever it entails minus whatever it presupposes. Thus, our S1 does not assert anything, because whatever it entails it also presupposes. This is rather unusual.

Consider the following verbs and other predicates:

think (that . . .), confirm (that . . .), know (that . . .), be surprised (that . . .), agree (that . . .), suspect (that . . .), accept (that . . .), assume (that . . .).

Which of them are like *regret* in that the sentence containing them presupposes that the content of the *that*-clause is a fact? Which of them are comparable to *deny* in making some other presupposition about the status of the content of the *that*-clause? Do you find cases that do not fall into either category?
    Example: Restate (that . . .) presupposes that the content of the *that*-clause has previously been stated, because both (a) and its negation (b) entail this.

(a)   Emilia restated that she was not guilty.
(b)   Emilia didn't restate that she was not guilty.

On the other hand, both (a) and (b) can be true whether or not Emilia was actually guilty. Thus *restate* belongs to the same category as *deny*.

Use the technique demonstrated in the example.

Class 1: The following verbs or predicates are like *regret* in that they presuppose that the complement describes a fact:

know (that . . .), be surprised (that . . .)

Note that *know* has an additional, non-factive use if the subject is first person: *I don't know that this is the best solution*, 'I wish to remain neutral as to whether this is the best solution, or I doubt that this is the best solution.'

Class 2: The following are like *deny* in that they make some other presupposition about the status of the content of the that-clause. Cattell (1978), 'The source of interrogative adverbs', *Language* 54:61–77, calls this class response stance verbs (the reason for this will be clear from the explanations). We give an indication of what the presupposition is, but there may be slight variation depending on register (e.g. colloquial versus 'legalese'). The main goal of the exercise is to notice the existence of such presuppositions and to classify verbs, rather than to assess all the connotations of each example.

confirm (that S1) – presupposition: The claim that S1 is true was made, or the issue whether S1 is true was raised, either explicitly or in a person's mind. Probably, the one who raised the issue is not the subject of *confirm* (if it is, *verify* is preferable).
agree (that S1) – presupposition: The opinion that S1 is true was expressed by someone other than the object of *agree*.
accept (that S1) – presupposition: The claim that S1 is true or the recommendation that S1 be realized was made by someone other than the subject of *accept*.

Class 3: The following verbs do not fall into either category: they do not make any presupposition about the status of the content of the that-clause. Cattell (1978) calls them volunteered stance verbs:

think (that . . .), suspect (that . . .), assume (that . . .)

. . . .

Are the following claims true or false?

(a)   The sentence *Everything is a brown cow* entails *Most things are cows*.
(b)   The sentence *All cows are purple* entails *All purple things are cows*.
(c)   The sentence *The student ate the cake* entails *The student ate*.
(d)   The sentence *The hammer broke the cup* entails *The hammer broke*.

- -

EXERCISE 7.4 ANSWERS

(a) is a tricky example. It is often assumed that the first sentence could be true even in a situation where there was nothing at all, because the sentence just says that everything there is is a brown cow. It does not say that there is anything. If we accept this, then (a) is false, because the second sentence can certainly not be true in a situation where there is nothing at all, since it says that more than half the things are cows. If there is nothing at all, then it cannot be that more than half the things there are are cows.

(b) is clearly false. It is coherent to imagine painting all cows and horses purple. Then the first sentence is true but the second is false.

(c) is clearly true. If the first sentence is true, the second one is too.

(d) is false. If the first sentence is true, the cup broke. The hammer could well be unbroken.

- -

EXERCISE 7.5

Consider some newly invented determiners: *wurg* and *berf*, so that you can say things like *Wurg daughters of Lear loved him* and *Berf fairies attend Hippolyta*. Let's define these new determiners as follows:

[Wurg N VP] is true just in case there are more things in ⟦VP⟧ than in ⟦N⟧. [Berf N VP] is true just in case ⟦VP⟧ is a subset of (is completely included in) ⟦N⟧.

With these definitions, answer the following questions:

(i) Is *wurg* conservative? Defend your answer.

(ii) Is there an English determiner that means the same thing as *wurg*? That is, how would you say something like *Wurg fairies wait upon the Queen* in English, without using the word *wurg*?

(iii) Is *berf* conservative? Defend your answer.

(iv) Is there an English determiner that means *berf*?

- -

EXERCISE 7.5 ANSWERS

(i) *Wurg* is not conservative. A sentence *Wurg A B* means $|A| < |B|$, which could be true. But the sentence *Wurg A are A that are B* means $|A| < |A \cap B|$. But the set $A \cap B$ cannot be larger than A. So the second sentence is always false. So these two sentences do not mean the same thing, and so the determiner is not conservative.

(ii) We know that English determiners are conservative, so the answer is: no. To say *Wurg fairies wait upon the Queen*, you need to say something like: *There are more things that wait upon the Queen than there are fairies.*

(iii) *Berf* is not conservative either. A sentence *Berf A B* means that B is a subset of A. This could be true, or it could be false. The sentence *Berf A are A that are B* means that $A \cap B$ is a subset of A. This second sentence is always true, and so means something quite different from the former sentence.

(iv)   We already know that determiners in English are conservative, so the answer has to be: no. This example is tricky though, because *Berf* is similar to the word *only* in English. A sentence like *Only dogs bark* means that the set of barking things is completely included in the set of *dogs*. But *only* is not really a determiner (see Exercise 7.7), so the right answer to this question is still: no.

· ·

Prepositional phrases are sometimes restrictive and intersective, the way that adjectival modifiers are. For example, *Every witch in the castle smiled* says that every element of 〚*witch*〛 ∩ 〚*in the castle*〛 is in 〚*smiled*〛. We can say:

EXERCISE 7.6

A prepositional phrase PP is intersective if [every N PP] means that the set of things that are in both 〚N〛 and 〚PP〛 is a subset of 〚VP〛.

Think of some prepositional phrases which are not intersective, and defend your view that they are not intersective.

· ·

As observed in the text, an adjective like *Danish* is intersective because a phrase like *Danish princes* can be treated as denoting the intersection of the things that are Danish, 〚Danish〛. with the things that are princes, 〚princes〛, while, on the other hand, an adjective like *oldest* cannot be treated that way, because the idea of a set of oldest things makes no sense. One thing can be both may oldest friend and the youngest prince, because *old* expresses a kind of relationship between a thing and a certain collection of things, like my friends or the princes, and the relationship can be different depending on what set is being considered.

In exactly the same way, a prepositional phrase like *from Denmark* is intersective, while prepositional phrases like *with the greatest years* or *with the largest weight* are not, because the latter are essentially relational. One thing can be my friend with the largest weight, but not the prince with the largest weight, so the idea of a set 〚with the largest weight〛 makes no sense.

EXERCISE 7.6 ANSWER

· ·

The claim that all determiners are conservative holds up quite well across languages. There are, however, a few apparent exceptions. One of them is the English word *only*, as in *only witches cast spells*.

EXERCISE 7.7

(a)   Explain why, if *only* is treated as a determiner here, it is not conservative.

(b)   Do the following data support the view that *only* is a determiner? Explain your answer:

the witches cast spells
three witches cast spells
the three witches cast spells
*the the witches cast spells
*the three four witches cast spells
only witches cast spells
only the witches cast spells
only the three witches cast spells
the three witches only cast spells
the three witches cast only spells

EXERCISE   (a)   The sentence *Only dogs bark* means that the set of barking things
7.7   has only dogs in it. It does not say that all dogs bark. So in general
ANSWERS   *Only A B* means that B is a subset of A. This is a sentence that might
                 or might not be true, depending on what goes in for A and B. The
                 sentence *Only A are A that B*, on the other hand, means that the things
                 that are both A and B are a subset of A, and that is something that is
                 always true. So we see that the second sentence does not mean the
                 same as the first, and so *only* is not conservative.
           (b)   These sentences show that the word *only* appears in various positions
                 where determiners cannot appear, and so it is safe to assume that *only*
                 is really something different.

EXERCISE   Most speakers of American English accept the following sentences:
7.8
           They baked a cake for me
           They baked me a cake
           They dug a ditch for me
           They dug me a ditch
           They mixed a drink for me
           They mixed me a drink

           Some other verbs seem to allow the [___ DP for-DP] but not the [___ DP
           DP] forms:

           A1.   a.   They opened the door for me
                 b.   *They opened me the door
           A2.   a.   They arranged the day for me
                 b.   *They arranged me the day
           A3.   a.   They caught the plane for me
                 b.   *They caught me the plane

           However, these last data are misleading. What is really going on is a little
           more subtle, and depends on the arguments involved:

A1.   c.   They opened me a beer
A2.   c.   They arranged us a wedding
A3.   c.   They caught me a butterfly

What do you think explains the contrasts between the (b) and (c) examples? (If you are not a native speaker of American English, you may want to consult with a speaker of this language to get a little more data.)

·   EXERCISE
This exercise requires some careful thought about how these constructions   7.8
are used.   ANSWER
    In A1.c, and in *They baked me a cake*, the thing denoted by the direct
object (the beer and the cake, respectively) is possessed by the subject (in
some sense) after the action takes place, while this is not so for A1.b. After
the door is opened for me, it is not mine. The idea that something like this
distinguishes these examples is confirmed by constructing some other examples to see if they continue to fit the same pattern:

A4.   a.   That made the day for me
A4.   b.   *That made me the day
A5.   a.   He shot a deer for me with his bow and arrow
A5.   b.   He shot me a deer with his bow and arrow

In some sense, the (b) forms seem to imply that the action denoted by the
verb creates a kind of possession relation.

·   EXERCISE
Compare the following data from English, Hausa, and Hungarian. Where   7.9
English has a pair of words, Hausa and Hungarian have only one. Discuss
how cognitive and linguistic distinctions compare in these languages:

English	Hausa	Hungarian
leather/skin	fata	bőr
meat/flesh	nama	hús
wood/tree	itače	fa

·   EXERCISE
The relevant distinction is between the living thing or part thereof (tree,   7.9
skin, etc.) and the dead thing or artifact (wood, leather, etc.). English, like   ANSWER
many other languages, lexicalizes it, i.e. has two separate lexical items. On
the other hand, Hausa and Hungarian do not lexicalize the distinction.
This shows that even though the distinction is cognitively straightforward
and may even be thought to be practically useful, there is no necessity for

a language to make it. It is a linguistic matter whether a language has it built into its lexicon. Thus, eventually, the distinctive feature that sets apart *tree* and *wood*, *skin* and *leather*, etc. is linguistic, not cognitive.

- -

EXERCISE 7.10

A motion event can be said to involve at least the following components, the fact of Motion, the Figure that moves, the direction in which the Figure moves, and the Manner in which the Figure moves. (The notion of a Figure goes back to Gestalt-psychology: it is the central element of the event.) Suppose that these are cognitive terms in which motion events can be described. Compare how English and Spanish express these components. Discuss what the results say about the claim that word meanings directly reflect cognitive distinctions.

The bottle floated into the cave.
La botella entró a la cueva flotando.
the bottle went+in prep the cave floating
'The bottle floated into the cave.'

I rolled the keg into the storeroom.
Metí el barril a la bodega rodándolo.
put+in-I the keg prep the storeroom rolling
'I rolled the keg into the storeroom.'

- -

EXERCISE 7.10 ANSWER

This exercise is based on Talmy (1985), 'Lexicalization patterns'. Spanish *entró* 'went+in' and *metí* 'put+in' conflate the notions of Motion and Direction in one lexical item. This lexicalization pattern is pervasive in Spanish (and in other Romance languages). English *float* 'move floatingly' and *roll* 'move rollingly' conflate the notions of Motion and Manner in one lexical item. Again, this lexicalization pattern is pervasive in English and in many other languages. Interestingly, both Spanish and English typically lack the pattern characteristic of the other. Thus, Spanish typically requires an adverb to express the Manner of Motion. English has many Motion+Direction conflations, but those are words of Romance origin: *enter*, *ascend*, etc.

The Figure–Motion–Direction–Manner distinction is cognitively straightforward. The fact that different languages map such distinctions to their lexical entries in systematically different ways indicates that it is a linguistic matter what distinction each language builds into its lexicon. On the other hand, Talmy found that the overwhelming majority of human languages exhibits one of the above two lexicalization patterns. That is, languages do not conflate arbitrary combinations of such distinctions. Whether the inventory of patterns that languages choose from is cognitively or linguistically determined is an important research topic in lexical semantics and cognitive linguistics.

· ·

Which of the following does the sentence *I regret that I lied to the queen*   **EXERCISE**
presuppose? In deciding, consider the truth conditions of both the above   **7.11**
sentence and its negation.

(a)   I regret that I lied to the queen.
(b)   I lied to the queen.
(c)   I am generally an honest person.
(d)   There is a queen.
(e)   A unique queen is identifiable in the context.

· ·

Does S1 *I regret that I lied to the queen* presuppose the following? We com-   **EXERCISE**
pare it with not-S1 *I do not regret that I lied to the queen.*   **7.11**
                                                                    ANSWER

(a) *I regret that I lied to the queen.*

No, because not-S1 does not entail (a).

(b) *I lied to the queen.*

Yes, because both S1 and not-S1 entail (b).

(c) *I am generally an honest person.*

No, this is an extralinguistic matter that may motivate my regrets, but it is
not even part of the linguistic pragmatic assumptions associated with the
proper use of the sentence.

(d) *There is a queen.*

Yes, both S1 and not-S1 entail this, because *the queen* is a definite DP, see
(40)–(41), p. 387 of textbook.

(e) *A unique queen is identifiable in the context.*

Yes, because *the queen* is a definite DP.

· ·

Below is a letter by someone who politely followed the rule that you do   **EXERCISE**
not say anything bad about a person in a letter of recommendation. But he   **7.12**
managed to smuggle in some important messages. Exactly what are these
and how did he do it?

Mr. X is a great person. He has recently stopped beating his neighbors and
kicked his habit of coming to work stone drunk.

. . . .

EXERCISE
7.12
ANSWER

The sentence *He has recently stopped beating his neighbors and kicked his habit of coming to work stone drunk* presupposes that he (Mr. X) beat his neighbors up until recently and also used to come to work drunk. What the sentence asserts is the positive fact that he no longer does these. It is up to the recipient of the letter to decide whether this indeed makes Mr. X a great person, as the letter's first sentence claims.

. . . .

EXERCISE
7.13

In chapter 4 of textbook we talked about the dependency between a wh-phrase and a gap in the sentence. Such a dependency may span more than one clause, e.g.:

How do you believe (that) I should behave – ?

In such long-distance dependencies the main clause verb is called a **bridge verb**. The above examples show that *believe* is quite a good bridge. Check whether the verbs in Exercise 7.3 are good bridges. In checking the acceptability of these wh-dependencies, retain the wh-word *how*, but adjust the tense and the mood of the verbs if necessary. Try to formulate a generalization concerning bridge-hood and presuppositions.

. . . .

EXERCISE
7.13
ANSWER

The exercise asks you to check whether a given verb is a good bridge verb by checking a long wh-dependency in which the wh-word is *how*.
     This test shows *think, suspect,* and *assume* to be good bridges like *believe*.

How do you think that he behaved?

On the other hand, *confirm, know, be surprised, agree,* and *accept* are not good bridges, e.g.

* How do you confirm that he behaved?

The generalization is that verbs that make a characteristic presupposition about the status of the content of the complement clause (factive or response-stance predicates) are not good bridges. This is confirmed by the observation that *deny*, another response-stance predicate discussed in the text, is not a good bridge, either:

* How do you deny that you behaved?

The good bridges are volunteered-stance predicates that have no comparable presupposition.
     This result indicates that the grammaticality of a syntactic operation, such as creating a certain kind of wh-dependency, may be contingent on

semantic factors. These semantic factors may play a role in grammar either through some syntactic intermediary, or by rendering the sentence uninterpretable gibberish.

To be on the safe side, note that not all wh-dependencies are blocked by bad bridges. For example:

Which sword do you deny that you stole?

Whether dependencies involving *what* are good or bad is contingent on exactly what *what* stands for (a particular object, a quality, an amount, etc.).

The complements of bad bridges are called weak islands, where 'weak' means 'selective'. Selectivity requires an explanation, but it remains a fact that the plus or minus presuppositional character of the matrix verb is a good predictor of its bridge-hood for the sensitive cases. This fact is the main point in this chapter.

. . . .

What do each of the following sentences presuppose? Form their negation by prefixing the sentence by *It is not the case that* . . .   **EXERCISE 7.14**

(a)   Othello, too, wept.
(b)   Even Othello wept.
(c)   Only Othello wept.
(d)   It was Othello who wept.

. . . .

(a)   Othello, too, wept. – It is not the case that Othello, too, wept.   **EXERCISE 7.14**
      presupp.: Someone other than Othello wept.
(b)   Even Othello wept. – It is not the case that even Othello wept.   **ANSWER**
      presupp.: Someone other than Othello wept, and Othello was less likely to weep than most other persons.
(c)   Only Othello wept. – It is not the case that only Othello wept.
      presupp.: Othello wept.
(d)   It was Othello who wept. – It was not [the case that it was] Othello who wept.
      presupp.: Someone wept, and it was a unique person or perhaps group.

In case discussion brings it up, it is interesting to observe that (i) *even* subsumes *too* plus a scalar judgment, and (ii) *only* and *it*-clefts distribute the same bits meaning differently. Both *only* and *it*-clefting have to do with unicity (exhaustivity), but the *only*-sentence asserts unicity, while the cleft presupposes it.

8
Semantics II: Scope

EXERCISE
8.1 Describe what the subject wide scope and the object wide scope readings of the following sentence are, and specify two situations: one in which the former is true but the latter is not, and one in which the latter is true but the former is not. Draw diagrams of the situations.

Exactly two squires greeted three of the earls.

EXERCISE
8.1
ANSWERS Subject wide scope reading (SW): There are exactly two squires who greeted three of the earls each, possibly different triplets.
   Object wide scope reading (OW): There are three particular earls each of whom was greeted by exactly two squires, possibly different pairs.
   A situation in which the SW reading is true but the OW reading is false is as follows:

S1   greeted   E1, E2, E3
S2   greeted   E3, E4, E5
S3   greeted   E5

Here exactly two squires, S1 and S2, greeted three of the earls each (hence SW is true). But there are only two earls each of whom were greeted by exactly two squires, E3 and E5 (hence OW is false).
   A situation in which the OW reading is true but the SW reading is false is as follows:

S1   greeted   E1, E2
S2   greeted   E1, E2, E3
S3   greeted   E3
S4   greeted   E4

Here three of the earls, E1, E2, and E3, were greeted by exactly two squires each (hence OW is true). But there is exactly one squire, S2, not exactly two, who greeted three of the earls (hence SW is false).

Comment: In this example, the two readings are logically independent: neither entails the other. We will shortly see examples where one reading entails the other.

Show that (41b) does not entail (41a), p. 410 of textbook. Follow the procedure outlined for (43), p. 410 of textbook, below.   **EXERCISE 8.2**

The principle: S1 entails S2 means that if S1 is true, S2 is inescapably true, too.

Then, S1 does not entail S2 means that we can construct a situation (**model**) in which S1 is true but S2 is false.

We now show that (43b) does not entail (43a). Assume that there are three fairies and ten Athenians, and consider the following situation:

F1	met	A1, A2, A3, A4, A5, A6, A7, A8, A9
F2	met	A1, A3, A5, A7, A9, A10
F3	met	A1, A2, A4, A6, A8, A10

In this situation, only one Athenian, A1, was met by each of the three fairies. Thus, it is true that there are few Athenians whom every fairy met (= (43b)). On the other hand, every fairy met many Athenians, at least six of the ten. Thus, it is false that for every fairy, there are few Athenians he/she has met (= (43a)). This means that (43b) does not entail (43a).

To show that (41b) does not entail (41a), p. 410 of textbook, we construct a model in which (41b) is true but (41a) is false. (This is easier than the model example in the exercise.)   *EXERCISE 8.2 ANSWERS*

(41a) There are two fairies each of whom talked with every Athenian.
(41b) For every Athenian, there are two possibly different fairies who talked with him/her.

Assume that there are altogether three Athenians:

F1	talked with	A1
F2	talked with	A1
F3	talked with	A2
F4	talked with	A2
F5	talked with	A3
F6	talked with	A3

164 *Exercises and Answer Key to Chapter 8*

Here each of A1, A2, and A3 (i.e. every Athenian) had two fairies talking with him/her (OW is true), but not a single fairy talked with every Athenian (SW is false).

EXERCISE 8.3

Show that (46b) entails (46a), p. 412 of textbook.

EXERCISE 8.3 ANSWERS

To show that (46b) entails (46a), p. 412 of textbook, we show that whenever (46b) is true, (46a) is true.

(46a)   For every fairy, there are two or more pies that she had a taste of.
(46b)   There are two or more pies that every fairy had a taste of.

Suppose P1, P2, and perhaps P3 are pies that every fairy had a taste of (the paradigm case in which (46b) is true). Then every fairy had a taste of P1, every fairy had a taste of P2, and every fairy had a taste of P3, hence (46a) is inescapably true, too.

EXERCISE 8.4

At most two witches is also a decreasing DP. Check whether this DP in direct object position can take inverse scope over negation or the subject. Model your examples on (37) and (40), p. 414 of textbook.

EXERCISE 8.4 ANSWERS

(a)   Richard III didn't murder at most two witches.   (after (37))

If (a) is acceptable at all, it does not mean 'There are at most two witches whom Richard III didn't murder'. It means 'It is not the case that Richard III murdered: he murdered three or more'.

(b)   Every fairy has met at most two witches.   (after (40))

This is clearly acceptable, but it does not mean 'There are at most two witches whom every fairy met'. It means 'For every fairy, the number of witches she met is at most two'.
   In sum, this decreasing DP in object position does not take inverse scope over preverbal negation or the subject.

EXERCISE 8.5

Every witch, two or more witches, and *two witches* are non-decreasing DPs. Check whether these DPs in direct object position can take inverse scope over (a) negation and (b) the subject. Use the data provided by (39), (45), and (46), pp. 407–9 and 411–12 of textbook, and supplement them with your own examples as necessary.

We are checking *every N*:

(39)   Two fairies have met every Athenian.
(a)   Oberon did not trick every Athenian.

Inverse scope over the subject is OK, see (39b), pp. 407–9 of textbook, but over negation it is not (unless *every* receives focus accent). (a) means 'not every', not 'every not'.

We are checking *two or more N*:

(46)   Every fairy had a taste of two or more pies.
(b)   This knight did not meet two or more requirements for the tournament.

Inverse scope over the subject is absent, see (46b), p. 412 of textbook, but over negation it is better: 'There are two or more requirements for the tournament that this knight did not meet'. Both examples improve if we use partitive *two or more of the N*, which does not affect the non-decreasingness of DP.

We are checking *two N*:

(45)   Every fairy had a taste of two of the pies.
(c)   Puck did not solve two of the problems.

Inverse scope over the subject (45b), p. 412 of textbook, and over negation ('There are two particular problems that Puck did not solve'), is equally good.

In sum, non-decreasing DPs typically have the ability to take inverse scope, although not necessarily over any kind of c-commanding operator.

. . . .

Are the following claims true or false? Defend your answers.

(a)   In the sentence, *Every student likes him*, the subject NP *every student* c-commands the object NP *him*.
(b)   In the sentence, *Every student likes him*, the subject NP *every student* can bind the object NP *him*.
(c)   In the sentence, *Every student likes himself*, the subject NP *every student* c-commands the object NP *himself*.
(d)   In the sentence, *Every student likes himself*, the subject NP *every student* can bind the object NP *himself*.
(e)   In the sentence, *Every student knows the teacher likes him*, the subject NP *every student* c-commands the NP *him*.
(f)   In the sentence, *Every student knows the teacher likes him*, the subject NP *every student* can bind the NP *him*.
(g)   In the sentence *I doubt that Brutus ever goes to dramas with no violence*, the NP *no violence* c-commands the NPI *ever*.

. . . .

EXERCISE
8.6
ANSWERS

(a)   True. We can see this by drawing the tree and seeing that the parent of the subject is the whole sentence S, and this includes the object.

(b)   False. Any speaker of English knows that *him* cannot mean each of the students. This special fact about non-reflexive pronouns was discussed, and Principle B was proposed, p. 403 of textbook, which says that a pronoun cannot be bound in the smallest sentence that contains it.

(c)   True, and this tree has the same shape as the tree in (a).

(d)   True. In fact, the subject *every student* must bind the object *himself*, according to Principle A, p. 403 of textbook.

(e)   True. We can see this by drawing the tree and seeing that the parent of the subject is the whole sentence S, and this includes the object of the embedded sentence.

(f)   True. Any speaker of English knows that *him* can mean each of the students. This is allowed by Principle B, p. 403 of textbook, since the subject *every student* is not in the smallest sentence that contains the pronoun.

(g)   False. We can see this by drawing the tree and seeing that the parent of *no violence* is the prepositional phrase, which does not include *ever*. The NPI *ever* can occur here because of the negative verb *doubt*.

. . . .

EXERCISE
8.7

Does the subject wide scope reading of the sentence below entail the object wide scope reading, or the other way around? Justify your claim by drawing diagrams of situations in which the two readings are true.

Two witches overturned every cauldron.

. . . .

EXERCISE
8.7
ANSWERS

The SW reading ('There are two witches who . . .') entails the OW reading ('For every cauldron, there are two witches who . . .'). Whenever SW is true, OW is inescapably true (assume there are just three cauldrons):

W1   overturned   C1, C2, C3
W2   overturned   C1, C2, C3

On the other hand, OW does not entail SW: below is one situation in which OW is true but SW is false:

C1   was overturned by   W1, W2
C2   was overturned by   W1, W3
C3   was overturned by   W4, W5

. . . .

EXERCISE
8.8

Paraphrase the following sentences in a way that clearly brings out their meaning difference. Can the difference be seen as one involving relative scope? If yes, which constituents interact in scope?

(a)   Hermia may marry a fat nobleman.

(b)   Hermia may marry any fat nobleman.

(a) Hermia may marry a fat nobleman.

    (i)   It is likely/allowed for Hermia to marry someone who turns out to be a fat nobleman.

    (ii) There is a particular fat nobleman whom Hermia is likely/allowed to marry.

(b) Hermia may marry any fat nobleman.

    (i)   It is likely/allowed for Hermia to marry someone who turns out to be a fat nobleman, and she may marry even the most unlikely one.

    (ii)* There is a particular fat nobleman whom Hermia is likely/allowed to marry.

Sentence (a) is ambiguous. If *may* takes scope over *a fat nobleman*, it means essentially that nothing excludes the possibility for Hermia's groom to turn out to be a fat nobleman. On the inverse reading, there exists a particular fat nobleman with a chance to be chosen by Hermia. Thus, we see that an indefinite may interact scopally with a modal.

Sentence (b) involves so-called free-choice *any*, which is commonly assimilated to indefinites with determiner *a(n)*. Free-choice *any* differs from *a(n)* in that it stresses the lack of any restriction on the choice of the individual. More important from our present perspective is the fact that it must be within the scope of a modal (an overt modal or an understood modal, as in *Any owl hunts mice*). Thus, the inverse reading (b) is absent.

Compare the sentences in which an indefinite DP contains the determiner 'a(n)' or 'some' with those in which it has no determiner (these are called **bare plurals**). What is the systematic difference in their scope interpretations?

(a) Every earl visited some ladies.
    Every earl visited ladies.

(b) Hamlet did not like a king.
    Hamlet did not like kings.

(c) Hamlet may meet an actor.
    Hamlet may meet actors.

The systematic difference is that indefinites DPs with *some* or *a(n)* can take inverse scope, but bare plurals on their comparable ('existential') reading cannot, an observation due to Carlson (1977), 'Reference to Kinds in English,' PhD, Amherst.

(a)   Every earl visited some ladies.
      OK   'there are some ladies whom every earl visited'
              Every earl visited ladies.
      *   'there are ladies whom every earl visited'

(b)   Hamlet did not like a/some king.
      OK   'there was a king (say Claudius) whom Hamlet did not like'
              Hamlet did not like kings.
      *   'there are kings whom Hamlet did not like'

(c)   Hamlet may meet an/some actor.
      OK   'there is an actor whom Hamlet may meet'
              Hamlet may meet actors.
      *   'there are actors whom Hamlet may meet'

The DPs whose determiner is *a(n)* or *some* can easily take wider scope than a quantifier, negation, or modal. Bare plurals do not take wider scope. (Greg N. Carlson used this fact to argue that bare plurals do not have a phonetically null indefinite determiner. If they did, we might expect bare plurals to interact scopally with other operators.)

EXERCISE
8.10

Do the following sentences allow the same relative scope interpretations for *a knight* and *every sword*? Propose a generalization.

(a)   A knight bought every sword.
(b)   A knight wanted to buy every sword.
(c)   A knight thought that I bought every sword.
(d)   A knight who bought every sword challenged Laertes.

EXERCISE
8.10
ANSWERS

(a) and (b) have readings on which *every sword* has *a knight* in its scope (the knights vary with the swords). (c) and (d) have no such readings. The generalization seems to be that a DP whose determiner is *every* cannot scope out of a tensed clause. (a) is monoclausal, (b) has an infinitival complement, but in (c) and (d), *every sword* is buried in a *that*-clause and a tensed relative clause, respectively. This generalization highlights yet another syntactic constraint on scope.

EXERCISE
8.11

Does scope influence the ability of a DP to license a negative polarity item or to bind a pronoun?
    The following examples are ambiguous with respect to the scope interpretation of *few sons* and *every knight*. Spell out the two readings in both cases.

(a)   Fathers of few sons have time to sing madrigals.
(b)   Prayers for every knight were said by this lady.

Now consider the following modifications of the examples:

(a')   Fathers of few sons have any time to sing madrigals.
(b')   Prayers for every knight were said by his lady.

Do the modified examples retain the same ambiguity? If not, what readings survive? Suggest an explanation, with reference to the conditions for NPI licensing and binding given in the text.

. . . .

(a)   Fathers of few sons have time to sing madrigals.

   (i)   Those fathers who have few sons each do have time to sing madrigals.
   (ii) There are few sons whose fathers have time to sing madrigals.

(b)   Prayers for every knight were said by this lady.
   (i)   This lady said prayers that each included every knight.
   (ii) Every knight is such that this lady said a prayer for him.

The modified examples are not ambiguous any more:

(a')   Fathers of few sons have any time to sing madrigals.
   (i)* Those fathers who have few sons each do have time to sing madrigals.
   (ii) There are few sons whose fathers have time to sing madrigals.

(b')   Prayers for every knight were said by his lady.
   (i)* His lady said prayers that each included every knight (where by *his lady*, we mean every knight's own lady).
   (ii) Every knight is such that his lady said a prayer for him (where by *his lady*, we mean every knight's own lady).

The negative polarity item *any time* must be within the scope of a decreasing operator. *Few sons* is a decreasing operator. But its scope is different in (a'i) and in (a'ii). In (a'i), *few sons* has scope only inside the subject DP. Therefore, it does not have scope over the NPI, and the NPI is not licensed. In (a'ii), *few sons* has scope over the subject DP and the whole sentence. Therefore it has scope over the NPI and licenses it.

A pronoun can be interpreted as dependent on (bound by) a quantificational DP like *every knight* under conditions very similar to those of reflexive binding: the dominant element of the relation must have scope over the dependent element. In (b'i), *every knight* has scope only inside the subject DP. Therefore it cannot bind *his*. In (b'ii), *every knight* has scope over the subject DP and the whole sentence; it can bind *his*.

In sum, the same notion of scope as is relevant for the relative scope of two DPs is relevant for NPI licensing and pronoun binding.

9
Semantics III: Cross-Categorial Parallelisms

<table>
<tr><td></td><td>Are the predicates below telic or atelic?

(a) Falstaff sneezed.
(b) Hamlet sweated.
(c) Juliet died.
(d) Romeo grieved.
(e) The water froze.</td></tr>
<tr><td>*EXERCISE 9.1 ANSWERS*</td><td>Telic: sneezed, died, froze (modifiable by *within*, not *for* phrases)
Atelic: sweated, grieved (conversely).

    Note: We intentionally chose one-word VPs. As Exercise 9.2 will point out, VPs, not individual Vs, can be classified as to telicity. Make sure that the examples stay as given.</td></tr>
<tr><td>**EXERCISE 9.2**</td><td>(a) Determine whether the following examples are telic or atelic:
    to work, to work oneself to death, to work on a plan, to work out a plan

    Use modification by *for five minutes / an hour / a year* (whichever is appropriate) as the primary test. Bear in mind the comments about irrelevant secondary meanings, made in the text.
    Example: *Lorenzo watched the race for an hour*: atelic
        **Lorenzo won the race for an hour* (unless it means that he was disqualified after that hour): telic

(b) On the basis of your results, suggest what categories should be classified as to telicity. V, VP, something else?</td></tr>
</table>

(a) (i)   Lorenzo worked for an hour.
    (ii) *Lorenzo worked himself to death for an hour.
    (iii) Lorenzo worked on a plan for an hour.
    (iv) *Lorenzo worked out a plan for an hour.

We see that bare *work* is atelic, but when combined with a direct or prepositional object, the result may be telic or atelic. If we were to say that *work*
is an atelic verb, we would have to maintain that even when it occurs as a
constituent of *work oneself to death*, which makes no sense.

(b) The answer to (a) indicates that VP is the smallest category that can
    reasonably be classified as to telicity. This squares with the findings
    in the text.

Recall the definition of *most* in chapter 7 of textbook:

[Most N VP] is true just in case the set of things in both [[N]] and [[VP]] is
larger than the set of things that are in [[N]] but not in [[VP]].

most A B = True   if and only if $(2 \times | A \cap B |) > | A |$

Complete (a) in the manner of (20)–(21), p. 432 of textbook:

(a) Most kings are whimsical: . . .

(a) Most kings are whimsical = There are more kings who are whimsical
    than kings who are not whimsical.

Complete the following, modeling the explanation of *seldom* after that of
few in (21), p. 432 of textbook:

(a) If/when you deal with Puck, you seldom have a good time: . . .

(a) If/when you deal with Puck, you seldom have a good time = the
    number of cases in which you deal with Puck and have a good time is
    small, **or** the number of cases in which you deal with Puck and have
    a good time is small compared to the number of cases in which you
    deal with Puck.

EXERCISE   Check to see whether adverbs of quantification are conservative. Recall the
9.5   definition from chapter 7 of textbook:

A relation Q named by a determiner is conservative if, and only if, for any properties A and B, relation Q holds between A and B if and only if relation Q holds between A and the things in (A ∩ B).

Paraphrase (a) in the manner required by the definition and decide whether the paraphrase is equivalent to the original sentence:

(a)   If/when you deal with Puck, you always have a good time: . . .

EXERCISE   (a)   If/when you deal with Puck, you always have a good time = The set
9.5   of cases in which you deal with Puck is a subset of those cases in
ANSWERS   which you have a good time = The set of cases in which you deal with
                     Puck is a subset of those cases in which you both deal with Puck and
                     have a good time.

   We see that the paraphrases of the original sentence conform to the equivalence required by conservativity. Adverbs of quantification are conservative.

EXERCISE   Note the fact in (a):
9.6

(a)   Relevant set inclusion:
      The set of cases in which you have a very good time is a subset of those in which you have a good time.

Now complete (b) and (c). For (b), what is the proposition that *If you deal with Puck, you seldom have a good time* needs to entail in order for *seldom* to be decreasing? Write it down and determine whether the entailment holds. For (c), demonstrate that *seldom* licenses an occurrence of *any* in the dotted part of the sentence:

(b)   Decreasing entailment:
      If you deal with Puck, you seldom have a good time
      = ? = > . . .

(c)   NPI licensing:
      If you deal with Puck, you seldom . . .

(b)   *Seldom* allows the entailment that is characteristic of decreasing operators:

If you deal with Puck, you seldom have a good time → If you deal with Puck, you seldom have a very good time.

(c)   *Seldom* indeed licenses the negative polarity item *any fun* in its scope:

If you deal with Puck, you seldom have any fun.

EXERCISE 9.6 ANSWERS

Recalling the discussion of what *deny* presupposes with respect to its clausal or gerundival complement, specify what set of cases constitutes the restriction of the adverbs in (25), p. 435 of textbook.

EXERCISE 9.7

Deny presupposes that the issue described in its that-complement has been raised. *The Fool always denies offending Lear* means that whenever the issue is raised whether the Fool offended Lear, the Fool denies it. In other words, the restriction of *always* is the set of cases in which the issue is raised (not the set of cases in which the Fool in fact offended Lear). Likewise for *usually* and *seldom*.

EXERCISE 9.7 ANSWERS

Suppose we have 5 knights. Knight 1 sees one lady twenty times a day, and the same for Knight 2. They bow to them dutifully. On the other hand, Knights 3, 4, and 5 see three ladies each, but only once a day. Knights 3, 4, and 5 neglect to bow.
    First, judge whether (42), p. 439 of textbook, is true in this situation. Next, explain what you counted in reaching your conclusion.

EXERCISE 9.8

The sentence is true. We count the events in which a knight sees a lady and check whether the knight bows. There are forty events of seeing-and-bowing, and only nine events of seeing-without-bowing.
    Notice that if we counted knight–lady pairs, we would get a different, and incorrect, result. The reason is that there are only two knight–lady pairs where the knight bows upon seeing the lady, whereas there are nine knight–lady pairs where the knight neglects to bow.

EXERCISE 9.8 ANSWERS

Explain why (47) is false in (50), pp. 441 and 442 of textbook.

EXERCISE 9.9

---

(47), p. 441 of textbook, asks you to consider boys who got a balloon. There are six such boys, but only two of them, Jaaku and Piita, broke their balloons.

EXERCISE 9.9 ANSWERS

| **EXERCISE** **9.10** | Assume with Bittner that (48) is interested in counting cases, and verify that (48) is false in (49) and true in (50), p. 442 of textbook. |

| *EXERCISE* *9.10* *ANSWERS* | In (49), p. 442 of textbook, there are 204 cases in which a boy got a balloon, and in only five of those did the boy break the balloon. Thus (48), p. 442 of textbook, is false in (49). |
| | In (50), p. 442 of textbook, there are again 204 cases in which a boy got a balloon, but in 200 of them he broke it. Thus (48) is true in (50). |

| **EXERCISE** **9.11** | Collect ten everyday measure expressions (that is, ones of the type *one bar of*, not of the type *one pound of*), together with the mass nouns that they are associated with. |
| | Example: *one bar of soap, chocolate* (but not *bread*). |

EXERCISE **9.11** **ANSWERS**	a jar of honey, jam, peanut butter
	a pile of dirt, clothes, books, sand
	a sliver of gold, wood
	a slab of marble, clay
	a bunch of flowers, trees, cash, bananas
	a stick of dynamite, celery, cinnamon
	a drop of water, wine, rain, common sense
	a pinch of salt
	a field of wheat, corn, poppies
	a bundle of newspapers, magazines, twigs, straw
	a stack of papers, books, forms, bricks

| **EXERCISE** **9.12** | Compare the behavior of mass and count terms in English with the other language(s) that you are a native speaker of or know well. Collect at least three cases where the counterpart of an English mass noun is a count noun, or vice versa. (See Sidebar 9.1, p. 423 of textbook.) |

| **EXERCISE** **9.12** **ANSWERS** | This exercise is recommended when enough students know a second language well enough to answer. There is no pre-set answer. |

| **EXERCISE** **9.13** | Some languages (e.g. Chinese) use measure expressions (called classifiers) even with nouns that are considered count in English. |

E.g.   yí   lì   mî   liǎng lì   mî
        one CL rice   two CL rice
        'one (grain of) rice'   'two (grains of) rice'

yí   zhāng zhuōzi   liǎng zhāng zhuōzi
one CL   table   two CL   table
'one (piece of) table'   'two (pieces of) table'

If you know a language with classifiers, give examples and explain how
they work.

. . . .

This exercise is recommended when enough students know a classifier
language well enough to answer. There is no pre-set answer.

**EXERCISE
9.13
ANSWERS**

. . . .

Determine whether the following nouns are basically mass, basically count,
or fully ambiguous. Note if the noun is basically mass but has secondary
(kind or serving) count uses; similarly, if a count noun has secondary mass
uses. Using full sentences will help to isolate the basic and the secondary
uses.

**EXERCISE
9.14**

Example: *pork*

(i)   I bought pork for dinner.
(ii)   I bought too much pork for dinner.
(iii)   I bought four pounds of pork for dinner.
(iv)   *I bought a pork for dinner.
(v)   *I bought four porks for dinner.
(vi)   You need a tender ground pork to stuff the dumplings with.
(vii)   ?This butcher offers several tasty porks.

Conclusion: *Pork* is basically a mass noun: see (i–v). It has a kind use,
which is count, see (vi), but this is hard to get with the plural, see (vii).

*bear, egg, sand, change, rug, lipstick, hair, milk, cement, advertisement,
advertising, fabric, metal, crack*

. . . .

Below are the judgments by one native speaker for the following contexts.
X means that the example is impossible in that context. Individual students'
judgments may differ a little. What is important is that in the end they
classify each word as basically count, basically mass, etc. on the basis of
these criteria, not speculation.

**EXERCISE
9.14
ANSWERS**

(i)   I saw too many . . . s
(ii)   I saw too much . . .
(iii)   I saw a . . .
(iv)   I saw four . . . s
(v)   You need a good . . . to [cook/paint/build/etc. with].
(vi)   This store offers several good . . . s (or something like this)

Word	(i)	(ii)	(iii)	(iv)	(v)	(vi)
bear		X				
egg						
sand	X		X	X		?
change/1 (coins)	X		X	X	X	X
change/2 (alteration)						
rug						
lipstick						
hair					X	X
milk	X		X?	X?	X	X
cement	X		X	X	X?	
advertisement	X					
advertising						
fabric						
metal	?			X?		
crack/1 (in floor)	X					
crack/2 (cocaine)	X		X	X	X?	X

. . . .

EXERCISE 9.15   Are the nouns *hose* and *chain* count or mass according to the grammatical tests? Do they refer in a cumulative or a quantized manner? Explain what is peculiar about them.

. . . .

EXERCISE 9.15 ANSWERS   The following data show that *hose* and *chain* behave like count nouns:

(a)   I bought a hose / a chain / four hoses / four chains.
(b)*   I bought much hose / much chain.

Hose and *chain* also interact with event structure as count nouns like *chair* do:

(c)   I built/destroyed a chain within an hour / * for an hour.
(d)   I built/destroyed chains * within a hour / for an hour.

But interestingly, even *a hose* and *a chain* refer cumulatively. If I take a hose and join it with another hose, I get a longer hose, not hoses; likewise with chains. Therefore, we will need a somewhat more sophisticated theory of the syntactic and semantic aspects of the count/mass distinction than the one we outlined in the text. Notice that *a hose* and *a chain* are not just isolated exceptions. They are similar to expressions like *a group of people* and *a set of exercises*: two groups of people merge into a larger group, etc. This type can be formed productively.

. . . .

The following pairs illustrate important argument structure alternations in English:

to teach Latin to Cleopatra, to teach Cleopatra Latin,
to stuff feathers into the pillow, to stuff the pillow with feathers

The semantic notions introduced in this chapter allow you to recognize a systematic difference between the members of these pairs. What is it?

. . . .

If I teach Latin to Cleopatra, that does not entail that Cleopatra acquires full command (or, a specific level of command) of Latin when I stop. If I teach Cleopatra Latin, that entails that she acquires such command. That is, the interpretation is cumulative in the first case and quantized (having a well-defined end point) in the second.

If I stuff feathers into the pillow, the pillow may not be full when I stop. If I stuff the pillow with feathers, it has to be full when I stop. Again, the interpretation of the first construction is cumulative and that of the second is quantized.

. . . .

Consider the following contrasts in the expression of English nominalizations. In some, but not all, cases, [the N of DP] can alternatively be phrased as [DP's N], with the same meaning:

the destruction of the city
the city's destruction

the exposure of the corruption
the corruption's exposure

the reenactment of the battle
the battle's reenactment

the performance of the play
the play's performance   but:

the admiration of the art work
*the art work's admiration

the discussion of the future
*the future's discussion

(a)   Collect further examples of both types.
(b)   It has sometimes been suggested that the type that allows both forms involves verbs signifying an action that causes a change in the entity it is directed at. Do the data conform to the generalization? If not, can you suggest another property that distinguishes the two types?

. . . .

**EXERCISE
9.17
ANSWERS**

(b)   The data given in the exercise do not conform to the suggested generalization, which is essentially in terms of thematic roles. It is true that to destroy the city is to cause a change in the city, while to admire the art work is not to change the art work. However, reenacting the battle or performing the play does not cause a change in the battle or the play. These latter examples are misfits. A better generalization seems to be that the [DP's N] nominalization pattern is possible only with telic VPs.

This can be corroborated by looking at the pattern that is grammatical with all nominalizations and checking whether it can be modified by *within* or by *for* phrases:

The destruction of the city within an hour was horrifying.
The exposure of the corruption within a month is desirable.
The reenactment of the battle within a year will shock the public.
The performance of the play within less than three hours is a shame.
*The admiration of the art work within a month flatters the artist.
*The discussion of the future within a week is necessary.

. . . .

**EXERCISE
9.18**

Underline the focus and the focus frame in each of the following sentences. The phrase in parentheses will also guide you in how to pronounce the sentence.

(a)   Ophelia threw white flowers into the water (not red flowers).
(b)   Ophelia threw white flowers into the water (not mice).
(c)   Ophelia threw white flowers into the water (not into the fire).
(d)   Ophelia threw white flowers into the water (instead of dropping them).
(e)   Ophelia threw white flowers into the water (instead of dancing a waltz).
(f)   Ophelia threw white flowers into the water (not Gertrude).

. . . .

The focus frame is always the whole sentence minus the focus.

(a)   focus: white
(b)   focus: white flowers
(c)   focus: water
(d)   focus: threw
(e)   focus: threw white flowers into the water
(f)   focus: Ophelia

. . . .

The (a) sentence contains intonational focus and the (b) sentence, a so-called cleft construction:

(a)   I think that *Oberon talks to PUCK.*
(b)   I think that *it is Puck that Oberon talks to.*

   Come up with various contexts in which the two sentences can be used and check whether it is possible to continue them in the following ways:

(c)   . . . although perhaps he does not talk to anyone.
(d)   . . . although perhaps he also talks to Titania.

   Summarize your results concerning whether intonational focus and clefts in English are identical with respect to carrying a presupposition and expressing exhaustive listing.

. . . .

Intonational focus is compatible with both continuations, *it*-cleft is not:

(a)   I think that *Oberon talks to PUCK*, although perhaps he does not talk to anyone.
       I think that *Oberon talks to PUCK*, although perhaps he also talks to Titania.

(b)   *I think *that it is Puck that Oberon talks to*, although perhaps he does not talk to anyone.
       *I think *that it is Puck that Oberon talks to*, although perhaps he also talks to Titania.

Thus, clefts seem to presuppose that the relevant property (here: being someone that Oberon talks to) holds of some individual, and they also seem to presuppose that it holds only of the individual or group named in the sentence. On the other hand, while intonational focus can be used in a similar way, this is not necessary; witness the possibility of the continuations. This shows that the two constructions, although they are close in meaning, are certainly not synonymous.

. . . .

EXERCISE
9.20

Intonational focus in English is somewhat elusive, but many languages place a contrastively (exhaustively) focused category into a particular syntactic position and/or mark it with a particle, in addition to making it intonationally prominent. The interpretation of such examples is rather similar to that of *it*-clefts in English. The following data from Vata and Hungarian illustrate these two possibilities (Hilda Koopman (1984), *The Syntax of Verbs*, Dordrecht: Foris).

Vata focus is marked by linear order and a focus particle (*mó*). The verb 'see' consists of a verb stem and another particle; this is irrelevant to us.

kòfí yê yòò   yé
Kofi see child-the part
'Kofi saw the child.'

yòò   mó   kòfí yê yé
child-the focus kofi saw part
'It is the child that Kofi saw.'

In Hungarian, the focused constituent is placed into an immediately preverbal position:

Kati látta a   gyereket.
Kati saw the child-acc
'Kati saw the child.'

Kati a   gyereket látta.
Kati the child-acc saw
'It was the child that Kati saw.'

If you are familiar with a comparable language, describe the syntax and the interpretation of its focus construction.

. . . .

EXERCISE
9.20
ANSWERS

The material in this exercise may be worth discussing in connection with focus, regardless of whether the exercise is assigned to students. The Hungarian and Vata data show that focus marking can be an integral part of the surface syntax of human languages. The data also show that syntactically marked focus is semantically more like *it*-clefts than intonational focus in English (according to the same tests as were used in the previous exercise).

11

Phonetics: The Sounds of Language

EXERCISE
11.1

For each set of three words, which one begins with a different speech sound? Consider only the *first* sound in each word.

Example: **scale - state - shall** – *shall* begins with a different sound

 (1) **countenance - king - cheer**
 (2) **sister - she - cease**
 (3) **equal - eyes - even**
 (4) **again - opponent - all**
 (5) **throne - thy - these**
 (6) **character - chaste - coldly**
 (7) **heart - where - who**
 (8) **jelly - giving - gentlemen**
 (9) **admiration - against - appears**
(10) **every - each - else**

EXERCISE
11.1
ANSWERS

The word that begins with a different sound is underlined.

 (1) **countenance - king - <u>cheer</u>**
 (2) **sister - <u>she</u> - cease**
 (3) **equal - <u>eyes</u> - even**
 (4) **again - opponent - <u>all</u>**
 (5) **<u>throne</u> - thy - these**
 (6) **character - <u>chaste</u> - coldly**
 (7) **heart - <u>where</u> - who**
 (8) **jelly - <u>giving</u> - gentlemen**
 (9) **<u>admiration</u> - against - appears**
(10) **every - <u>each</u> - else**

EXERCISE 11.2

How many speech sounds does each of the following English words contain? For each sound, say whether it is a consonant (C) or a vowel (V).

Example: **still** = 4 sounds, CCVC (there is only one *l* sound even though there are two letters)

(1) **yet**
(2) **seems**
(3) **boot**
(4) **have**
(5) **privy**
(6) **walks**
(7) **dumb**
(8) **theme**
(9) **health**
(10) **grizzly**

EXERCISE 11.2 ANSWERS

(1)	**yet**	3 sounds: CVC
(2)	**seems**	4 sounds: CVCC
(3)	**boot**	3 sounds: CVC
(4)	**have**	3 sounds: CVC
(5)	**privy**	5 sounds: CCVCV
(6)	**walks**	4 sounds: CVCC
(7)	**dumb**	3 sounds: CVC
(8)	**theme**	3 sounds: CVC
(9)	**health**	4 sounds: CVCC
(10)	**grizzly**	6 sounds: CCVCCV

Note: In accord with chapter 11 of textbook, none of the vowels above is counted as a diphthong (two sounds). If the instructor chooses to count more vowels of English as diphthongs, some answers could be different (e.g. (3)).

EXERCISE 11.3

For each set of three words, one of them has the stress on a different syllable than the other two. Mark that word. If you are not sure where the stress in a word is, look it up in a dictionary.

Example: **question - scholar - tonight** – mark 'tonight'

(1) **expressed - surprised - triumph**
(2) **luxury - malicious - ministers**
(3) **porcupine - secrecy - illusion**
(4) **possess - answer - gracious**
(5) **extravagant - revolution - disposition**

The word with the main stress on a different syllable is underlined.

(1) **expressed - surprised - <u>triumph</u>**
(2) **luxury - <u>malicious</u> - ministers**
(3) **porcupine - secrecy - <u>illusion</u>**
(4) **<u>possess</u> - answer - gracious**
(5) **<u>extravagant</u> - revolution - disposition**

Underline the vowel in the stressed syllable in each word. (If two letters spell the vowel sound, underline both of them.)

Example: **foolishly** – f<u>oo</u>lishly

(1)   **extravagant**
(2)   **intermission**
(3)   **encounter**
(4)   **hospitality**
(5)   **unworthy**
(6)   **reputation**
(7)   **unwillingly**
(8)   **childishness**
(9)   **philosophy**
(10) **messengers**

The vowel in the stressed syllable in each word is underlined.

(1)   **extrav<u>a</u>gant**
(2)   **interm<u>i</u>ssion**
(3)   **enc<u>ou</u>nter**
(4)   **hospit<u>a</u>lity**
(5)   **unw<u>o</u>rthy** *(also, according to later in the chapter, <u>or</u>)*
(6)   **reput<u>a</u>tion**
(7)   **unw<u>i</u>llingly**
(8)   **ch<u>i</u>ldishness**
(9)   **phil<u>o</u>sophy**
(10) **m<u>e</u>ssengers**

Each of the following English words contains two instances of the letter *s* or the letter *c*. The letter *s* can spell either the sound [s] or [z]. The letter *c* can spell either the sound [s] or [k]. For each word, decide whether the two letters are spelling the same sound, or two different sounds.

Example: **sea̲son** the two *s*'s are pronounced differently, as [s] then [z].

(1) **Francis̲co**
(2) **pa̲stors̲**
(3) **re̲solves̲**
(4) **s̲ometimes̲**
(5) **s̲urpris̲ed**
(6) **dis̲posi̲tion**
(7) **wis̲doms̲**
(8) **se̲cre̲cy**
(9) **s̲pirits̲**
(10) **se̲ns̲ible**

EXERCISE	(1)	**Francis̲co**	different	s	k
11.5	(2)	**pa̲stors̲**	different	s	z
ANSWERS	(3)	**re̲solves̲**	same	z	z
	(4)	**s̲ometimes̲**	different	s	z
	(5)	**s̲urpris̲ed**	different	s	z
	(6)	**dis̲posi̲tion**	different	s	z
	(7)	**wis̲doms̲**	same	z	z
	(8)	**se̲cre̲cy**	different	k	s
	(9)	**s̲pirits̲**	same	s	s
	(10)	**se̲ns̲ible**	same	s	s

EXERCISE 11.6

Each of the following words contains a silent letter. If this letter were removed from the spelling, the spelling would still represent how the word is pronounced. Pronounce each word, decide which letter is not sounded, and circle it.

Example: **answer**: *w* is silent (*anser* would still be a possible spelling for this word).

(1) **guard**
(2) **designed**
(3) **black**
(4) **witch**
(5) **wrung**

EXERCISE 11.6 ANSWERS

The silent letter is underlined.
(1) **gu̲ard**
(2) **desi̲gned**
(3) **blac̲k** (*or* k̲)
(4) **wit̲ch**
(5) **w̲rung**

For each word, a choice of broad transcriptions is given. Indicate which one is consistent with pronunciation of the word and with the set of IPA symbols for broad transcription used in this chapter and listed in (3), pp. 487–807 textbook.

**EXERCISE
11.7**

Example: *cat*   **(a)** /cat/   **(b)** /kat/   **(c)** /kæt/   **(d)** /cæt/   Answer is (c).

(1)	**see**	(a) /see/	(b) /si/	(c) /cee/	(d) /sy/
(2)	**Fuji**	(a) /fuji/	(b) /fuge/	(c) /fudʒi/	(d) /fudʒe/
(3)	**class**	(a) /class/	(b) /klass/	(c) /clæs/	(d) /klæs/
(4)	**you**	(a) /you/	(b) /ju/	(c) /jou/	(d) /yu/
(5)	**spa**	(a) /spa/	(b) /spæ/	(c) /spo/	(d) /ʃpa/
(6)	**she**	(a) /she/	(b) /ʃe/	(c) /shi/	(d) /ʃi/
(7)	**sir**	(a) /sir/	(b) /sɚ/	(c) /ʃir/	(d) /ser/

(1)	**see**	(b) /si/
(2)	**Fuji**	(c) /fudʒi/
(3)	**class**	(d) /klæs/
(4)	**you**	(b) /ju/
(5)	**spa**	(a) /spa/
(6)	**she**	(d) /ʃɪ/
(7)	**sir**	(b) /sɚ/

*EXERCISE
11.7
ANSWERS*

Give the regular English orthography for the following words, which are given in a fairly broad transcription but with a few extra symbols. Even if the pronunciation given here is not the same as yours, you should be able to figure it out. If you are not sure of the orthography, look the word up in a dictionary.

**EXERCISE
11.8**

Example: **[mʌtʃ]** is *much*

(1)   [naɪt]
(2)   [ˈmjuzɪk]
(3)   [ˈbælkəni]
(4)   [gost]
(5)   [ˈmɚsi]
(6)   [ˈmerɪdʒ]
(7)   [ˈferiz]
(8)   [ˈberli]
(9)   [ˈtʃrædʒɚi]
(10) [ˈkʌntrimɪn]

EXERCISE 11.8 ANSWERS			
	(1)	[naɪt]	night
	(2)	['mjuzɪk]	music
	(3)	['bælkəni]	balcony
	(4)	[gost]	ghost
	(5)	['mɚsi]	mercy
	(6)	['merɪdʒ]	marriage
	(7)	['feriz]	fairies
	(8)	['berli]	barely
	(9)	['tʃrædʒəri]	tragedy
	(10)	['kʌntrimɪn]	countrymen (or, countryman)

EXERCISE 11.9

Give broad transcriptions of the following words, as best you can for your own pronunciation. Or, look the words up in a dictionary and give that pronunciation in IPA symbols. Do not mark stress unless your instructor tells you to.

(1) **xerox**
(2) **utopia**
(3) **direct**
(4) **photo**
(5) **triumph**

EXERCISE 11.9 ANSWERS

Possible broad transcriptions:

(1)	**xerox**	ziraks
(2)	**utopia**	jutopiə
(3)	**direct**	dɚɛkt, dərɛkt, dajrɛkt
(4)	**photo**	foto, foɾo
(5)	**triumph**	trajəmf, tʃr-, aɪ-, -ʌm-, -mpf

EXERCISE 11.10

Compare the pronunciations in (5), p. 494 of textbook, with those in a dictionary. First, copy out the pronunciation(s) as given in the dictionary. Then, if necessary, convert these into IPA by referring to the pronunciation key at the beginning of the dictionary. Compare your IPA-pronunciations with the ones in the table to see whether the author's pronunciations are recognized by the dictionary.

EXERCISE 11.10 ANSWERS

Answers will vary depending on what dictionary students select. There is no pre-set answer.

Give the term corresponding to the definition given.

Example: **the soft part of the roof of the mouth** = soft palate

(1)   **end of the tongue blade**
(2)   **airspace between uvula and larynx**
(3)   **bottom part of tongue forming front wall of pharynx**
(4)   **cartilage box at bottom of pharynx holding the vocal cords**
(5)   **articulator which is active or passive, and moved by the jaw**

(1)	**end of the tongue blade**	tip
(2)	**airspace between uvula and larynx**	pharynx
(3)	**bottom part of tongue forming front wall of pharynx**	root
(4)	**cartilage box at bottom of pharynx holding the vocal cords**	larynx
(5)	**articulator which is active or passive, and moved by the jaw**	lower lip

Give the term corresponding to the definition given.

Example: **both lips** – bilabial

(1)   **tongue blade to ridge above upper teeth**
(2)   **tongue body to soft palate**
(3)   **make noise in a gap**
(4)   **plosives and fricatives as a group**
(5)   **vocal cord vibration**

(1)	**tongue blade to ridge above upper teeth**	alveolar (full IPA = laminal alveolar)
(2)	**tongue body to soft palate**	velar
(3)	**make noise in a gap**	fricative
(4)	**plosives and fricatives as a group**	obstruents
(5)	**vocal cord vibration**	voicing

Provide the IPA symbol whose definition is given. Only IPA terms are used.

Example: **voiced alveolar plosive** = [d]

(1)   voiceless velar plosive
(2)   bilabial nasal
(3)   voiced labiodental fricative
(4)   alveolar lateral approximant
(5)   glottal plosive
(6)   alveolar tap or flap
(7)   voiced postalveolar fricative
(8)   velar nasal
(9)   voiceless glottal fricative
(10) voiced dental fricative

EXERCISE			
11.13	(1)	voiceless velar plosive	k
ANSWERS	(2)	bilabial nasal	m
	(3)	voiced labiodental fricative	v
	(4)	alveolar lateral approximant	l
	(5)	glottal plosive	ʔ
	(6)	alveolar tap or flap	ɾ
	(7)	voiced postalveolar fricative	ʒ
	(8)	velar nasal	ŋ
	(9)	voiceless glottal fricative	h
	(10)	voiced dental fricative	ð

EXERCISE   Give the term corresponding to the definition given.
11.14

Example: **made with the tongue overall forward** = front

(1)   made with the lips pulled together and forward
(2)   vowel composed of a sequence of two vowel sounds
(3)   made with the tongue maximally low
(4) ·made with the tongue maximally high
(5)   made with the tongue in an intermediate position in the front–back dimension

---

EXERCISE			
11.14	(1)	made with the lips pulled together and forward	rounded
ANSWERS	(2)	vowel composed of a sequence of two vowel sounds	diphthong
	(3)	made with the tongue maximally low	open (or, low)
	(4)	made with the tongue maximally high	close (or, high)
	(5)	made with the tongue in an intermediate position in the front–back dimension	central

Provide the IPA symbol whose definition is given.

Example: **mid central unrounded vowel** = [ə]

(1) **high (= close) front unrounded vowel**
(2) **lower high front unrounded vowel**
(3) **higher mid (= close-mid) back rounded vowel**
(4) **low (= open) back unrounded vowel**
(5) **high back rounded vowel**
(6) **higher low front unrounded vowel**
(7) **high front rounded vowel**
(8) **lower mid front unrounded vowel**
(9) **high central rounded vowel**
(10) **lower high back rounded vowel**

(1) **high (= close) front unrounded vowel**	i	*EXERCISE*
(2) **lower high front unrounded vowel**	ɪ	*11.15*
(3) **higher mid (= close-mid) back rounded vowel**	o	*ANSWERS*
(4) **low (= open) back unrounded vowel**	a (or, ɑ)	
(5) **high back rounded vowel**	u	
(6) **higher low front unrounded vowel**	œ	
(7) **high front rounded vowel**	y	
(8) **lower mid front unrounded vowel**	ɛ	
(9) **high central rounded vowel**	ʉ	
(10) **lower high back rounded vowel**	ʊ	

Give a symbol with a diacritic according to the description provided.

Example: **aspirated voiceless bilabial stop at the beginning of** *pat* = [pʰ]

(1) **syllabic alveolar nasal at the end of** *sweeten*
(2) **voiced dental stop in** *breadth*
(3) **nasalized high front unrounded vowel in** *lean*
(4) **unreleased final voiced velar stop in** *hag*
(5) **partially voiceless alveolar fricative in** *buzz*

(1) **syllabic alveolar nasal at the end of** *sweeten*	n̩	*EXERCISE*
(2) **voiced dental stop in** *breadth*	d̪	*11.16*
(3) **nasalized high front unrounded vowel in** *lean*	ĩ	*ANSWERS*
(4) **unreleased final voiced velar stop in** *hag*	g̚	
(5) **partially voiceless alveolar fricative in** *buzz*	z̥	

EXERCISE 11.17

Add in arrows to indicate the intonational rises or falls described.

Example: *Virtue? A fig!* with a rise on the first word and a fall on the last

    ↗   ↘

Virtue? A fig!

(1) *It cannot be.* with a fall on *be*
(2) *Put money in thy purse.* with a fall on *purse*
(3) *Thou art sure of me.* with a rise and fall on *sure*
(4) *Do you hear, Roderigo?* with rises on *hear* and *Roderigo*
(5) *How, is this true?* with a fall on *how* and a rise on *true*

EXERCISE
11.17
ANSWERS

            ↘
(1) *It cannot be.*

                ↘
(2) *Put money in thy purse.*

            ↗↘
(3) *Thou art sure of me.*

          ↗   ↗
(4) *Do you hear, Roderigo?*

        ↘   ↗
(5) *How, is this true?*

. . . .

EXERCISE 11.18

Give the regular English orthography for the following words, which are given in a broad transcription. The pronunciations given may not be like yours, but the words should be identifiable nonetheless.

(1) bʊk
(2) onli
(3) pepɚ
(4) aʊt
(5) rimaɪnd (or rəmaɪnd)
(6) stap
(7) hɛd
(8) θɪŋk

(1)	bʊk	book	
(2)	onli	only	
(3)	pepɚ	paper	
(4)	aʊt	out	
(5)	rimaɪnd (or rəmaɪnd)	remind	
(6)	stap	stop	
(7)	hɛd	head	
(8)	θɪŋk	think	

Give broad transcriptions for the following pairs of English words. The focus here is on what makes the two words in each pair different. Use a dictionary if you like, but use IPA symbols. (Since each student may transcribe his or her own pronunciations, there can be no single correct answer here.)

(1) **spot - Scot**
(2) **weary - worry**
(3) **cue - few**
(4) **lose - loose**
(5) **man - men**
(6) **woman - women**
(7) **attend - Athens**
(8) **size - seize**
(9) **show - shoe**
(10) **put - putt**

Sample answers. Differences are underlined.

(1)	**spot - Scot**	spat	sk̲at
(2)	**weary - worry**	wi̲ri	wʊ̲ri
(3)	**cue - few**	k̲ju	f̲ju
(4)	**lose - loose**	luz̲	lus̲
(5)	**man - men**	mæ̲n	mɛ̲n
(6)	**woman - women**	wʊ̲mən	wɪ̲mən
(7)	**attend - Athens**	ə̲tɛnd	æ̲θ̲ə̲nz
(8)	**size - seize**	sa̲ɪz	si̲z
(9)	**show - shoe**	ʃo̲	ʃu̲
(10)	**put - putt**	pʊ̲t	pʌ̲t

Give the regular English orthography for the following words, which are given in a narrow transcription. Again, these pronunciations may not be like yours.

(1) [ˈpʰlẽnti]
(2) [bʊk˺]
(3) [tʃrækʰ]
(4) [ˈmoɾɚ]
(5) [sẽnts] (some speakers will have more than one possible answer for this!)

- -

EXERCISE
11.20
ANSWERS

(1)	[ˈpʰlẽnti]	plenty
(2)	[bʊk˺]	book
(3)	[tʃrækʰ]	track
(4)	[ˈmoɾɚ]	motor
(5)	[sẽnts]	cents, scents, sense, since

- -

EXERCISE
11.21

Give a broad transcription for the following words, which are given in a narrow transcription.

(1) [ˈwʌ̃ndɚfl̩]
(2) [ˈʔæpl̩]
(3) [pʰʊʔt]
(4) [meɪ]
(5) [wãt˺] (hint: what unpronounced sound would cause the vowel to be nasalized?)

- -

EXERCISE
11.21
ANSWERS

(1)	[ˈwʌ̃ndɚfl̩]	wonderful
(2)	[ˈʔæpl̩]	apple
(3)	[pʰʊʔt]	put
(4)	[meɪ]	may
(5)	[wãt˺]	want

- -

EXERCISE
11.22

Compare the sounds in each set below. In each set, all but one are in a single row or column on the IPA chart. Give the name of that row or column, and circle the sound which does not belong.

(1) m n r ŋ
(2) p t k v d g
(3) p t s l n
(4) f v s z h k
(5) i e u ɛ æ

- -

EXERCISE
11.22
ANSWERS

(1)	m n r ŋ	all: nasals	except: r
(2)	p t k v d g	all: plosives	except: v
(3)	p t s l n	all: alveolar	except: p
(4)	f v s z h k	all: fricatives	except: k
(5)	i e u ɛ æ	all: front vowels	except: u

The same as Exercise 11.22, but here all but one sound in each set belong to a class of sounds that goes beyond a single row or column of the chart – classes such as *labial, coronal, dorsal, obstruent, sonorant, approximant, stop, fricative, voiced, voiceless, rounded, unrounded* – or within a single row or column, such as *voiced stops, labial stops*. Give the name of the class of sounds, and circle the sound which does not belong.

EXERCISE 11.23

(1) β v ð z ʒ h
(2) i e æ u ʌ
(3) m l r j w
(4) m n k l r j
(5) θ f ð s z ʃ ʒ

(1)	β v ð z ʒ h	all: voiced fricatives	except: h
(2)	i e æ u ʌ	all: unrounded vowels	except: u
(3)	m l r j w	all: approximants	except: m
(4)	m n k l r j	all: voiced consonants	except: k
(5)	θ f ð s z ʃ ʒ	all: coronal fricatives	except: f

EXERCISE 11.23 ANSWERS

Here are the basic sounds of Burera, an Australian language. Compare this set with the basic sounds of English to answer the questions that follow.

EXERCISE 11.24

/p t c k m n ɲŋ ɾ l r (as in English) j w i ɛ a ɔ u/

a. Which sounds of Burera are not basic in English (as in (3) in the chapter, pp. 487–8 of textbook)? You do not need to define these, just indicate them.
b. What labial sound(s) of English are not in Burera?
c. What coronal sound(s) of English are not in Burera?
d. What dorsal sound(s) of English are not in Burera?
e. What glottal sound(s) of English are not in Burera?

a. c ɲ ɾ
b. b f v
c. d θ ð s z ʃ ʒ tʃ dʒ
d. g
e. h

EXERCISE 11.24 ANSWERS

12

Phonology I: Basic Principles and Methods

EXERCISE 12.1	Find minimal pairs for the following sounds: [i] vs. [e], [p] vs. [b], [θ] vs. [ð], [v] vs. [u].

EXERCISE 12.1 ANSWERS

[i] vs. [e] *seen/sane, free/fray, seal/sale, E/A,* and many others

[p] vs. [b] *pill/bill, cup/cub, ample/amble,* and many others

[θ] vs. [ð] *thigh/thy, ether/either,* and various morphologically related pairs: *mouth* (noun)/*mouth* (verb), *sheath/sheathe, wreath/ wreathe, loath/loathe, sooth/soothe, swath/swathe, teeth/teethe*

[ʊ] vs. [u] *look/Luke, soot/suit, full/fool, bull/Bool, pull/pool, nook/nuke, cook/kook, should/shoed, wood/wooed, stood/stewed, could/cooed.* Some of these are miminal pairs only in some dialects of English.

. . . .

EXERCISE 12.2

English Allophones

In English, [k] and [ḵ] (plain velar and fronted velar stops respectively) are allophones of the same phoneme. Consider the following data:

kitten	['ḵɪtn]	cop	[kap]	crack	[kræk]
keen	[ḵin]	cool	[kul]	clock	[klak]
cake	[ḵek]	cope	[kop]	quick	[kwɪk]
cat	[ḵæt]	cook	[kʊk]	extract	[ɛk'strækt]
lucky	['lʌḵi]	cup	[kʌp]	Exxon	['ɛksan]

(a) What is the environment in which [ḵ] is found? If you don't immediately see the answer, carefully follow the procedure laid out above, collecting and writing down the environments in which [k] and [ḵ] occur. It also may help to examine the English vowel chart under (3), p. 520 of textbook.

(b) What is the environment in which [k] is found?

(c) Decide on the basis of your answer to the previous question what should be the underlying form of the phoneme. Write a phonological rule, using words, that derives the contextual allophone.

(d) Look at the following data and write an improved version of your rule, using features. [g̟] is a fronted voiced velar stop. You may use [+fronted] as a feature to distinguish [k̟, g̟] from [k, g].

gill	[gɪl]	got	[gat]	grog	[grag]
geese	[g̟is]	goose	[gus]	glimmer	['glɪmr̩]
game	[g̟em]	go	[go]	Gwendolyn	['gwɛndələn]
gag	[g̟æg]	good	[gʊd]	eggs	[ɛgz]
soggy	['sag̟i]	Gus	[gʌs]	Muggsy	['mʌgzi]

(e) Provide underlying forms and a phonological derivation for *keen, clock, soggy,* and *eggs.*

· ·

(a) Before front vowels.

(b) Elsewhere.

(c) /k/
k becomes [k̟] when a front vowel immediately follows.

(d) $\begin{bmatrix} \text{+stop} \\ \text{+velar} \end{bmatrix} \rightarrow [\text{+fronted}] / \underline{\quad} \begin{bmatrix} \text{+vowel} \\ \text{+front} \end{bmatrix}$

(e)
keen	*clock*	*soggy*	*eggs*	
/kin/	/klak/	/'sagi/	/ɛgz/	underlying forms
k̟in	—	'sag̟i	—	Velar Fronting
[k̟in]	[klak]	['sag̟i]	[ɛgz]	output

· ·

Lango

Lango is a Nilotic language spoken in Uganda. Here are phonetic symbols found in the data below that may be unfamiliar:

[á]	High tone (on the vowel [a])
[à]	Low tone
[â]	Falling tone
[ǎ]	Rising tone
[tɕ, dʑ]	voiceless and voiced palatal affricates (Note: these are single sounds, not sequences of sounds.)
[ɾ̥]	voiceless alveolar flap
[ɸ]	voiceless bilabial fricative
[ç]	voiceless palatal fricative
[x]	voiceless velar fricative
[ɲ]	palatal nasal

Consonants transcribed as double are simply **held longer**; they are not 'rearticulated.' Think of them as single long consonants. [ttç] and [ddʑ] are long affricates, held for a long time with an affricated release.

(1)	[pì]	'because of'
(2)	[kètç]	'hunger'
(3)	[tɔ́ŋ]	'spear'
(4)	[búttçó]	'to yell at'
(5)	[tçɔ̀]	'men'
(6)	[ʔɔ̀t]	'house'
(7)	[dɔ̀ttɔ̀]	'to suck'
(8)	[pə̀ppì]	'fathers'
(9)	[pójó]	'to remember'
(10)	[ljèt]	'hot'
(11)	[bókkó]	'to make red'
(12)	[júttçú]	'to throw'
(13)	[èŋɔ́ɾó]	'lion'
(14)	[ókkɔ́]	'completely'
(15)	[déɸô]	'to collect'
(16)	[dèk]	'stew'
(17)	[tçùɸâ]	'bottle'
(18)	[gwèk]	'gazelle'
(19)	[kókkó]	'to cry'
(20)	[ɲáɸô]	'laziness'
(21)	[ɾétç]	'fish'
(22)	[bóɾə́]	'to me'
(23)	[dìppó]	'to smash'
(24)	[dwéɾê]	'months'
(25)	[kóddó]	'to blow'
(26)	[tçín]	'intestines'
(27)	[gíɾé]	'really'
(28)	[lòçə̀]	'man'
(29)	[kwɔ̀çê]	'leopards'
(30)	[kál]	'millet'
(31)	[màçê]	'fires'
(32)	[àbíçèl]	'six'
(33)	[dáxô]	'woman'
(34)	[tçùtç]	'pitch black'
(35)	[tójô]	'dew'
(36)	[wókkí]	'a few minutes ago'
(37)	[dìə̀xə̀]	'wet'
(38)	[máxâtç]	'scissors'
(39)	[pé]	'snow, hail'
(40)	[kɔ́ppɔ̀]	'cup'
(41)	[pàttçó]	'to peel'

(42) [pámâ]   'cotton'
(43) [mɔ̀r̥ɔ̀xà]   'car'
(44) [bə̀p]   'to deflate'
(45) [lwìttê]   'to sneak'
(46) [ɲàp]   'lazy'
(47) [bwɔ̀ttɔ̀]   'to retort insultingly'
(48) [tèttó]   'to forge'
(49) [tɕám]   'eating'
(50) [tɔ̀p]   'to spoil'
(51) [tɕɔ́k]   'near'
(52) [pàɸó]   'father'
(53) [ɲwèttɕó]   'to run from'
(54) [bót]   'to'
(55) [dèppó]   'to collect'
(56) [gɔ̀t]   'mountain'
(57) [j̀ìtɕ]   'belly'
(58) [bìttó]   'to unshell'
(59) [dɔ̀k]   'to go back'
(60) [kòp]   'matter'
(61) [tîn]   'today'
(62) [kít]   'kind'
(63) [àkká]   'purposely'
(64) [tɕàk]   'milk'
(65) [dʑ̩ɔk]   'pagan god'

(a)   Fill in all the consonants found in the problem in the following phon-
      etic chart. You may treat [w] as labial and [j] as palatal. Not all slots in
      the chart get filled.

			labial	alveolar	palatal	velar
stops and affricates	voiceless	short				
		long				
	voiced	(all short)				
fricatives	(all voiceless)	(all short)				
nasals	(all voiced)	(all short)				
liquids	laterals	(voiced)				
	flaps	voiceless				
		voiced				
glides	(all voiced)	(all short)				

(b)   This problem deals just with the sounds [p, pp, ɸ, t, tt, ɽ (NOT ɾ), tɕ, ttɕ, ɕ, k, kk, x]. For these sounds only, follow the procedure laid out in the text: collect and write down the environments in which each occurs.

(c)   Describe in words the environments in which [p, pp, ɸ, t, tt, ɽ, tɕ, ttɕ, ɕ, k, kk, x] occur. To the extent that this is possible, state your description in general terms, rather than one sound at a time.

(d)   Are [pp, tt, ttɕ, kk] in complementary distribution with [p, t, tɕ, k]? Are [ɸ, ɽ, ɕ, x] in complementary distribution with [p, t, tɕ, k]? What is the problem that this gives rise to? Does appealing to phonetic similarity help?

(e)   Here are further data that can help solve the problem. These data involve alternations; the same stem appears with or without a suffix. (Do not try to handle the tonal alternations, just consider the final consonants of stems.)

(i)	[dĕp]	'gather-imperative'	[ìdɛ́ɸò]	'you gathered'
	[măt]	'drink-imperative'	[ìmáɽò]	'you drank'
	[dătɕ]	'drop-imperative'	[ìdáɕò]	'you dropped'
	[gĭk]	'stop-imperative'	[ìgíxò]	'you stopped'
(ii)	[jît]	'ear'	[jîɽê]	'his/her ear'
	[lăk]	'tooth'	[làxê]	'his/her tooth'
(iii)	[ɲàp]	'lazy'	[ɲáɸô]	'laziness'

What do the alternations tell you about the correct phonemicization of Lango?

(f)   State phonological rules that derive the right allophones, using words.

(g)   Provide the phonemic forms (underlying representations) for [pàppì] 'fathers', [dĕp] 'gather-imperative', [ìdĕɸò] 'you gathered', and [lòɕà] 'man'.

. . . .

EXERCISE 12.3 ANSWERS

(a)

			labial	alveolar	palatal	velar
stops and affricates	voiceless	short	p	t	tɕ	k
		long	pp	tt	ttɕ	kk
	voiced	(all short)	b	d	dʑ	g
fricatives	(all voiceless)	(all short)	ɸ		ɕ	x
nasals	(all voiced)	(all short)	m	n	ɲ	ŋ
liquids	laterals	(voiced)		l		
	flaps	voiceless		ɽ		
		voiced		ɾ		
glides	(all voiced)	(all short)	w		j	

(b)

Phone	Env.	#	Phone	Env.	#	Phone	Env.	#
p	[__ì	1	pp	à__ì	8	Φ	é__ô	15
p	[__ə̀	8	pp	ì__ó	23	Φ	ù__â	17
p	[__ó	9	pp	ɔ́__ɔ̀	40	Φ	á__ô	20
p	[__é	39	pp	ɛ̀__ó	55	Φ	à__ó	52
p	[__à	41						
p	[__á	42						
p	ə̀__]	44						
p	à__]	46						
p	ɔ̀__]	50						
p	[__à	52						
p	ò__]	60						
t	[__ɔ́	3	tt	ɔ̀__ɔ̀	7	ɾ̥	ə̀__ó	13
t	ɔ̀__]	6	tt	ì__ê	45	ɾ̥	ó__ə̀	22
t	è__]	10	tt	ɔ̀__ɔ̀	47	ɾ̥	é__ê	24
t	[__ó	35	tt	è__ó	48	ɾ̥	í__é	27
t	[__è	48	tt	ì__ó	58	ɾ̥	ɔ̀__ɔ̀	43
t	[__ɔ̀	50						
t	ó__]	54						
t	ɔ̀__]	56						
t	[__î	61						
t	í__]	62						
tɕ	è__]	2	ttɕ	ú__ó	4	ç	ò__ə	28
tɕ	[__ɔ̀	5	ttɕ	ú__ú	12	ç	à__ê	29
tɕ	[__ù	17	ttɕ	à__ó	41	ç	à__ê	31
tɕ	ɛ́__]	21	ttɕ	ɛ̀__ó	53	ç	í__ɛ̀	32
tɕ	[__í	26						
tɕ	[__ù	34						
tɕ	ù__]	34						
tɕ	â__]	38						
tɕ	[__á	49						
tɕ	[__ɔ́	51						
tɕ	ì__]	57						
tɕ	[__à	64						
k	[__è	2	kk	ó__ó	11	x	á__ô	33
k	ɛ̀__]	16	kk	ó__ɔ́	14	x	à__ə̀	37
k	ɛ̀__]	18	kk	ó__ó	19	x	á__â	38
k	[__ó	19	kk	ó__í	36	x	ɔ̀__à	43
k	[__ó	25	kk	à__á	63			
k	[__w	29						
k	[__w	29						
k	[__á	30						
k	[__ɔ́	40						
k	ɔ́__]	51						
k	ɔ̀__]	59						
k	[__ò	60						
k	[__í	62						
k	à__]	64						
k	ɔ__]	65						

(c) • Long consonants occur only between vowels.
   • Fricatives occur only between vowels.
   • The voiceless flap [ɾ̥] occurs only between vowels.
   • Single stops and affricates occur elsewhere, which in practice means initially or finally.

(d) [pp, tt, ttɕ, kk] are in complementary distribution with [p, t, tɕ, k].
   [ɸ, ɾ̥, ç, x] are in complementary distribution with [p, t, tɕ, k].

   They are NOT in complementary distribution with each other, so they can't all be allophones of the same phoneme. We can either say that [pp, tt, ttɕ, kk] are allophones of /p, t, tɕ, k/, or that [ɸ, ɾ̥, ç, x] are allophones of /p, t, tɕ, k/, but NOT BOTH.

   Appealing to phonetic similarity does not help. We might think that [ɸ, ɾ̥, ç, x] are too different from [p, t, tɕ, k] to be in the same phoneme (recall the discussion of English [h] and [ŋ]), but in fact [ɸ, ɾ̥, ç, x] are quite similar to [p, t, tɕ, k], as they occur at the same places of articulation and have the same voicing. They differ only in the stop/fricative or stop/flap distinction. [pp, tt, ttɕ, kk] are likewise quite similar to [p, t, tɕ, k], differing only in length.

(e) It has to be [ɸ, ɾ̥, ç, x] that are allophones of /p, t, tɕ, k/, because [ɸ, ɾ̥, ç, x] are what /p, t, tɕ, k/ turn into when the appropriate environment (= surrounded by vowels) is created by suffixation.

(f) *Flapping*
   Short /t/ is flapped between vowels.

   Spirantization
   Short stops and affricates become fricatives between vowels.

   We can either order Flapping before Spirantization, or specify that Spirantization does not affect alveolars. Yet another possibility is to allow Spirantization to create alveolar fricatives, then add a later rule that converts alveolar fricatives to flaps.

(g) [pə̀ppì]   'fathers'   /pə̀ppì/
   [dĕp]   'gather-imperative' /dɛp/
   [ìdĕɸò]   'you gathered'   /ìdɛpò/
   [lòçə̀]   'man'   /lòtɕə̀/

. . . .

EXERCISE   **Rule Ordering in 'Vancouver'**
12.4   In a dialect spoken by many English speakers, there is an allophonic rule whereby the phoneme /æ/ gets diphthongized in a particular way before /ŋ/. Individual speakers vary, but this diphthong is often pronounced

something like [æi]. The effects of the diphthongizing rule can be seen in pairs such as the following:

pan	/pæn/	[pæn]		*pang*	/pæŋ/	[pæiŋ]
fan	/fæn/	[fæn]		*fang*	/fæŋ/	[fæiŋ]
gander	/'gændr̩/	['gændr̩]		*anger*	/'æŋgr̩/	['æiŋgr̩]

Note that in all of these cases, the [æ]'s and [æi]'s are actually nasalized, because of the Vowel Nasalization given earlier under (50), p. 545 of text-book. The nasal tildes have been left out for legibility.

The special allophone of /æ/ before /ŋ/ can be derived by a rule that looks like this:

Pre-/ŋ/ Diphthongization: /æ/ → [æi] / ____ ŋ

Most speakers of English also have an optional rule of /n/ Assimilation, which causes /n/ to to shift to the place of articulation of an immediately following consonant:

/n/ Assimilation: /n/ → [same place] / ____ C (in casual speech)

Some examples of this rule are as follows:

input	['ɪnpʊt] or ['ɪmpʊt]
unprepared	[ʌnprə'perd] or [ʌmprə'perd]
unbelievable	[ʌnbə'livəbəl] or [ʌmbə'livəbəl]
I live in Minnesota	[aɪ 'lɪv ɪn mɪnə'sorə] or [aɪ 'lɪv ɪm mɪnə'sorə]
phone call	['fonkɔl] or ['foŋkɔl]
concourse	['kankors] or ['kaŋkors]
con game	['kan‚gem] or ['kaŋ‚gem]
in college	[ɪn 'kalɪdʒ] or [ɪŋ'kalɪdʒ]

Note that among other changes, this rule shifts /n/ to [ŋ], when the following consonant is velar.

Determine what the following data tell us about the RELATIVE ORDERING of Pre-/ŋ/ Diphthongization and /n/ Assimilation. To prove an order-ing securely, give full derivations for both orders (as in (102), pp. 569–70 of textbook), and point out which outcome matches the observed facts. Where a rule applies optionally, include both possibilities in your derivations.

Word	Phonemic Form	Pronunciation
pancake	/'pænkek/	['pænkeɪk] (careful speech) or ['pæŋkeɪk] (casual speech) but not *['pæɪŋkeɪk]
Vancouver	/væn'kuvr̩/	[væn'kuvr̩] (careful speech) or [væŋ'kuvr̩] (casual speech) but not *[væɪŋ'kuvr̩]
Dan Gurney	/'dæn'grni/	['dæn'grni] (careful speech) or ['dæŋ'grni] (casual speech) but not ['dæɪŋ'grni]
sank	/'sæŋk/	['sæɪŋk] only
anchor	/'æŋkr̩/	['æɪŋkr̩] only
Rangoon	/ræŋ'gun/	[ræɪŋ'gun] only
pang cake 'cake eaten to assuage pangs of hunger'	/'pæŋkeɪk/	['pæɪŋkeɪk] only

· · · · · · · · · · · · ·

EXERCISE 12.4 ANSWERS

The following derivations order Pre-/ŋ/ Diphthongization BEFORE /n/ Assimilation, and get the right result:

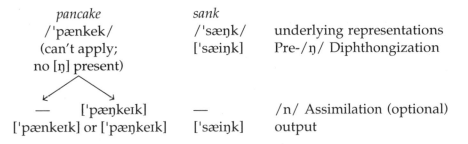

pancake	*sank*	
/'pænkek/	/'sæŋk/	underlying representations
(can't apply; no [ŋ] present)	['sæɪŋk]	Pre-/ŋ/ Diphthongization
— ['pæŋkeɪk]	—	/n/ Assimilation (optional)
['pænkeɪk] or ['pæŋkeɪk]	['sæɪŋk]	output

The following derivations order Pre-/ŋ/ Diphthongization AFTER /n/ Assimilation, and get the wrong result:

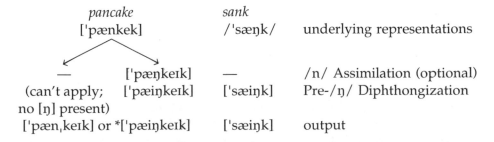

pancake	*sank*	
['pænkek]	/'sæŋk/	underlying representations
— ['pæŋkeɪk]	—	/n/ Assimilation (optional)
(can't apply; no [ŋ] present) ['pæɪŋkeɪk]	['sæɪŋk]	Pre-/ŋ/ Diphthongization
['pæn͵keɪk] or *['pæɪŋkeɪk]	['sæɪŋk]	output

Under this ordering, we optionally derive an output that is impossible, *['pæɪŋkeɪk]. Since the previous ordering derives all and only the correct outcomes, it must be the right one

· ·

More on Choctaw   EXERCISE

The discussion in section 12.10.2, pp. 557–60 of textbook, only scratches   12.5
the surface of Choctaw phonology. Here, we delve slightly deeper. To do
this problem you should carefully re-read the section.

Choctaw is phonologically unusual in having three audible degrees of
vowel length. Thus far, we have only included examples with short and
long vowels. But there are also OVERLONG vowels. These occur as distinct
phonemes. In this problem, we will transcribe short, long, and overlong
vowels like this: [a], [aː], [aːː].

The overlong vowels have a strong influence on the pattern of Rhythmic
Lengthening. Recall that in words that phonemically have only short vowels,
the EVEN-NUMBERED, NON-FINAL short vowels undergo the rule, and surface
as long.

Now consider some inflectional paradigms for stems that include overlong vowels.

[hopoːːni]	'cook'
[hopoːːni + li]	'cook-I.subj' = 'I cook'
[tʃi + hoːpoːːni]	'you.obj-cook' = '(he) cooks you'
[tʃi + hoːpoːːni + li]	'you.obj-cook-I.subj' = 'I cook you'
[hopoːːni + tʃi]	'cook-causative' = '(he) makes (him) cook'
[tʃi + hoːpoːːni + tʃi]	'you.obj-cook-causative' = '(he) makes you cook'
[hopoːːni + tʃiː + li]	'cook-causative-I.subj' = 'I make (him) cook'
[tʃi + hoːpoːːni + tʃiː + li]	'you.obj-cook-causative-I.subj' = 'I make you cook'

[taloːːwa]	'sing'
[taloːːwa + li]	'sing-I.subj' = 'I sing'
[taloːːwa + tʃi]	'sing-causative' = '(he) makes (him) sing'
[tʃi + taːloːːwa + tʃi]	'you.obj-sing-causative' = '(he) makes you sing'
[taloːːwa + tʃiː + li]	'sing-causative-I.subj' = 'I make (him) sing'

[ʃoːːli]	'hug'
[ʃoːːli + li]	'hug-I.subj' = 'I hug'
[tʃi + ʃoːːli]	'you.obj-hug' = '(he) hugs you'
[tʃi + ʃoːːli + li]	'you.obj-hug-I.subj' = 'I hug you'
[taːːni]	'get out of bed'
[taːːni + li]	'get.out.of.bed-I.subj' = 'I get out of bed'
[taːːni + tʃi]	'get.out.of.bed-causative' = '(he) makes (him) get out of bed'
[tʃi + taːːni + tʃi]	'you.obj-get.out.of.bed-causative' = '(he) makes you get out of bed'

[taːni + tʃiː + li]   'get.out.of.bed-causative-I.subj' = 'I make (him) get out of bed'

[tʃi + taːni + tʃiː + li]   'you.obj-get.out.of.bed-causative-I.subj' = 'I make you get out of bed'

[faːpatʃi]   'push in a swing'

[faːpatʃiː + li]   'push.in.a.swing-I.subj' = 'I push (him) in a swing'

[tʃi + faːpatʃi]   'you.obj-push.in.a.swing' = '(he) pushes you in a swing'

[tʃi + faːpatʃiː + li]   'you.obj-push.in.a.swing-I.subj' = 'I push you in a swing'

You can see that in some of these forms, the pattern of Rhythmic Lengthening is different for words that have overlong vowels. To make this clear, examine the following pairs, focusing on the bold face vowels:

With overlong vowels	*Without overlong vowels*
[tʃi + hoːpoːni + tʃiː + li] 'you.obj-cook-causative-I.subj' = 'I make you cook'	[tʃi + haːbinaː + tʃi + li] 'you.obj-receive.as.a.present-causative-I.subj' = 'I cause you to receive as a present'
[taːni + tʃiː + li] 'get.out.of.bed-causative-I.subj' = 'I make (him) get out of bed'	[pisaː + tʃi + li] 'see-causative-I.subj' = 'I make (him) see'
[faːpatʃiː + li] 'push.in.a.swing-I.subj' = 'I push (him) in a swing'	[habiːna + li] 'receive.as.a.present-I.subj' = 'I receive as a present'
[ʃoːli + li] 'hug-I.subj' = 'I hug (him)'	[pisaː + li] 'see-I.subj' = 'I see'

(a)   True or false: 'Rhythmic Lengthening does not apply to a word if the word contains an overlong vowel.' Justify your answer with reference to the data.

(b)   State in words a corrected version of the Rhythmic Lengthening rule that will derive the correct results for all the words given.

(c)   Provide the underlying form and a phonological derivation for [hopoːni + tʃiː + li] 'cook-causative-I.subj' = 'I make (him) cook'.

(d)   True or false: 'The contrast between [aː] and [aːː] is distributionally limited, as it is never found in initial syllables.' Explain your answer.

(e)   What would you expect to be the Choctaw form that means 'I make you sing'; that is, 'you.obj-sing-causative-I.subj'? Explain your answer with a full morphological and phonological derivation.

· ·

(a)   False. It DOES apply, but in different locations. For instance, the long
      vowels of [tʃi + hoːpoːːni + tʃiː + li] must be derived by Rhythmic
      Lengthening, since the same vowels show up as short in other
      allomorphs of the same morphemes.

(b)   Lengthen all the non-final even-numbered vowels in a sequence of
      underlying short vowels.

(c)   hopoːːni + tʃi + li   underlying form
      hopoːːni + tʃiː + li   Rhythmic Lengthening (sequence of short
                            vowels: /i . . . i . . . i/)
                            Note: /oːː/ is overlong, and not eligible.
      [hopoːːnitʃiːli]   output

(d)   True. [aː] cannot contrast with [aːː] in an initial syllable, because
      [aː] is always derived from /a/ by Rhythmic Lengthening. Rhythmic
      Lengthening targets only even-numbered, and hence never initial,
      syllables.

(e)   /taloːːwa/   stem meaning 'sing'
                              Morphology:
      /tʃi + taloːwa + tʃi + li/   addition of affixes:
                                  /tʃi-/ = 'you.obj.'
                                  /-tʃi/ = 'causative'
                                  /-li/ = 'I.subj.'
                              Phonology:
      tʃi + taːloːːwa + tʃiː + li   Rhythmic Lengthening
        [tʃitaːloːːwatʃiːli]   output

13

Phonology II: Phonological Representations

EXERCISE 13.1

Give the feature composition of the sounds /e/, /ĩ/, /s/, /ŋ/, /ʃ/, /w/, /ɣ/ using the features discussed in section 13.1.2, pp. 581–4 of textbook.

EXERCISE 13.1 ANSWERS

	/e/	/ĩ/	/s/	/ŋ/	/ʃ/	/w/	/ɣ/
labial							
coronal	−	−	+	−	+	+	−
dorsal	+	+	−	+	−	+	+
continuant	+	+	+	−	+	+	+
consonantal	−	−	+	+	+	−	+
nasal	−	−	−	+	−	−	−
high	−	+	−	+	−	+	+
low	−	−	−	−	−	−	−
voice	+	+	−	+	−	+	+
sonorant	+	+	−	+	−	+	−
strident	−		+	−	+	−	−
anterior	−	−	+	−	−	+	−

EXERCISE 13.2

The voicing alternations of Hungarian obstruents involve not only voiced {b, d, g . . . } becoming voiceless {p, t, k, . . . } but also voiceless {p, t, k, . . . } becoming voiced {b, d, g . . . }. Consider the following data and formulate a feature analysis – extending the statement of (9), p. 585 of textbook – so that it will characterize all voicing alternations in the language, the ones in (8), pp. 584–5 of textbook, as well as those seen below:

ljuk	'hole'	ljugbɔn	'in the hole'
nɔp	'sun'	nɔbbɔn	'in the sun'
sɛrteːʃ	'pig'	sɛrteːʒbɔn	'in the pig'
golf	'golf'	golv bɔjnokʃaːg	'golf championship'

Now consider the additional data below:

list	'flour'	lizdbɛn	'in the flour'
bɔrɔtsk	'apricot'	bɔrɔdzgbɔn	'in the apricot'
tɛkst	'text'	tɛgzdbɔn	'in the text'

Make sure your statement will accurately characterize all alternations. The data are limited and thus compatible with a number of interpretations and analyses: choose the most general one even if your analysis makes predictions that you cannot verify at this point. (Do not consider the *bɔn/bɛn* alternations – they reflect an unrelated phenomenon.)

(a)   [−sonorant] → [−voice] / ___ [−voice]
(b)   [−sonorant] → [+voice] / ___ [+voice, −sonorant]

Rule (b) above applies *repeatedly* to all strings in which its structural description is met.

A feature-based analysis is capable of modelling certain aspects of linguistic knowledge that go beyond the sounds attested in one's native language. With this in mind we asked a Hungarian colleague and co-author of this book how she pronounces in Hungarian the phrase 'in (the city of) Bath'. The suffix -*ban* [bɔn] is used in Hungarian to indicate location (cf. Exercise 13.2). Note that the English place name *Bath* [baθ] contains a voiceless interdental fricative [θ] that is unattested in Hungarian. Our colleague had never used the expression *Bath-ban* in Hungarian and had not heard anyone use it either. She uttered [baθ] for *Bath* in isolation but [baðbɔn] for *Bath-ban*, using [ð], the voiced counterpart [θ]. Explain the significance of this fact for feature-based and segment-based analyses of voicing assimilation. Does your answer to Exercise 13.2 predict the attested [baðbɔn] or the form our colleague rejected, namely [baθbɔn]?

The data are as predicted by the answer given above to Exercise 13.2. Every sound that is a voiceless obstruent, whether or not this sound is native to Hungarian, becomes voiced when preceding a voiced obstruent. Thus [θ] is not native to Hungarian but alternates as predicted by the voicing rule. The significance of this is that it supports the feature-based analysis proposed in the textbook: a list-based analysis of voicing alternations in Hungarian will predict that only native Hungarian sounds, not [θ], will alternate as to voicing.

EXERCISE 13.4	Consider the alternations in vowel length in the Yokuts words seen below. (Yokuts is a California Indian language. Data come from Stanley Newman (1944), *Yokuts Language of California*, New York: Viking Fund Publications in Anthropology, no. 2). Posit underlying representations for roots and suffixes. Make assumptions about possible Yokuts syllables and about how the Yokuts words below are divided into syllables. State what these assumptions are and use them to explain the distribution of long and short vowels. You will need a rule of the form [+syllabic] → [−long]/ in some context defined in terms of syllable structure. Ignore the alternation between i and zero. The dash (-) indicates morpheme boundaries, which do not necessarily coincide with syllable boundaries:

Nonfuture	Imperative	Dubitative	Future	Gloss
ṣap-hin	ṣap-ka	ṣa:pal	ṣa:p-en	burn
lan-hin	lan-ka	la:nal	la:n-en	hear
ʔa:mil-hin	ʔa:mil-ka	ʔaml-al	ʔaml-en	help
xat-hin	xat-ka	xat-al	xat-en	eat
paʔiṭ-hin	paʔiṭ-ka	paʔṭ-al	paʔṭ-en	fight

Nonfuture	Passive			Gloss
pana:-hin	pana-t			arrive
hoyo:-hin	hoyo-t			name

EXERCISE 13.4 ANSWERS	We assume that surface syllables in Yokuts have the following possible forms: CV, CVC, CV:. Underlying syllables may also contain CV:C. The alternations are caused by long vowels shortening in closed syllables:

[+syllabic, +long] → [−long]/ _C]$_\sigma$ i.e. when followed by a C in the same syllable.

EXERCISE 13.5	Read aloud the following sentences focusing on the noun phrases in bold characters:

(a)   He is **the editor of a book**.
(b)   He is **the book's editor**.
(c)   He is **the book editor**.

Mark primary and subsidiary stresses. Provide grid structures for all three noun phrases.

(a) **the editor of a book** [ˌɛɾɪtər əvə ˈbʊk]: main stress on last syllable, secondary stress on first

layer 2					x	
layer 1 x					x	
layer 0 x	x	x	x	x	x	
	σ	σ	σ	σ	σ	σ
	ʔɛ	ɾɪ	tər	əv	ə	bʊk

(b) **the book's editor** [ˌbʊks ˈʔɛɾɪtər]: main stress on last syllable, secondary stress on first

layer 2	x		
layer 1 x	x		
layer 0 x	x	x	x
	σ	σ	σ	σ
	bʊks	ʔɛ	ɾɪ	tər

(c) **the book editor** [ˈbʊk ˌʔɛɾɪtər]: main stress on first syllable, secondary stress on last

layer 2 x			
layer 1 x	x		
layer 0 x	x	x	x
	σ	σ	σ	σ
	bʊk	ʔɛ	ɾɪ	tər

Observe the differences in the location of main stress between (a–b) and, on the other hand, (c) in Exercise 13.5. Identify the general class of nominal expressions that are characterized by the stress pattern of (c) as distinct from (a–b).

All noun phrases have primary stress on their last stressed syllable. Noun compounds consisting of two nouns have primary stress on the first noun.

EXERCISE 13.7

The definite article /l/ of Moroccan Arabic is realized in four different ways depending on the structure of the noun it is attached to: [l], [lə] and an allomorph we call C, which consists of substituting for [l] a copy of the first stem consonant (data from Mohammed Guerssel (1978), 'A condition on assimilation rules', *Linguistic Analysis*, 4: 225–54). Identify in feature terms (a) the class of nouns that requires the C allomorph and (b) the class of nouns that requires the [lə] allomorphs. The form of the noun in isolation is identical to the string that follows the morpheme boundary:

l allomorph	lə allomorph	C allomorph
l-uqid 'the matches'	*lə-ktab* 'the book'	*t-tuma* 'the garlic'
l-kamyu 'the truck'	*lə-brˤa* 'the letter'	*z-zbəl* 'the garbage'
l-biru 'the office'	*lə-qfəl* 'the lock'	*ʃ-ʃamʃ* 'the sun'
l-firan 'the mice'	*lə-fʒəl* 'the radish'	*ʒ-ʒrad* 'the locust'
	lə-ksˤida 'the accident'	*d-dfal* 'the saliva'
		s-sma 'the sky'

Note: The symbol ˤ indicates that the preceding sound is pharyngealized.

EXERCISE 13.7 ANSWERS

(a)   Nouns beginning with a [coronal] sound require the C allomorph.

(b)   Nouns beginning with two consonants, the first of which is [−coronal], require the [lə] allomorph.

EXERCISE 13.8

We present below two rather different looking sets of facts from Sanskrit and Ancient Greek respectively. Your task is to identify, with the help of feature analysis, the common principle that underlies both sets of facts.

In Sanskrit, the segments {pʰ, tʰ, ʈʰ, kʰ, tʃʰ, bʰ, dʰ, gʰ, dʒʰ} do not occur word-finally or before obstruents. The Sanskrit consonantal phonemes are: {p, t, ʈ, tʃ, k, b, d, ɖ, dʒ, g, pʰ, tʰ, ʈʰ, tʃʰ, kʰ, bʰ, dʰ, gʰ, dʒʰ, s, ʂ, ç, m, n, ɽ, l}.

In Greek, the segments {pʰ, tʰ, kʰ} do not occur word-finally or before obstruents. The Greek consonantal phonemes are: {p, t, k, b, d, dz, g, pʰ, tʰ, kʰ, s, m, n, r, l}.

The answer to this problem must consist of a statement about the distribution of aspirated or unaspirated segments. Use the feature [±aspirated]. The same general statement is valid for the two languages considered, despite the difference of segmental inventories.

EXERCISE 13.8 ANSWERS

Sounds that are [+aspirated] do not occur word-finally or before obstruents in either Greek or Sanskrit.

. . . .

Speakers of Cuna, an Indian language spoken off the coast of Panama, disguise their speech by a form of backwards talk they call *Sorsik Sunmakke* 'talking backwards'. Consider the following data and formulate an explicit rule or rules that transform regular Cuna words into their correspondents in Sorsik Sunmakke. You will need to make explicit assumptions about how Cuna words are divided into syllables.

EXERCISE 13.9

Cuna	sorsik sunmakke	gloss
dage	geda	come
saban	bansa	belly
argan	ganar	hand
ina	nai	medicine
goe	ego	deer
inna	nain	chicha (some plant or animal)

. . . .

Cuna words are divided into syllables as follows: V.CV, VC.CV, V.V. The rule of Sorsik Sunmakke is that the last syllable and the first syllable exchange places. We write the rule as follows:

EXERCISE 13.9 ANSWERS

σ1 σ2 → σ2 σ1

. . . .

Translate the following statements in the rule notation introduced here and in chapter 12 of textbook, using annotated brackets or constituent structure trees or reference to # boundaries, where appropriate. Characterize the segment classes mentioned below by some combination of feature values that is minimally sufficient to distinguish them from segments that do not undergo the rule.

EXERCISE 13.10

(a) All nasal consonants become velar when followed by a velar consonant in the same syllable. Thus nk → ŋk, unless they belong to distinct syllables.
(b) Word-final mid rounded vowels become [+tense].
(c) A syllable-initial stop is aspirated.

. . . .

(a) [+nasal] → [dorsal] / __[dorsal, −syllabic]

$$\underset{\sigma}{\underbrace{\qquad\qquad}}$$

EXERCISE 13.10 ANSWERS

(b) [−high, −low, +round] → [+tense] / __]$_{word}$
(c) [−sonorant, −continuant] → [+aspirated] / [$_\sigma$ __]

· ·

EXERCISE
13.11

Consider the following compound nouns:

(a)   *láw degrèe*
(b)   *láw schòol*
       lánguage requìrements
(c)   *lánguage requìrement chànges*
       (meaning: changes in the language requirements)
       pípe òrgan lèsson
       láw schòol chùm
       (meaning: a friend from law school)
(d)   *làw degrèe lánguage requìrements*
       làbor ùnion fínance còmmittee
       flỳ-ròd tróut fìshing

Re-read section 2.7 of chapter 2, pp. 67–9 of textbook, and assign constituent structures to all compounds based on what they mean. Now formulate a general rule for assigning main stress in compounds based on the constituent structure.

· ·

EXERCISE
13.11
ANSWERS

Constituent structure:
(a) and (b) forms:

[[láw] [degrèe]]
[[láw] [schòol]]
[[lánguage] [requìrements]]

(c) forms are left-branching compounds: they consist of a compound whose first member is itself a compound:

[[[lánguage] [requìrement]] [chànges]]
[[[pípe] [òrgan]] [lèsson]]
[[[láw] [schòol]] [chùm]]

(d) forms are both right-branching and left compounds: they consist of compounds whose first and second member consists of a compound:

[[[làw] [degrèe]] [[lánguage] [requìrements]]]
[[[flỳ][ròd]] [[tróut][fìshing]]]

Rule for assigning main stress in compounds:
Consider the bracketed structure of the compound. There are two types of compound, those whose components consist of single nouns (e.g. [pipe] [organ]) and those composed of further compounds ([pipe organ] [lesson]).

Step 1: Assign stress within simple compounds, consisting of two nouns only.

The first element in such compounds carries more stress than the second: assign to the main stressed syllable of the first element an additional asterisk.

Therefore [[pipe] [organ]] will be stressed as below:

layer 2 x			
layer 1 x	x		
layer 0 x	x	x	
	σ	σ	σ
	paɪp	ʔɔr	gən

Step 2: Now assign stress within compounds whose component parts are themselves compounds.

For such compounds the rule is that the second element of the compound carries primary stress if it is itself a compound. Otherwise the first element carries main stress.

Thus [[[pipe] [organ]] [lesson]] continues to receive stress on the stressed syllable of the first element ([[pipe] [organ]]), since the second element is a simple compound:

layer 2 x					
layer 1 x	x		x		
layer 0 x	x	x	x	x	
	σ	σ	σ	σ	σ
	paɪp	ʔɔr	gən	lɛs	ən

But [[[flỳ][ròd]] [[tróut][fìshing]]] will receive main stress on its second element ([[tróut][fìshing]]) because this element is itself a compound. Within this element, the rule of Step 1 applies and thus the stronger stress within each constituent compound is on the first noun of that compound:

layer 3		x			
layer 2 x		x			
layer 1 x	x	x	x		
layer 0 x	x	x	x	x	
	σ	σ	σ	σ	σ
	flaɪ	rɑd	traʊt	fɪ	ʃɪŋ

14

Phonology III: Explanation and Constraints in Phonology

Consider the following alternations between [t] and [s] in English:

(a)
pirate	[paɪrət]	*piracy*	[paɪrəsi]
vacant	[veɪkənt]	*vacancy*	[veɪkənsi]
secret	[sikrət]	*secrecy*	[sikrəsi]
president	[prɛzidənt]	*presidency*	[prɛzidənsi]
accurate	[ækjurət]	*accuracy*	[ækjurəsi]
fluent	[fluənt]	*fluency*	[fluənsi]

Write a phonological rule of the sort you learned in chapters 12–13 of textbook, to account for this data. Make clear what you consider to be the underlying representation for each pair of alternants. The alternations illustrated above obtain only for certain combinations of stems and suffixes in English: however, for the purpose of this exercise you can ignore this fact and formulate your rules and principles as if the process being analyzed is fully general.

Now consider the forms in (b):

(b)
modest	[madɛst]	*modesty*	[madɛsti]
honest	[anəst]	*honesty*	[anəsti]
pederast	[pɛdəræst]	*pederasty*	[pɛdəræsti]

If the rule that applied in (a) had been able to apply to forms like *modest*, we would observe *[madɛssi], with the second [s] coming from the

underlying /t/ of [madɛst]. Based on the discussion of phonological principles provided in this chapter, explain in one sentence why the rule does not
apply to forms like (b). The right answer is not to restate the rule so as to
exclude /s/ from occurring in its left context but rather to think of possible
unwelcome consequences of that rule's application to the sequence /st/.

Underlying representations are identical to the unsuffixed stems:

EXERCISE
14.1
ANSWERS

pirate	[paɪrət]
vacant	[veɪkənt]
secret	[sikrət]
president	[prɛzidənt]
accurate	[ækjurət]
fluent	[fluənt]

The rule for the first part is:

[coronal, −sonorant] → [+continuant, +strident] / ___ [−consonantal, +high, −back]

This rule does not apply to forms like those in (b) because the Not-Too-Similar Principle would be violated if the rule were to take effect.

Unsuffixed	*Suffixed satisfies Not-Too-Similar*	*violates Not-Too-Similar*
[madɛst]	[madɛsti]	*[madɛssi]
[anəst]	[anəsti]	*[anəssi]
[pɛdəræst]	[pɛdəræsti]	*[pɛdəræssi]

The answer then is that the rule above applies only when its output structure satisfies the Not-Too-Similar Principle. Otherwise the rule does not apply.

Consider the following alternations occurring in Afar, a Cushitic language:

EXERCISE
14.2

Accusative	Nominative/Genitive	Gloss
xamíla	*xaml-í*	swampgrass
ʔagára	*ʔagr-í*	scabies
darágu	*darg-í*	watered milk

Postulate underlying representations for the three roots. Write a rule
that accounts for the root alternations. (There are several possible formula-
tions compatible with this limited data.)

Now consider the following forms, which are representative of a general restriction on the application of the rule you have written. (The sound [dˤ] is a pharyngealized /d/.)

Afar form	Gloss
midˤadˤ-í	fruit-Nominative/Genitive
sababá	reason
xarar-é	he burned

Formulate a principle – akin to one discussed in the textbook – that explains why your rule did not apply to forms like the above. Make explicit the relation between the rule and the principle by explaining what are the types of representations that must satisfy your principle: underlying representations, intermediate, surface representations or some combination of these?

EXERCISE 14.2 ANSWERS

The underlying representations for the three forms are: *xamíla, ʃagára, darágu*. The vowel deletion rule can be written as:

[+syllabic] → Ø/σ C _ σ′

(In English: a vowel deletes if followed by a stressed syllable and preceded by at least one syllable.)

The vowel deletion is blocked from applying in forms where its application would create surface violations of the Not-Too-Similar Principle.

EXERCISE 14.3

(1)   Consider the following alternations in English:

A		B	
damn	[dæm]	*damnation*	[dæmneɪʃən]
condemn	[kəndɛm]	*condemnation*	[kɑndəmneɪʃən]
hymn	[hɪm]	*hymnal*	[hɪmnəl]
solemn	[sɑləm]	*solemnity*	[səlɛmnɪti]
column	[kɑləm]	*columnar*	[kəlʌmnər]

Divide the words in column B into root and suffix and identify the underlying representation of each root. Write a rule in the format of (20), p. 621 of textbook, which accounts for the stem alternations. Like the rules in (20), your rule must consist of two parts: a principle, i.e. a generalization about possible surface sequences of consonants in English words; and a procedure by which underlying representations violating this principle yield surface forms that comply with it.

(2)   Following the same procedure account for the following alternations. Consider only the changes in the stem consonants and do not attempt to characterize the vowel changes.

A		B	
sign	[saɪn]	*signatory*	[sɪgnətori]
design	[dizaɪn]	*designation*	[dɛsɪgneɪʃən]
malign	[məlaɪn]	*malignity*	[məlɪgnɪti]
assign	[əsaɪn]	*assignation*	[æsɪgneɪʃən]
impugn	[ɪmpjun]	*pugnacious*	[pʌgneɪʃəs]

(*Note*: there are two classes of vowel-initial suffixes in English, only one of which is illustrated above. To simplify your task, you should ignore the behavior of the other class of vowel-initial suffixes, exemplified by the suffixes -*ing* and -*er*.)

---

(1)   Underlying representations of the stems appear before the suffix -*ation*:

A		B	
damn	[dæm]	*damn-ation*	[dæmn-eɪʃən]
condemn	[kəndɛm]	*condemn-ation*	[kandəmn-eɪʃən]
hymn	[hɪm]	*hymn-al*	[hɪmn-əl]
solemn	[saləm]	*solemn-ity*	[səlɛmn-ɪti]
column	[kaləm]	*column-ar*	[kəlʌmn-ər]

Phonotactic principle *mn: No word final sequence *mn* is permitted.

Rule that enforces the principle:
(i)   Find every underlying string that violates the *mn Principle.
(ii)   In every such string DELETE THE SECOND ELEMENT of the consonant sequence that violates the principle.

(2)   These data are accounted for as follows by reference to a similar principle and a similar rule.

Phonotactic principle *gn: No word final sequence *gn* is permitted.

Rule that enforces the principle:
(i)   Find every underlying string that violates the *gn Principle.
(ii)   In every such string DELETE THE FIRST ELEMENT of the consonant sequence that violates the principle.

It is possible to generalize and formulate a single principle and a single rule for both cases:

Phonotactic principle *[+voice, −cont] n: No word final sequence *[+voice, −cont] n is permitted.

Rule that enforces the principle:
(i)   Find every underlying string that violates the *[+voice, −cont] n Principle.
(ii) In every such string DELETE THE NASAL ELEMENT of the consonant sequence that violates the principle, or, if sequence contains two nasals, then the final element.

EXERCISE 14.4

Consider the alternating shape of the English plural and third singular suffixes, which surface as [z] in forms like *bugs* [bʌgz], *cans* [kænz], as [s] in forms like *packs* [pæks], *laughs* [læfs], *licks* [lɪks] and as [əz] in forms such as *squishes* [skwɪʃəz], *reaches* [ritʃəz], *buses* [bʌsəz]. Gather a fuller set of forms to determine what the generalizations are regarding the distribution of these allomorphs. Then formulate an analysis of these alternations in the format indicated in (20), p. 621 of textbook. Determine whether the rules in (20) and the principles they refer to are applicable to this new data set and, if not, how they need to be modified to properly apply to the new data.

EXERCISE 14.4 ANSWERS

The answer appears in section 14.4 of textbook.

EXERCISE 14.5

Consider the alternations below, which are caused by the addition of the suffixes [jən], [jəl], and [juəl] to stems ending in /s/ and /z/.

(a)   Suffix [jən] (as in *rebellion* [rəbɛljən])

confess	[kənfɛs]	*confession*	[kənfɛʃən]
obsess	[absɛs]	*obsession*	[absɛʃən]
fuse	[fjuz]	*fusion*	[fjuʒən]

(b)   Suffix [jəl] (as in *serial* [sirjəl])

race	[reɪs]	*racial*	[reɪʃəl]
office	[afɪs]	*official*	[əfɪʃəl]
substance	[sʌbstəns]	*substantial*	[sʌbstænʃəl]

(1) Formulate one or more rules to account for these alternations. The rules should mention only phonological information (features and segments), not morphological information (i.e. not which affixes participate in triggering a given process). State a broad generalization about possible sound sequences in English words which motivates the application of the process above. Formulate this generalization as a constraint, of the same type as the constraints discussed above in (9), (14), and (26), pp. 612, 614, and 626 of textbook. (Hint: try pronouncing *obsession*, as a simple juxtaposition of the verb *obsess* and the suffix [jən], without modifying either the root or the affix.)

(2) State what is the relation between the alternations above and the alternations in (c) below.

(c) | *miss* | [mɪs] | *miss you* | [mɪʃju] |
bless	[blɛs]	*bless you*	[blɛʃju]
let	[lɛt]	*let you*	[lɛtʃju]
cut	[kʌt]	*cut you*	[kʌtʃju]

You will need to assume that some rules apply only word-internally, while others apply both within and across word boundaries. The sequence transcribed [ʧ] – e.g. in [lɛʧju] – is a palatoalveolar affricate. Palatoalveolars in general (i.e. [ʃ], [ʒ] and [ʧ], [ʤ]) are [+coronal] segments differentiated from alveolars by the feature [±anterior]: alveolars are [+anterior] and palatoalveolars are [−anterior]. In addition, palatoalveolar affricates (i.e. [ʧ], [ʤ]) differ from alveolar stops in that they contain two subparts, an actual stop portion and a palatoalveolar fricative [ʃ]. Therefore they contain the feature sequence [−continuant] [+continuant]. Your rules must reflect the feature composition of the output segments.

(3) Now consider the alternations in (d):

(d) Suffix *-ion* (as in *rebellion*)
digest	[daɪdʒɛst]	*digestion*	[daidʒɛsʧən]
exhaust	[ɛgzɔst]	*exhaustion*	[ɛgzɔsʧən]
suggest	[sədʒɛst]	*suggestion*	[sədʒɛsʧən]

Suffix *-ial* (as in *editorial*)
| *beast* | [bist] | *bestial* | [bisʧəl] |

Suffix *-ian* (as in *Egyptian* [idʒɪpʃən], *Lilliputian* [lɪləpjuʃən])
| *Christ* | [kraɪst] | *Christian* | [krɪsʧən] |

Explain why the rules that apply word-internally to derive [ʃ] from [tj] – as in /lɪləpjut-jən/ → [lɪləpjuʃən] – fail to apply in the forms in (d). Why is it that we say [sədʒɛsʧən], not *[sədʒɛsʃən] and [krɪsʧən], rather than *[krɪsʃən]? And how can the analysis be modified to account for this fact?

EXERCISE 14.5 ANSWERS

(1)   **General principle:** the sequences [sj], [ʃj] are not permitted.

*[+strident][−cons, −syllabic, +high, −back]

Rules:

(i)   Find every underlying string that violates the principle above.

(ii)   Strings identified in this way are modified as follows:

(a)   THE [+STRIDENT] BECOMES [−ANTERIOR].

(b)   THE GLIDE IS DELETED.

(2)   The rules written for (1) must be generalized as below:

General principle: the sequences [sj], [ʃj] are not permitted.

*[+coronal][−cons, −syllabic, +high, −back]

Rules:

(i)   Find every underlying string that violates the principle above.

(ii)   Strings identified in this way are modified as follows:

(a)   THE [+CORONAL] SOUND BECOMES [+STRIDENT, +CONTINUANT, −ANTERIOR].

IF IT WAS [−CONT], IT MAINTAINS THE [−CONT] VALUE AND ADDS TO IT [+CONT].

(IN THIS WAY IT BECOME AN AFFRICATE.)

(b)   THE GLIDE IS DELETED.

And rule (b) turns out not to apply when the glide is word-initial.

EXERCISE 14.6

Read Exercise 13.3 and item (8) from chapter 13, pp. 584–5 of textbook. Reformulate the analysis of Hungarian voicing alternations by writing a principle similar to the English Voice Agreement Principle but appropriate for the Hungarian data and a rule similar to the English (20b), p. 621 of textbook. Bear in mind that no sequence of obstruents disagreeing in the feature [±voice] is permissible word-internally in this language. Formulate the corresponding rules using the format in (20).

EXERCISE 14.6 ANSWERS

Consider the underlying form /rɔb solgɔ/:

This can be modified as follows to avoid violations of Voice Agreement:

Insert a vowel between the consonants: /rɔb solgɔ/ → [rɔbəsolgɔ]
Delete one of the voice-disagreeing obstruents: /rɔb solgɔ/ → [rɔsolgɔ]
Turn one of the voice-disagreeing obstruents into a sonorant: /rɔb solgɔ/ → [rɔmsolgɔ]

EXERCISE 14.7

Read again Exercise 14.3 and your solution to it. In your solution, you had formulated a principle stating that certain sequences of consonants are not acceptable in the surface structures of English words. This principle leads to modifications of the underlying representations that would violate it. For instance, underlying *condemn* /kəndɛmn/ surfaces as [kəndɛm] when it is not followed by a vowel-initial suffix like *-ation*. This change of under-lying word-final /-mn/ to surface [m] raises an interesting difficulty to the analysis proposed so far in chapter 14 of textbook. Your task in this exercise is to discover this problem. A later section in the chapter will propose a solution. To identify the problem you must consider the faithfulness con-straints that have been stated so far in this chapter as well as the constraint you had postulated above.

Form a tableau in which all these constraints are represented and where the following candidates for underlying /kəndɛmn/ are evaluated. Note that only Candidate 1 is the actual surface form that should emerge from a correct analysis.

Underlying	Candidate 1	Candidate 2	Candidate 3	Candidate 4	Candidate 5
kəndɛmn	kəndɛm	kəndɛmd	kəndɛmen	kɔndɛmn	kəndɛn

Discuss the problem you have discovered by reference to your tableau.

Let's assume that there is a constraint such as *[mn]/__]$_{word}$ which explains why a form like underlying /kəndɛmn/ cannot surface as such. The prob-lem is that the form which actually surfaces from underlying /kəndɛmn/ is not being uniquely selected by our existing constraints. [kəndɛm], [kəndɛn], and [kəndɛmən] satisfy the constraints stated so far and, in light of the change observed in the past tense and plural forms (where [ə] is inserted to break up an impossible cluster), there is no reason not to expect the ungrammatical [kəndɛmən] as the surface realization of [kəndɛm]. The table below demonstrates this point: only Candidates 2 and 4 violate any constraint. Candidates 1, 3, and 5 emerge as equally well formed, and this is incorrect. (*Note*: We record Candidate 2 as violating Recover obstruency because a sonorant has been turned into an obstruent: the constraint penalizes any change from a sonorant to an obstruent or the other way around.)

	[mn]/__]$_{word}$	*Recover Obstruency*	*Recover the morpheme*	*Not-Too-Similar*
1 kəndɛm				
2 kəndɛmd		*		
3 kəndɛmən				
4 kəndɛmn	*			
5 kəndɛn				

EXERCISE 14.8	Read again Exercise 14.5 which discusses the process whereby underlying sequences such as /sj/ become surface [ʃ] in word-internal position: e.g. underlying /kənfɛs-jən/ becomes surface [kənfɛʃən]. Identify at least five candidates, i.e. five distinct potential surface forms corresponding to /kənfɛs-jən/, which avoid in one way or another the forbidden sequence [sj]. If the candidates you list violate principles discussed so far, state what these principles are, in the form of a tableau. Identify candidates distinct from the surface form that do not violate any of the principles stated so far, and propose either phonotactic constraints or faithfulness constraints which are being violated by these candidates.

EXERCISE 14.8 ANSWERS	Here is a tableau containing six candidates of underlying /kənfɛs-jən/:

/kənfɛs-jən/	*[+coron, –son] j	Recover Obstruency	Recover the morpheme	Not-Too-Similar
1 kənfɛʃən				
2 kənfɛsjən	*			
3 kənfɛʃjən	*			
4 kənfɛsən				
5 kənfɛnjən		* (s turned to n)		
6 kənfɛs			*(–jən suffix deleted)	

Candidate (1) is the one that should surface. Candidates (2), (3), (5), and (6) violate one or another of the constraints indicated. However, Candidate (4) violates no constraint so far and we must suggest a constraint that will differentiate it from (1). Candidate (4) separates the underlyingly adjacent sequence /sj/ and can be excluded by an additional constraint we may call Recover the segment, which prohibits deleting underlying segment.

EXERCISE 14.9	Yokuts – an almost extinct California American Indian language (Stanley Newman (1944), *Yokuts Language of California*, New York: Viking Fund Publications in Anthropology, no. 2) – possesses two types of sonorant consonants in its phonemic inventory: plain voiced sonorants – as in (a) – and glottalized sonorants – as in (b). The glottalized sonorants are produced with vocal folds tense and constricted for part of their length. The feature differentiating the two types of sonorants is [±constricted glottis]: the glottalized series is [+constricted glottis].

(a)   Plain voiced sonorants, [–constricted glottis]: m, n, l, w, j
(b)   Glottalized sonorants, [+constricted glottis]: m̰, n̰, l̰, w̰, j̰

Part I

The plain sonorants occur within Yokuts words in any position: word-initially, word-finally, between a vowel and a consonant or between a consonant and a vowel. Some examples of voiced sonorants occurring in Yokuts words appear in (c): the relevant sounds are in bold characters.

(c)	word-initial:	*me:kit* 'was swallowed',
		wowlal 'may stand up'
	between vowels:	*gijit* 'was touched', *ʔamilka* 'help!'
	word-final:	*xathin* 'ate', *logwol* 'may pulverize'
	between vowel and	
	consonant:	*ʔamilka* 'help!', *logiwka* 'pulverize!'
	between consonant	
	and vowel:	*ʔamlal* 'may help', *gijmi* 'helping'

However, the glottalized sonorants do not occur word-initially or after a consonant. Relevant examples appear in (d):

(d)	word-initial:	_____
	between vowels:	*caw̰a:hin* 'shout', *neṇa:hin* 'make quiet'
	word-final:	*xaja:haḻij* 'one who is placed'
	between vowel and	
	consonant:	*jaw̰la:hin* 'follow', *ʔeḻka:hin* 'sing'
	between consonant	
	and vowel:	_____

Formulate a principle of the form *Feature combination x is disallowed in position Y*, which summarizes as succinctly as possible the restriction on the occurrence of glottalized sonorants in Yokuts. Bear in mind that this is not a rule: the data being characterized involves no alternations, but rather just the systematic absence of a sound class from certain positions within the word.

Part II

Now consider the alternation in (e)–(f): some Yokuts suffixes – such as /ʔiṇaj/ and /ʔaʔ/, all of which begin with a glottal stop [ʔ] – cause a sonorant in the preceding root to become glottalized. When this happens, the suffix-initial glottal stop deletes. However, not all sonorants can undergo this process (cf. (g)) and some roots containing sonorants remain unaffected. The sonorants that fail to undergo the process are identifiable by their position: examine the data and state how they can be identified. Explain how the data examined in part 1 sheds light on this fact. Discuss the form *lihm-ʔiṇaj* and explain why it does not surface as either **lihṃ-iṇaj* or as **ḻihm-inaj*.

(e)   Underlying form of the suffix /ʔiṇaj/ appears in:
      dub-ʔiṇaj 'while leading by the hand'   (root *dub* 'lead by the hand')

(f)   Glottal stop of /ʔiṇaj/ realized as sonorant glottalization in:
      c'oẉ-iṇaj   'while grasping'   (root *c'oow* 'grasp')
      hiẉt-iṇaj   'while walking'   (root *hiwiit* 'walk')
      taṇ-iṇaj   'while going'   (root *taan* 'go')
      Initial glottal stop of /ʔaʔ/ realized as sonorant glottalization in:
      t'ojx-aʔ   'give medicine'   (root *t'ojx* 'medicine')
      ʔaṃl-aʔ   'help, get aid'   (root *ʔaml* 'help')

(g)   Glottal stop of /ʔiṇaj/ is not realized as sonorant glottalization in:
      lihm-ʔiṇaj 'while running'   (root *lihm* 'run')
      Glottal stop of suffix /ʔaʔ/ is not realized as sonorant glottalization in:
      wiṣ-ʔaʔ   'straighten'   (root *wiṣ* 'straight')
      ʔugn-ʔaʔ   'drink'   (root *ʔugn* 'drink')
      picw-ʔaʔ   'catch'   (root *picw* 'catch')

Extra credit: Formulate explicitly the process that turns underlying forms like /t'ojx-ʔaʔ/ into surface *t'ojx-aʔ* 'give medicine'.

EXERCISE 14.9 ANSWERS

Part I
The needed principle is:

Glottalized sonorants are disallowed in contexts where they do not follow vowels.

Part II
Glottalizing suffixes cannot create glottalized sonorants in positions where they do not follow vowels: the suffix glottalization process applies only when its output satisfies the constraint formulated in part I. Thus the form [lihm-ʔiṇaj] cannot give rise to [ḷihm-iṇaj] (because the derived glottalized sonorant [ḷ] would be word-initial, hence not following a vowel. Nor can it give rise to [lihṃ-iṇaj] because the [m] in this form does not follow a vowel either.

   Extra credit: Associate the feature [+constricted glottis] which represents the consonant [ʔ] to the nearest stem sonorant, subject to the constraint stated in part I.

EXERCISE 14.10

Consider again the data of Hungarian voicing alternations presented in chapter 13 (item (8), pp. 584–5 of textbook, and Exercises 13.2–13.3). In Exercise 14.6 you have formulated a voicing agreement principle that motivates the existence of the voicing alternations. In order to enforce this principle, the voicing value of the stem-final obstruent is modified to agree with the voicing value of the suffix-initial obstruent. Consider now the fact that there are many other ways which could have insured that surface strings comply with the Voicing Agreement Principle. For instance a vowel could have been inserted between the two obstruents that disagree in voice: e.g. underlying /rɔb solgɔ/ 'slave' could have been realized as [rɔbəsolgɔ] with a buffer [ə] separating the two obstruents. This representation satisfies the Voice Agreement Principle through a different modification of the underlying structures from the one actually adopted in Hungarian.

Identify three other procedures through which the language could have insured, but did not, that obstruent sequences agree in surface voice value. Show how underlying representations would be modified if these other means had been adopted to satisfy the Voice Agreement Principle that is active in Hungarian.

- -

Hungarian Voice Agreement:
Obstruent sequences may not differ with respect to [±voice].

Rule that enforces the principle:
(i)   Find every underlying string that violates the Hungarian Voice Agreement Principle.
(ii) In every such string MODIFY THE VOICE VALUE of the first obstruent in the sequence.

- -

Read Exercise 13.4 from chapter 13. Reformulate the analysis of Yokuts vowel length alternations by writing a principle limiting the occurrence of long vowels to certain contexts. Long vowels do not occur before CC sequences or before word-final Cs. Write the principle – making use of syllable notation – and the rule, using the format in (20), p. 621 of textbook.

- -

Yokuts long vowel principle:
Long vowels are not permitted in closed syllables: $^*V{:}/\_C]_\sigma$

Rule that enforces the principle:
(i)   Find every underlying string that violates the Yokuts Long Vowel Principle.
(ii) In every such string SHORTEN THE VOWEL occurring in the closed syllable.

- -

Consider the following pairs of underlying and surface representations, discussed earlier in textbook:

	Spelling	Underlying	Surface
(a)	*squishes*	[skwɪʃ-z]	[skwɪʃəz]
(b)	*buses*	[bʌs-z]	[bʌsəz]
(c)	*licks*	[lɪk-z]	[lɪks]
(d)	*laps*	[læp-z]	[læps]

For each of the underlying forms above consider the following alternative candidates:

	Candidate class 1	Candidate class 2	Candidate class 3
(a)	[skwɪʃz]	[skwɪʃ]	[skwɪnz]
(b)	[bʌsz]	[bʌs]	[bʌnz]
(c)	[lɪkz]	[lɪk]	[lɪŋz]
(d)	[læpz]	[læp]	[læmz]

Identify the constraint violated by each class of candidates. Write four tables, one for each word considered, in the format of (32), p. 635 of textbook, in which you record the constraint violations of each one of the alternative candidates considered and you compare them with the actual surface form of the word.

· ·

EXERCISE 14.12 ANSWERS

Candidate class 1 violates Not-Too-Similar. Candidate class 2 violates Recover the morpheme. Candidate class 3 violates Recover Obstruency.

· ·

EXERCISE 14.13

Now consider a new class of unsuccessful candidates:

	Underlying	Candidate class 4
(a)	/skwɪʃ-z/	[skwɪz]
(b)	/bʌs-z/	[bʌz]
(c)	/lɪk-z/	[lɪz]
(d)	/læp-z/	[læz]

Formulate a new faithfulness principle that is violated by this class of failed candidates. Write one table for each of the four words: compare the actual surface representation of the word with the corresponding class 4 candidate in terms of your constraint. The result should be that the actual surface form does not violate your proposed principle whereas the class 4 candidate does.

. . . .

Candidate class 4 can be ruled out because it violates the constraint Recover the segment.

EXERCISE
14.13
ANSWERS

. . . .

In Sidebar 14.4 on Recover Adjacency, p. 639 of textbook, it was pointed out that the adjacency between segments belonging to the same morpheme may be more strictly preserved than that of segments that are concatenated by a morphological operation. Thus the Sierra Miwok vowel insertion rule separates consonants that were adjacent underlyingly but which belonged to separate morphemes; however, it does not separate underlyingly adjacent segments belonging to the same morpheme. In this language, and others, we must distinguish two related versions of Recover Adjacency: a specific one that holds of morpheme-internal position, shown below, and the general version stated earlier in (33b), p. 638 of textbook, which does not differentiate morpheme-internal clusters from others.

EXERCISE
14.14

Recover Adjacency (morpheme-internal) segments that are adjacent in the underlying representation of a single morpheme must be adjacent in the surface representation.

In Sierra Miwok, the constraint written above is undominated (not violated by any surface form), whereas the general constraint in (33b) is in fact violated in cases of vowel insertion. Equipped with this information, propose a solution to the problem identified earlier in Exercise 14.7.

. . . .

The solution to the problem raised by Exercise 14.7 is to invoke the morpheme-internal constraint Recover Adjacency. This constraint is not violated in the cases of schwa-insertion that apply between stems and suffixes (e.g. [mɛndəd] from /mɛnd-d/) but it would be violated if schwa were inserted to break up morpheme-internal clusters, i.e. in hypothetical forms like candidate 3 below [kəndɛmən]:

EXERCISE
14.14
ANSWERS

	*[mn]/__]_word_	Recover Obstruency	Recover Adjacency
1 kəndɛm			
2 kəndɛmd		*	
3 kəndɛmən			*
4 kəndɛmn	*		
5 kəndɛn			

Note finally that we can extend Recover Adjacency so that it will rule out candidate (5): we formulate this extension as follows:

Recover Adjacency (morpheme-internal; extended): Segments that are adjacent in the underlying representation are adjacent on the surface; and segments that are adjacent in the surface representation, if present underlyingly, are underlyingly adjacent.

The second clause of the extended constraint rules out (5): in this form [ɛ] and [n] are adjacent in the surface representation, despite the fact that they were not adjacent underlyingly.